SOUTHSIDE PROVISIONAL

From Freedom Fighter to the Four Courts

Kieran Conway

ORPEN PRESS

Published by
Orpen Press
Lonsdale House
Avoca Avenue
Blackrock
Co. Dublin
Ireland

email: info@orpenpress.com
www.orpenpress.com

Paperback ISBN 978-1-909895-55-3
ePub ISBN 978-1-909895-56-0
Kindle ISBN 978-1-909895-57-7
PDF ISBN 978-1-909895-58-4

Printed in Dublin by SPRINT-print Ltd

In memory of Kevin and Imelda Conway

And, to the IRA volunteers and republican supporters referred to herein

Contents

Chapter 1

There was nothing in my past to suggest that I might one day join the IRA. My parents both came from Fine Gael backgrounds and, in so far as they bothered with politics at all, they voted with their histories. My earliest republican memories are of the celebrations surrounding the 1916 Rising commemoration in 1966 and the blowing up of Nelson's Pillar the month before. De Valera, the ancient president, surrounded by grey men in hats and grey coats. While I saw pieces of it on television, it meant nothing to me; the fact that it was being celebrated by adults placing it past consideration. Nor, beyond a vague bemusement, was I moved one way or another by the disappearance of the Pillar. The first stirrings of trouble in the North, the rise of Paisley and a murderous Ulster Volunteer Force, passed me by.

I went to a Catholic middle-class secondary school, Blackrock College, and shared the normal teenage interests of the 1960s: English pop music, English football and English teenage culture generally. I knew no one who didn't cheer when England won the World Cup in 1966; no one for whom London or Liverpool wasn't a spiritual capital. Ireland, and Gaelic Ireland in particular, was hopelessly backward; the culture a strange anachronism. The language was, for me, particularly hateful and one of the few points where as a teenager my sentiments matched those of my father, whose sole political involvement aside from voting for Fine Gael was support for the Language Freedom Movement, a ginger group that campaigned against compulsory Irish in the 1960s. Along the 46A bus route on which I would travel occasionally was graffiti condemning free trade with Britain. Even this seemed stupid. Protectionism merely meant we were denied Opal Fruits and Mars bars and wore clothes inferior to those available to our English counterparts.

Everything about the country seemed mean and petty compared to the great liberal oasis across the water. My father, a civil engineer, had worked for the British colonial service in Malaya, and at the age of nine I had gone to an English prep-type boarding school there. The school was co-ed and civilised and I don't remember raised voices, far less the casual brutality then endemic in the Irish Catholic educational system. At home on leave and staying with my mother's family in County Mayo, a teacher from the local Christian Brothers sent another child out to cut a branch off a tree with which to beat me. My offence: the slighting of a visiting priest by failing to leap to my feet at the requisite speed. Great welts and bruising on my nine-year-old hands; I was, for him, some sort of hated symbol with my perfect manners and little English voice.

The family, which by now included my younger brother and sister (a second sister arrived some years later), came home for good when I was eleven and I was sent to board with the Jesuits in Mungret, County Limerick, my father's home county. They were less brutal than the Brothers but more controlled. In Mungret you could only be beaten by designated priests at designated times; the teachers literally marked your card with the issue of a chit that had to be cashed in within, as I recall, seven days. But that would come later. In the first year I engaged fully with the priests, did well in class and became deeply immersed in Catholicism, my favourite reading the lives of the saints. Adolescent rebellion arrived on cue in second year and, as I began to smoke and hang around with some of the tougher boys, I entered into a standard cycle of punishment and resentment. With my school results in free-fall, my parents decided to move me to where they could keep a better eye on things.

Blackrock College, where I was sent at the age of thirteen, was big and overblown, with six streams to each year. It was the sort of school in which it was easy to get lost and I certainly did, settling into the unchallenged ease of middle-stream classes. I announced myself an atheist at fifteen, sparring with the teacher during religion class and shocking my friends when I refused to go to confession during the fifth-year retreat. I stopped going to Mass, walking the seafront below Glasthule on Sundays while waiting for the others to come out, thrilling at the play of the mortal sin on my possibly still immortal soul.

I drifted into sixth year unmarked, as I thought, by the school. Then, at the age of sixteen, my favourite teacher, Seamus Grace, asked us in English class what we were reading. I had recently broken up with my long-term girlfriend and, between that and my desolate atheism, was hard at work honing my sensibility. When my turn arrived, I told the teacher, quite proudly since most of the class read comics, that I had read, amongst others, Ian Fleming. He responded, 'I'm surprised at you, Conway', words that shocked and stung me. He then gave us a list of novelists, at the top of which were Graham Greene and George Orwell, and I went on to read them in great bouts of intensity. They were immediate influences, respectively validating my teenage instincts about, on the one hand, God, death and love, and, on the other, money, politics and the sharp unfairness of the ordered world. News broadcasts regarding Rhodesia, South Africa and Vietnam began to make some sense as it slowly dawned on me that there were noble adults and live causes that were supported by them.

Literature became my new world, its suffering men my heroes. I walked Killiney Hill late at night arguing life, religion and politics with friends. I was in love with all humanity – well, in the abstract anyway. My sympathy never did quite stretch to the 1960s' remnants of conservative Gaelic Ireland. Brendan Bowyer and the assorted hillbillies for us were musical throwbacks to the 1950s and no match for the Beatles or the Rolling Stones, far less the depths of Bob Dylan and, later, Leonard Cohen. However, while we may have affected to despise the culchies and their showbands, it didn't stop us hanging around the Ierne and other Dublin ballrooms where we would try to con the country shop girls and student nurses that we were university students, it being thought they were easier than the sophisticates from the Loretos and other Dublin convent schools.

When I left school in the summer of 1967, a group of us went to work in the Smedley canning factory in Spalding, Lincolnshire, living in Nissen huts on an old World War II RAF base. We had to pass through London to get there and, while we waited for a train to take us north, went down to Carnaby Street, where on a damp Sunday morning we stood and marvelled at the checked hipsters and coloured shirts and jackets on display in the windows. This was the first time I had relatively serious money and could manage more than the couple of beers possible in Dublin on a Saturday night. We downed gallons of bitter and Double Diamond, and drank ridiculous multiples of vodka, whiskey, gin and rum, as we vied with each other to see who could drink the most. One of the lads, with me in tow, braved the local chemist to buy Durex to bring home. 'What size do you want?' asked the elderly male chemist, sending my friend away red-faced in defeat. Though he recovered sufficiently to succeed elsewhere, I passed on the purchase, quite certain I knew no girls who were that advanced.

That year, the jobs were dominated by Northerners. The night cleaners were students in Queen's University; the rest of the best jobs went to boys from Belfast Royal Academy and the other rugby-playing Northern Protestant schools. If you couldn't be English, you could at least be Protestant. Even at home, they had money and an edge. I would see the Glengara girls walking through Dun Laoghaire on their way home from school, pretty noses in the air, telling me I'd no chance. Our different education systems gave the Northerners a year on us, and a year at that age is a lot. From my place on the lowly pea-line I'd watch the night cleaners after they came on shift, long-haired and bearded, the powerful hoses held casually in their hands like weapons. I would see them in the canteen engaged in easy banter with the Northern girls who served the food; see them out downing pints on Saturday nights. Even fecking Belfast was cooler than Dublin and, if not quite English, the Northerners were at least British. Not that my Brit- or Anglophilia was unqualified. We had to watch out for the working-class locals who were always on the look-out for stray Irish college boys, from North or South, making their way back to the factory. But I was no stranger to this version of class warfare; we had it every other weekend in Dun Laoghaire, where we were routinely chased, and sometimes caught, by the hard cases from Sallynoggin and the other local corporation estates.

From home the news reached me that I had failed Latin in the Leaving Cert, which was then a requirement for university entrance. I returned briefly to fall out with my father then took off again to work on a Guinness hop farm in Worcestershire. There, I learned to drink a variety of strong local ciders instead of beer and marvelled at the refined Englishness of those who frequented the folk music club. After another short sojourn in Dublin, in a by now severely strained household, I headed off to England once again with a couple of pals, this time to make some money with the intention of travelling on to Istanbul, the then hippy destination. The project quickly came off the rails as we squandered what little money we had, running into problems right away. Having arrived in London, we encountered the generous British social welfare system – famously popular with Irish students – and were soon ensconced in a freezing chalet at the rear of a block of flats close to Russell Square with enough cash in our pockets to feed us for the week until we reported back to the social welfare office. Naturally we drank the lot and spent the couple of days before our next appearance on dry bread and water. Fortunately we soon discovered how simple it was to get casual work through the various agencies, so we worked when we needed the cash and spent the rest of the time meandering through London, meeting up with the unusual sorts who frequent inner-city bars during daylight hours and eyeing up the girls who walked in and out of London University, part of which sat close to our base, and around Leicester Square and King's Road, famous venues from the pop songs of the time.

After my friends left, I stuck it out alone in London for a few weeks more before heading back home to Dublin, all but penniless. There, I got work as an encyclopaedia salesman, wandering the windswept north Dublin corporation estates and the overheated towers of Ballymun, our savage sales pitch that the targets should give their children the chance of something better than the mess that was their own lives. I then worked sporadically in hotels and pubs until the summer arrived. I repeated Latin before heading off to pack peas again, this time in Peterborough, before finally coming home to go to University College Dublin.

Teenage rebel or not, I had always taken for granted that I would go to university, though to do just what was another matter. I left school shortly before the impact of free education and the annual points race began to be felt within the middle classes. Nineteen sixty-eight was,

I think, the first year in which a single honour was required for entrance to UCD, with perhaps two for Trinity. This qualified you to study just about anything and, though there were other minimal requirements, middle-class kids did as they wished, queuing up on registration day for anything from Medicine through Architecture to Science or Arts, sometimes switching queue and so career on spotting a friend. By now I had read my way through my teacher's list and wanted to do English but my father wouldn't hear of it. BAs were for girls in his view and, lacking sufficient conviction to fight my corner, I was bullied into registering for Law.

I started college in the autumn of 1968 against the backdrop of student revolts in the US, France and Germany and, to a much lesser extent, Britain. Students were awake to politics, and the world's unfairness, at least abstractly. The message was shifting from taking dope and dropping out to revolution. The radical individualism of 1967 was being eclipsed by variations on anarchism and communism, all of them resolutely anti-Soviet and captured in the title of Daniel Cohn-Bendit's manifesto, *Obsolete Communism: The Left-Wing Alternative*. After Prague, there was as little sympathy with Moscow's perceived Soviet imperialism as with Washington's more standard version, though Castro, Mao and Ho Chi Minh remained revolutionary heroes.

First-year law students back then studied English, History and Philosophy in addition to Law subjects. In English we studied Joyce's *A Portrait of the Artist*, much of it set in the university grounds, and I too longed to forge the uncreated conscience of my race. UCD was still very much the Catholic university, and Scholastic philosophy was what was taught there. It was crushingly boring, though the year was briefly enlivened by a short series of lectures introducing Jean-Paul Sartre and existentialism. Existentialism was all the rage in the late 1960s and Sartre's message of untrammelled freedom, coupled with the notion of taking absolute responsibility for your situation, has never lost its appeal to me. No matter what you were supposed to be studying, books of poetry, high fiction, history or politics were real fashion items, to be read, passed around, discussed and of course displayed to impress, with Fanon, Marcuse, Freud and, for the psychedelics, Timothy Leary and Aldous Huxley among the top hits. I was a dedicated follower of the fashion and even managed to read some of them. In politics I was a lot more influenced by Bertrand Russell than Marx, completely taken with the egalitarian principles and predictions laid out in works of his like *In Praise of Idleness* and *Proposed Roads to Freedom*, so readable when set against the Marxist canon.

The teaching of history was supposed to be undergoing a revolution but I didn't notice, save that by taking the subject beyond the foundation of the State in 1921 it couldn't fail to raise questions about the status quo. My politics at the time were vague and disorganised; I was still much more interested in girls, drink and smoking the bit of hash that was going around. This was the year of the so-called Gentle Revolution in UCD and I went on the many protest marches down to the Dáil, my confidence in an alternative Ireland growing with each attack on the ridiculous adult world of Lynch and Cosgrave. John Feeney ran Grille, a left-wing Christian outfit; the other leading lights I remember – no doubt because their celebrity endured – were Kevin Myers and Ruairi Quinn. The latter subsequently became a career politician, but he seemed wild and exciting to me then. I was friendly with his younger brother and one night, when we were protesting outside the Dáil, Ruairi wandered up and – disgusted by the speaker's calling for peaceful protest rather than encouraging us to torch the place – said witheringly, 'This is no place for a revolutionary.' I was impressed but kept some distance in my first year and didn't join up for anything.

***

Meanwhile, things had taken a far from gentle turn in the North, where student revolutionaries from Queen's University and a group around Eamonn McCann in Derry were setting the pace. On 5 October 1968, a series of Northern civil rights actions culminated in an RUC baton charge on the assembled marchers in Derry, itself the exemplar of the anti-Catholic bias of the Northern statelet. Film footage of the brutality was flashed around the world, which suddenly woke up to the existence of what looked very much like an apartheid state on Britain's doorstep, one moreover for which Britain was responsible. In embarrassed response, the reformist Northern Prime Minister Terence O'Neill (he of the remarkable insight that Catholics would behave like Protestants if 'people' would only treat them properly) in December made his famous 'Crossroads' speech in which he, not inaccurately, set out a path and counterpath to the future and, a couple of days later, helpfully fired his right-wing Home Affairs Minister, William Craig. Pleased with O'Neill, the Northern Ireland Civil Rights Association (NICRA) then announced a moratorium on marches, which People's Democracy – the Queen's student organisation – promptly said it would disregard.

The students planned a long march from Belfast to Derry to open the New Year, modelled on the civil rights march to Montgomery, Alabama in 1966, which had done so much to show up the racism of the American Deep South and force federal intervention. The parallels were striking: with reforming unionists threatening to treat with the Catholics, there was a growing supremacist backlash led by Ian Paisley, and a proliferation of loyalist paramilitary organs appeared, pledging to defend the union against change by whatever means were necessary. The student march was duly harassed and harried as it crossed the North, and at Burntollet bridge near Derry it was attacked by Protestant thugs, many of them off-duty B Specials, who laid about them while the RUC looked on, presaging events the following August when entire streets in nationalist areas of Belfast were torched by loyalist mobs while the RUC stood by.

Burntollet had been preceded by rioting in Derry and was followed by a veritable police riot as drunken RUC men took revenge on the Bogside, so ending the brief honeymoon between O'Neill and NICRA and forcing the latter back onto the streets. And while O'Neill had indeed introduced limited reforms, the most dangerous moment for bad government, as de Tocqueville noted, is when it sets about reform, and so it proved. The driving forces behind the coming revolt – People's Democracy, the group in Derry, and plenty of present and ex-IRA men – saw an opportunity coming and, being revolutionaries, were completely uninterested in reforms, insisting from the outset that the State was incapable of reforming itself. This, of course, was a self-fulfilling prophecy which would be substantiated in time, assisted into being by the actions of the very ones who had prophesied it.

Early summer saw me back in Spalding. Two years older, I was this time given heavy work on a machine called the breaker and worked with tough Hungarian students, who gave the handful of quiet and dignified Czechs permitted out that year a hard time over their alleged shortcomings in standing up to the Soviet invasion of 1968. Things were changing and I thought the Northerners no longer as friendly as they had been, though political discussion was carefully skirted. Needing to repeat an exam, I arrived back in Dublin and was there throughout the month of August while Belfast, in particular, burned.

Again the trouble began in Derry when an enlarged contingent of the loyalist Apprentice Boys organisation arrived to march along the Derry Walls and remind those in the Bogside below of their inferior status. Fierce rioting broke out, but the Bogsiders – led by a defence committee headed by veteran IRA man Seán Keenan – had put up barricades and these were now defended with bricks, stones and petrol bombs. Unable to breach the barricades, the RUC responded with the first use of CS gas in the North, and the Battle of the Bogside was on.

The following night Taoiseach Jack Lynch came on television, Churchill-style, to demand the introduction of UN peacekeepers, together with early negotiations on reunification, and to announce that he had moved Irish troops to the border and could no longer 'stand by' and see the innocent 'injured and perhaps worse'. Invasion seemed briefly on the cards, and to no one more so than the nationalists and loyalists in the North. I had joined the Irish army reserve (FCA) while in school, ceasing to attend after a drill sergeant stamped on my ankles, and wondered if I would be called up.

The trouble spread as calls for nationalists to take to the streets, to draw the RUC away from Derry, were answered throughout the North. A man was shot dead by B Specials following a rally in Armagh and, in Belfast, crowds came out to stone the RUC barracks on the Falls Road and loyalist mobs later surged down the side streets in the wake of RUC men and B Specials, burning Catholic homes as they went. Defensive fire from the republican side led to the death of one loyalist and resulted in a ferocious overreaction from the RUC, who brought up armoured cars with heavy machine guns and opened up on the

Divis Flats complex, killing nine-year-old Patrick Rooney as he lay in his bed. Meanwhile, in the Ardoyne area, two Catholics were killed by wild RUC gunfire as a Protestant mob followed an RUC baton charge into Hooker Street, again torching Catholic homes and businesses as they went.

In Derry the RUC proved unable to breach the barricades, repulsed by the courage and ingenuity of the young men hurling missiles and petrol bombs from their vantage point on top of Rossville Flats. As the rioting entered into its third day, British troops were deployed to clapping and cheering from the locals, many of whom believed that the troops had been summoned to protect them from the RUC. Calls from Bernadette Devlin and others to refuse to welcome the soldiers – since Stormont, which the army had been brought in to protect, still remainded – fell, in the circumstances, on mainly deaf ears.

Belfast, meanwhile, continued to burn. By dawn the following day the RUC were withdrawing to barracks, blaming the IRA for the trouble and claiming to have intelligence that there would be further attacks, together with armed incursions from the South. But the IRA was a paper tiger, for, despite the warning signs, few weapons were available and IRA activity in the Falls area was limited and chaotic, with just a handful of volunteers eventually opening fire on the loyalist crowd. Shortly after midday, James Chichester-Clark – who had taken over from O'Neill as premier in May – requested troops, whose arrival on the streets, as in Derry, was greeted with relief by the nationalist residents.

Stormont had very much wanted to avoid bringing in the troops, believing there would be constitutional repercussions – as had been threatened by the British Prime Minister, Harold Wilson – but there were none, and Stormont continued to take many of the security decisions that followed. Meanwhile, Lynch's speech had served to mislead both sides: encouraging nationalists while enraging loyalists, and contributing to the showdown that resulted in the deaths of eight people, injuries to 750 more, and the displacement of some 1,500 Catholic families and a smaller number of Protestant ones. These deaths and the torching of Catholic streets also resulted in the birth of the Provisionals; its *raison d'être* the failure of the then IRA leadership to properly defend nationalist Belfast. Little of this, however, was then apparent and, certainly in the South, the republicans were being fêted as the heroes of the day.

For a week or so, Dublin had a rolling demonstration, with republicans as the star turns. I attended marches and protests at which Northern and Sinn Féin leaders berated the Southern government and demanded arms. Luke Kelly of the Dubliners, a member of the Irish Workers' Party (the name of the then Southern Communist Party), was one of those who spoke from republican platforms. The Dubliners had helped to effect a huge cultural change in beating out a musical genre that was at once both thoroughly Irish and cool as well. Men were openly recruited for the IRA at a meeting at the GPO and, at Collins Barracks, Tomás Mac Giolla, then president of Sinn Féin, addressed the crowd and soldiers inside, saying, 'The weapons are in the FCA and the Free State Army. Now is the time when we must say if you are not prepared to use them, will you give them to us', as the crowd waved tricolours and shouted 'We want guns.' With its fringe vandalism and the occasional police baton charge, August 1969 had changed everything, including, as it turned out, me.

Chapter 2

Back in UCD for second-year Law, the Great Hall was a showcase of revolutionary choice. There were Young Socialists, the Irish Communist Organisation (ICO), varying Maoists, small groups of anarchists and syndicalists, the Republican Club and independents like John Feeney's Grille, as well as the mainstream, beyond consideration, student branches of Fianna Fáil and Fine Gael. The various left groups squabbled fiercely over Stalin and Trotsky, the fault lines between them a bewildering mix of philosophy, history and personality. Meanwhile the sacrifice of the Czech pacifist hero Jan Palach, who burned himself alive in January 1969 in Wenceslas Square in imitation of the saffron-robed Buddhist monks in Vietnam, was for some reason no longer enough. In the US, the Black Panthers had long superseded Martin Luther King, assassinated in April 1968, in the affections of the young – the Black Power salutes of Tommie Smith and John Carlos at the Mexico Olympics later that year simply confirming the shift. In a curious turn, Che Guevara was now everyone's hero, and armed rather than passive resistance what was called for. Suddenly one was required to kill as well as be willing to die. My own metamorphosis from fledgling flower child to would-be revolutionary had gone by, entirely unnoticed by me.

Inspired by left-wing national liberation movements from Vietnam to Cuba, we were all quite certain that the 1970s would be socialist. Even the Labour Party claimed it stood for a socialist republic, though it would go on to coalesce with one or other of the centre-right parties repeatedly over the next 40 years. I had watched the 1969 general election in June with huge attention, appalled at the electorate's putting Fianna Fáil back in power, its overlooking of new-look Labour, with its intellectual colossuses like David Thornley and Conor Cruise O'Brien – home-grown counterparts of the Russells and Sartres who so impressed me. However, any thoughts I might have had of a future with Labour's youth group disappeared with August 1969, and the republicans seemed to me the only possible choice for anyone remotely serious about revolution.

As I went into second year, there was a semi-fascist government in the North whose behaviour was sanctioned by British imperialists, while power in the South was in the hands of Vichy-like collaborators with the British. I thought myself blessed to be living in revolutionary times and quickly joined the UCD Republican Club, its leading light someone who had been a year ahead of me in Blackrock. Politics, and revolutionary politics in particular, seeks willing hands and I was there for everything, selling the *United Irishman* in the Great Hall on Fridays, dealing with the derision and counter-arguments of the ICO and Maoists, the charges that we were revisionist, reformist, Stalinist, Trotskyite, adventurist, petite bourgeois – whatever the cutting counter of the day was. I fought my way through Irish and world history and the works of socialism, my father noting wearily from time to time that James Connolly wasn't going to get me my exams. Struggling with Marx, Lenin and Trotsky, as well as the anarchist and syndicalist writers, I worked hard trying to hold my own amidst this strange new vocabulary, and studied even less Law than I had in my first year.

Cheap pamphlets were widely available, while Pelicans as well as college textbooks were casually 'liberated' from various Dublin bookshops – for reasons that are beyond me, we were an unforgivably light-fingered generation. James Connolly's *Labour in Irish History* was the central tome, Connolly himself the home-grown Lenin to whom everyone paid homage. The novice republican, though, had more ground to cover. There was Wolfe Tone, to be judged, as with the French revolutionaries, historically, by the highest standards of his own time; the Young Irelanders, John Mitchel and Fintan Lalor; the Fenians; and the men of 1916 and thereafter. We had to track through 1916 and the War of Independence, the Civil War, the Fianna Fáil betrayal, and the great ideological battles of the 1930s, while defending, too, the anti-ideological republicans of the 1940s and 50s.

The characters came alive for me and I admired equally Frank Ryan, who fought in Spain against Franco, and Seán Russell, who went to Nazi Germany to seek aid against Britain during World War II. Republicanism, for me as for many others, quickly acquired that transcendent, quasi-religious character captured in the use of quotations like 'for those who believe, no explanation is necessary; for those who don't, no explanation will suffice', a line which, it turns out, has its origins in the Catholic hagiography *Song of Bernadette*. Once, I simply walked off the Law Society debating platform I had shared with Austin Currie – of the soon-to-be-formed SDLP – entirely untroubled by the verbal thrashing I had just received at his hands, far less by my failure to touch the audience.

***

The Republican Club was putatively Stalinist, finding justification in the 'stages theory', which dictated that national liberation was the prerequisite of revolution, thus excusing the presence of bourgeois adventurers among our ranks should our opponents be able to point to any. Outside, the IRA – our parent so to speak – was doing the real business. Republicans were forcibly delivering social justice, providing muscle not only for civil rights demonstrations in the North but for Dublin Housing Action Committee sit-ins as well. They were active in Land Leagues, the anti-ground-rents campaign and protests against privately owned beaches and private fishing rights. In May 1968 the IRA in Limerick had destroyed a fleet of buses being used to move scab labour into a US multinational. In Galway, a giant, foreign-owned fishing boat had been bombed to safeguard Ireland's natural resources for native fishermen, while German-owned farms were being burned out in Counties Meath and Louth. All these were portrayed by us as revolutionary acts, as direct attacks on imperialism. Armed with Marx's eleventh thesis on Feuerbach – 'Philosophers thus far have only interpreted the world; the point however is to change it' – we had a ready reply to the insults of the Young Socialists and others.

Republican policy at the time was to construct a national liberation front, together with Irish communists and others. The Republican

Club had regular meetings with the Connolly Youth Movement, a communist youth organisation which consisted of genuine working-class young fellows, thus giving us an additional cachet amongst the middle-class university left. The seriously Stalinist Irish Communist Organisation was the only other college group that impressed me. Though republican back then, the ICO later metamorphosed into the British and Irish Communist Organisation and went on to provide the intellectual basis for left-wing 'two nationism', according to which the loyalists had as solid a claim to British nationality as the republicans to Irish nationality. Later again – because the British state was deemed to be more advanced in Marxist terms than the Irish one – they became de facto unionists and articulated positions that became popular among sections of the left in the South, eventually capturing those who were about to become the Official IRA themselves.

My ideological base was firming up, but of course I was arguing in the small incestuous world of the hard left and disdained discussion with the beyond-hope careerists in Fianna Fáil and Fine Gael. Patrick Pearse became a particular favourite, in spite of the then beginning of the assault on his reputation that would culminate some years later in Ruth Dudley Edwards' vicious work. I began to drift, finding it difficult to fit Pearse within the hard boundaries of the debate, but unwilling to yield up his wonderful sense of self-sacrifice and love of nation. Displaced Catholicism perhaps. We had seminars for which papers were dutifully prepared and I proposed doing mine on Pearse, against opposition from within the Republican Club itself, some of whose members had themselves become embarrassed by Pearse. Meanwhile, our leaders were real-life heroes of the 1940s and 50s. Cathal Goulding, Seán Garland and Seamus Costello were living, visible, here-and-now revolutionaries, who had done prison time, or carried the scars of British bullets on their bodies, unlike the dead and distant heroes of the other left-wing groups. My confidence grew as, through discussion and study, I hammered out cast-iron certainties.

In revolutionary politics, availability is everything and shortly before Christmas 1969 I was asked to be secretary of the Republican Club. By now, rumours of a split in the IRA and the formation of the Provisionals were hitting the papers, but the Provisionals had no presence in the university and thus initially passed me by. They served, though, as a handy butt, in that when our revolutionary bona fides came under challenge, we could always point to the split as the place where we had shed our 'bourgeois element', along with the 'Trotskyists' and assorted 'Fianna Fáil adventurists'. The language of the time is something I look back on now appalled, and in wonder at how we could all have taken ourselves so seriously.

Meanwhile, there were aspects of republicanism that continued to embarrass me, in the shape of its attachment to the Irish language and sports. The *United Irishman* always carried a piece in Irish as well as some Gaelic sports coverage on the back page and one Friday I was accosted in the Great Hall by John Feeney, who demanded to be told what Gaelic football or the Irish language had to do with revolution. Not much in my view, but I did manage, in a dig at Feeney's Christian Marxism, to wonder out loud what God himself had to do with revolution either, so just about holding my own.

The ard fheis at which Sinn Féin split – ostensibly over participation at Westminster and the two partitionist assemblies in Ireland – took place in January 1970 at the Intercontinental Hotel on the same weekend as a large anti-apartheid march directed against the South African rugby team, who were playing Ireland in nearby Lansdowne Road. I attended some of the latter and most of the former as one of the lucky two from UCD with Republican Club visitor cards. Though I saw Seán MacStiofáin and other Provisional leaders speak out, they didn't, for me, hold the charge that the better-known Gouldings, Garlands and Costellos possessed. The media was expecting a walk-out and indeed it did take place that evening. Fortuitously, RTE had filmed the ard fheis breaking for lunch and this lunchtime clip, in which I was clearly visible, was the one shown on television that night, thereby producing an impression among those I knew that I was a Provisional.

Around this time, too, I began to make efforts to join the IRA, firstly by approaching the best-connected person in the Republican Club. He was horrified and made it perfectly clear that the IRA was not for the likes of us but for the working-class lads from Coolock, Ballyfermot and Finglas. I pressed on and what seemed to be a considered response did eventually come back, the gist of which was a repeat of the previous advice. The IRA had enough foot soldiers; there was serious revolutionary business to be done and the role envisaged for students like myself was that we would get our degrees and then be assisted, infiltrated, into the civil service, media and trade unions. Entryism of this kind did in fact occur and it presented the student rebels of my time with an easy choice, allowing them to enjoy the excitement of subversion while taking none of the risks. I tried separately, through a contact in the Labour Party – who had introduced me to a leading IRA and Sinn Féin member in a Dublin pub – but from him I received an even starker response: to even *want* to join the IRA was indicative of my immature adventurism. My place, my role in the coming revolution, was to be an entirely different one. I was devastated.

In February, John Taylor, the then unionist Minister of State for Home Affairs, came South to address one of the student societies in UCD. Taylor was a comparative sophisticate for a unionist, a regular visitor to the South, and a thoroughly unpleasant opportunist who subsequently gained a well-deserved reputation for political game-playing, and even then you could sense him striking a pose. He enraged us by deliberately conflating revolutionary republicanism with the failures of the de Valera regime, contrasting the North with its industry and British standard of living with the pastoral, agricultural, priest-ridden South. In advance of the meeting, I and a group of Maoists, anarchists and one or two Republican Club members had armed ourselves with a dozen eggs and a few tomatoes; when Taylor rose to speak, I too stood up and made a short unscheduled speech, to the horror of some of the Republican Club members present. My message for Taylor was that we intended, Frank Ryan-like, to deny him the freedom to deliver his fascist views and, having announced this, we let fly at him with the eggs and tomatoes. Taylor grabbed a chair and managed to deflect most of the material while my friends and I were duly set upon by a bunch of agricultural students and half-kicked, half-thrown out of the hall.

The action established my standing as a leading republican in UCD, and among the remaining Club members as a loose cannon, but there was not a lot they could do about it and, as the second term dragged on and exams beckoned, there was little enough happening in UCD in any event.[1] The Taylor incident got some publicity in the press and there were expressions of outrage at a visitor to the university being denied free speech. I sent unapologetic letters to the *Irish Times* and *Irish Independent* justifying the action by reference to what was happening in the North with Taylor's help. I got dirty looks from a couple of our own members, as well as from some law students from the North, but many more seemed to feel that we had given Taylor what he deserved. The strangest response came from another law student who head-hunted me for Fine Gael, which was then in the heyday of its Just Society phase and claiming to be 'socialist' as well. Offering that I had demonstrated initiative and a preparedness to work hard, he suggested that my political future would be more secure within an established party since, according to him, those who had reached officer board level within either Fianna Fáil or Fine Gael at university had, if they wanted it, invariably gone on to become Dáil deputies. Even in the halcyon days of student revolution, it seems, personal ambition was the motor driving student politics; the revolutionaries, in Orwell's phrase, little more than social climbers with bombs in their pockets.

On Easter Sunday 1970 I took part in the march to Deansgrange Cemetery, one among the dozens of events in which republicans assemble at graveyards throughout Ireland to celebrate the 1916 Rising and relate it to the present day. Cathal Goulding spoke there, his emphasis on the need to promote revolution in the South, and afterwards my girlfriend and I struggled with the UCD Republican Club banner on the walk home. The following Friday Garda Richard Fallon was shot dead on Arran Quay by Saor Éire members (an offshoot of the Dublin IRA unit) following a bank robbery, having arrived, unarmed, on the scene and confronted the robbers. The reaction was extraordinarily muted and testifies to the confused politics of the time, when it was quite fashionable to be anti-State.[2] Indeed, there were rumours –

[1] I vetoed a proposal some weeks later to give George Colley, then a government minister, the same treatment during his appearance at one of the student societies. Colley's daughter, Anne, was a fellow law student, and I knew a line from Graham Greene which said it was unforgivable to embarrass a father in front of his child.
[2] Though the front page of the *Irish Times* the following day carried a complaint from a Special Branch member that they had 'always been painted as the villains, the ones

which have persisted to this day – that the weapon used was one of a consignment purchased with the help of government money and that the escape of the on-the-run robbers had been assisted by a government minister.

Pouring fuel on the rumours, the Arms Crisis erupted into public view just weeks later when Lynch sacked two ministers, Charlie Haughey and Neil Blaney, for allegedly attempting to import arms for the Official IRA. A third, Kevin Boland, resigned in sympathy, while Justice Minister Micheál Ó Móráin had also resigned a couple of days previously, supposedly for health reasons. These men were hate figures for the left generally. Haughey's self-regard and ambition were obvious even back then, while Conor Cruise O'Brien had exposed his personal corruption in relation to land dealing during the 1969 general election. Ó Móráin had memorably described the Labour candidates in that election as a collection of 'left-wing political queers from Trinity College', while Blaney was the Fianna Fáil strategist who bore most responsibility for the red scare tactics that proved so effective against them. Boland, meanwhile, was the scourge of the Dublin Housing Action Committee, as well as the man responsible for the rigging of electoral boundaries that resulted in Fianna Fáil increasing its share of seats despite a fall in its share of the vote.

The Arms Crisis, which deepened some weeks later when criminal charges were brought against Haughey, Blaney and others, meant little to me. I detested Fianna Fáil and was quite happy with the Officials' line, that a section of that party were involved in efforts to further the split in the IRA by promoting the interests of right-wing Provisionals who, in return, would confine themselves exclusively to the North. It wouldn't have been a bad strategy. The Provisionals in Belfast were somewhat insular in view of what had happened there, and it was not unreasonable that they would seek and accept arms or cash from any

---

who are brutal', they continued to receive bad press with complaints of heavy-handed behaviour in the aftermath of the shooting coming from various civil liberties groups. Meanwhile, a statement from Saor Éire following Fallon's State funeral could scarcely have been more hard-line. Denying establishment claims that Garda Fallon was killed while protecting the public, it said that on the contrary, 'He died protecting the property of the ruling class who are too cowardly and clever to do their own dirty work.'

quarter. The Southern government, meanwhile, feared the republicans might make rapid progress on the back of what was happening in the North and were determined not to assist in their own destabilisation. They were also fed up with being castigated as Green Tories – complete with the promise that we'd be coming after them next – by the likes of Bernadette Devlin, who, when given the keys to the city in New York, had promptly handed them over to the Black Panthers, in the process outraging much of Irish America as well as conservatives at home.

In the circles in which I moved, the killing of Garda Fallon was treated as pretty much his own fault and at worst an unfortunate tragedy. On the Friday night of the killing I sat in a pub in Dun Laoghaire as the news came in and heard real working men at the bar railing angrily against the IRA. I was wearing a Connolly badge on my then de rigueur combat jacket, a sure giveaway, and thought the men might have a go at me. Though mildly shocked, I was already well on my way over to the other side and could easily see how the killing might have happened. Shortly afterwards, I duly failed my Law exams and headed off to England once more.

***

I arrived in London and linked up with a friend from Blackrock College. He was an advanced sort of fellow who was apprenticed in the wine trade and worked in a wine shop on King's Road in Chelsea. This was an exotic location for an Irish Catholic just turned twenty and I enjoyed it greatly. My friend worked with a pair of homosexual brothers, one as brazen as could be, the other barely out of the closet, and the banter was terrific, though they both seemed to have lives of endless abuse and sadness. My pal was on his way to Israel to work on a kibbutz, but meanwhile he introduced me to his political circle. The Irish National Liberation Solidarity Front (INLSF) was a quasi-Maoist outfit, a typical London micro-group, with an assortment of ex-Connolly Association and other Marxists, and we all addressed each other as 'Comrade'. It was fronted by a South African, who was quite an orator, and the vice-chairman was a Belfast housepainter who subsequently joined the IRA. Though certain this was not my political home, I attended INLSF meetings and occasionally helped sell their paper, and while suspect for defending Bernadette Devlin, I was forgiven on account of my relative youth and because I was actually Irish. Ideological impurity was the great enemy, especially Trotskyism in its various guises, though I cannot now remember whether its paper really once carried the headline 'Irish people demand to know the true facts about renegade Trotsky', or if Brendan Holland and I later imagined that one up in Long Kesh.

I was still formally pro-Official – the split having by then fully crystallised – but was on the political move, from necessity more than anything else, since there seemed to be no prospect whatsoever of my getting to join the IRA. When you deliberate, the die is cast, as Sartre once said, and the INLSF was regularly ripping into the Officials; fortuitously, around this time another left-wing paper carried material painting the Provisionals as a movement combining disparate influences, vaguely anarchist, but in any case revolutionary, or at least potentially so, in contrast to the hopeless Moscow-style reformism of the Officials. This argument made it possible to outflank the Officials on the left, using lines with which I was familiar from university, and I began to look more closely at the Provisionals.

The Provisionals had given five reasons for the split. The first and most striking was opposition to the proposal to abandon abstentionism: the refusal to take up parliamentary seats in what were considered to be partitionist assemblies established by the British. This had, for a long time, been the defining position from which the republican movement claimed the unbroken legitimacy that gave it the moral authority to wage war and take lives. The Provisional leaders argued that to abandon abstentionism would not only undermine the republican claim to legitimacy but would also inexorably lead to reformism and absorption into the system, as it had always done in the past. Abstentionism was presented by the Provisionals as a revolutionary principle, and it served them well, ensuring that the undivided energy of the movement was, from the earliest days, directed towards revolutionary objectives.

The Provisionals objected, secondly, to the proposal to establish a national liberation front, which really amounted to an organisational

alliance with the communists, together with such left-wing independents as might trail along. Again, this was a proposal that could
be attacked from right or left. Though the Provisional leaders were
critical of the 'extreme socialism' of the Officials, it was just about
possible to ignore the embarrassing rhetoric, particularly since they
were also anti-Moscow and insistent that the road to socialism should
be an Irish one. Thirdly, they objected to the methods of internal discipline which had been used to silence dissidents, a placeholder for the
Leninist democratic centralism then practised within the movement.
Ironically, this would also come to characterise the Provisionals in the
1980s and 90s, but there was no sign of it back in 1970 when simple
membership entitled you to a place in a conversation of equals which
allowed you to argue just about any position. Fourthly, there was an
unbridgeable difference over Stormont, with the Officials arguing for
its retention and reform, and the Provisionals for its abolition. The fifth
reason, military policy – for which read the then leadership's failure to
adequately defend Catholics in Belfast during the August 1969 attacks
– spoke for itself. In the North this was the most important reason of all
and it may well be that there would have been a breakaway movement
even without the other factors. Events in the North, together with the
attempt to abandon abstentionism, created a coalition of republicans,
North and South, who for one reason or another opposed the reformist agenda of the Officials.[3]

The Provisional leadership, some of whom had waited all their adult
lives for this moment, were determined to seize it and agreed a three-
stage strategy at an early meeting of the Army Council in January 1970

---

[3] The 'deep' Official Republican and NICRA strategy was to seek to remove Protestant
advantage through a civil rights campaign that would result in 'British' standards of
equality for all. This would destroy the rationale for unionism and by 'showing' the
loyalists that the small advantages they had enjoyed were no longer dependent on
their support for unionism, bring them to realise their class interest lay in collabora-
tion with their Catholic neighbours. Among the problems with this was that – should
the theory prove correct – if and when the loyalists arrived blinking into the light,
there was no reason at all why they should seek to join the much less economically
successful South. Indeed, on the contrary, any normalisation within the North might
just as well result in the thus far alienated Catholics becoming reconciled to both the
Northern state and the British link – as may now be happening.

(though obviously I knew nothing of this at the time). In the first phase the IRA would prepare for the defence of nationalist areas to ensure that what had occurred in 1969 would never happen again. In the second, defence would be combined with retaliation against whomever it required, and the strategy would conclude with a full-blown armed offensive against the British presence in Ireland. An intense programme of recruitment, training and arms procurement, meanwhile, was to take place in order to put the IRA in a position to deliver. This was a strategy designed with Belfast, in particular, at its centre and it is clear in retrospect that the IRA leadership there showed great patience in not allowing itself to be drawn into confrontations it was unable to handle. Of course it takes two to tango, and both the loyalists and the British would now behave in a manner that can be seen to have served IRA strategic interests in ways that are simply beyond parody.

The first physical force response to the troops came from the loyalists, who reacted to British proposals for reform with riots and gunfire on the Shankill Road in October 1969; one RUC man died, ironically the first police casualty of the so-called Troubles. Two blameless Protestant civilians were also shot dead, the earliest in a long series of controversial killings by the British army that would follow.

Meanwhile, the British enjoyed an extended honeymoon period with nationalists, during which British government ministers received ecstatic welcomes on walkabouts and soldiers dated Catholic girls – though the latter practice would go on to produce predictable resentments amongst young nationalist males. Most Catholics were hugely relieved that the British army had saved them from the loyalists and, in the then climate, anti-imperialist chit-chat was unlikely to cut much ice with the intended recipients.

By Easter 1970, though, the nationalist mood was shifting. A commemoration in Derry was followed by trouble outside the local RUC barracks and things took an even more dramatic turn in the Ballymurphy area of Belfast, after nationalists there took exception to an exercise in Orange coat-trailing facilitated by British troops. Rather than hold the line between the two sets of troublemakers, the British chose to wade in against the residents with batons and the indiscriminate firing of volleys of CS gas. Three days and nights of fierce rioting took place, with loyalists piling into Ballymurphy in the wake of the Scottish soldiers – much as they had done behind the RUC the previous August, which the IRA wisely stayed in the background, too weak at this stage to engage the army. This was a radicalising moment for Northern nationalists, who now saw that little enough had changed, with bigoted Scotsmen simply replacing the hated RUC as the primary aggressors. Though, like much else that would follow, the result of accident rather than any predetermined plan, the Ballymurphy riots were a key turning point, and when the British commander in the North, General Ian Freeland, announced that in future petrol bombers would be shot, the IRA promptly said that this would fetch the appropriate response from it.

In their anxiety to shore up Chichester-Clark, the British decided to allow further loyalist marches to skirt close to nationalist areas. Their partiality became even more marked after local right-wing successes in the British general election in June, which saw Edward Heath and the Conservatives come to power. Chichester-Clark was by then under intense pressure, not just from his own right wing, but from outside the party, and especially from Ian Paisley, the anti-Catholic demagogue, whose sinister machinations contributed perhaps more than any other single individual to the events that engulfed the North.

But by now the IRA was ready to take action. On 27 June, separate loyalist marches went by Ballymurphy and Ardoyne, sparking an anti-British riot in the former and exchanges of gunfire with IRA men in the latter. In the course of the gun battle three loyalists were shot dead, producing instant support for the Provisionals, who were now seen locally as having delivered on their promise that there would be no repeat of August 1969.

A loyalist mob later gathered on the fringes of the Catholic Short Strand enclave in east Belfast and, while the British army ignored them, they launched an armed attack on St Matthew's Catholic Church. The then brigade officer commanding (O/C), Billy McKee, had made his way across to Short Strand earlier that evening before the British blocked the bridge over the river – cutting it off from the rest of nationalist Belfast – and now he stayed to personally lead the defence of the area. While the army remained on the edges, gun battles raged and, as dawn broke, it was clear that the armed loyalists had been repulsed. Three loyalists and an IRA auxiliary were shot dead, McKee himself suffered a number of gunshot wounds, but the church and the streets of Short Strand still stood. The Battle of St Matthew's was the event that marked the rebirth of the IRA, which was credited with having saved the area from a loyalist mob while the British army and RUC stood by. Ourselves alone – no one else could be relied on. The Provisionals had delivered in a gun battle which could hardly have helped them more had it been choreographed, shot for shot, by McKee himself.

Though an act of omission of monumental stupidity by the British, still further evidence of British crassness came just one week later when an arms search in the Lower Falls Road area produced a sequence that was allowed to spiral wildly out of control, as minor riot fetched up army reinforcements, causing further rioting. When the British withdrew to the periphery to regroup, the Official IRA opened up on them and, outraged, Freeland decided to 'secure' the area, imposing a curfew of doubtful legality which lasted for 36 hours. During this time the area was blanketed in CS gas, three civilians were shot dead by trigger-happy soldiers, and a fourth was killed when an army vehicle crushed him against a wall. There was much gratuitous violence by the army as well as deliberate damage to property, incidents of theft and looting, and even allegations of indecent assault. What became known locally as the Siege of the Lower Falls was lifted when hundreds of women descended on the area with supplies of food, and then left with IRA weapons concealed in prams and in their clothing. The conviction that the British were irredeemably pro-unionist was copper-fastened when two Stormont ministers were pictured grinning from ear to ear in the open back of an army Land Rover as they were driven in triumph through the putatively subjugated Falls and, with this clear signal, the year-long honeymoon between nationalist Belfast and the British army was at an end.

Chapter 3

Just days after the Falls Curfew, the INLSF gave me my physical entrée to the North. Among the assorted revolutionaries in London, there was an Englishman – let's call him Albert – who may well have been a British agent or provocateur, but who had been in both Derry and Belfast in 1969 and had republican contacts with whom he promised to put me in touch. I arrived on the Liverpool boat a couple of days before the 12 July Orange marches and spent a night with the Salvation Army before meeting up with Albert. He introduced me to a man called Charlie who lived in Coates Street, in one of the handful of houses which had survived the August 1969 riots when much of the street was burned down. Charlie's house was bang on the peace line, directly opposite a British army barracks where west Belfast girls were still attending soldiers' discos.

Albert went off and did whatever it was he was doing, but left altogether after a couple of days. I stayed on with Charlie for a week or so, being brought from bar to bar and learning something of the geography of Belfast. Although serious trouble was anticipated, it was a quiet enough week in the North and I spent a good part of it in the Castle Street bars where I drank pints of porter – which had by then disappeared from Dublin – at ten old pence a pint, and argued furiously with men twice and three times my age who still believed the South, and Charlie Haughey in particular, would come to their rescue. On 12 July I awoke to the thud of the Lambegs and went to the edge of the city centre to watch the parade go by, and later – in an act of mindless bravado – walked across the Shankill to reach Ardoyne. Charlie had some level of involvement with the Officials and introduced me to various people of doubtful influence with a view to helping me join the IRA – either IRA would have done.

The importance of my first stay in Belfast was that I now had my own contact there as Charlie said I was more than welcome to stay with him any time. Clean out of money, I headed home to Dublin some days later, where relations with my father were furiously strained by my refusal to repeat my failed exams. I got part-time work and in the evenings watched Wimbledon with a couple of old school friends while I considered my next move.

On 31 July the British army shot dead Danny O'Hagan, a nineteen-year-old who was allegedly throwing petrol bombs, marking a further escalation in things. I went to the Gardiner Street offices of the Officials and told a surprised Mick Ryan, then a senior Official, that I was ready to fight and asked where to report. Ryan had no reply for me and I stalked off furiously to make my own way to Belfast, this time with a small box of .22 ammunition a friend had managed to get, which I gave to Charlie as a peace offering for the Officials. The killing of Danny O'Hagan was a turning point in the North. This time, the restraints that had been still visible a couple of weeks earlier were gone and, with both sides spoiling for a fight, riots took place across the city at various levels of intensity. I was in the thick of it in the Divis Flats where I got my first taste of CS gas, hurling rocks, and advancing and retreating with the other youths with vinegar-soaked handkerchiefs held to our faces. The Flats were held for a time, while the soldiers shouted up sectarian slogans they had borrowed from the Shankill, but the rioting eventually ceased, apparently on Official IRA orders. I watched from the darkness inside one of the flats as British soldiers casually smashed in all the windows along the walkways, and then heard local curate Father Murphy announce through a British army megaphone, against the evidence of my own eyes, that it was the IRA who had done it.

Through the Divis riots I had met my first Provisionals and for a few days it looked as if I might get to join the Belfast Brigade. I was interviewed twice in houses in the Falls Road area, the second time by an older man who said they would love to have me, but a couple of days later the answer came back that I would have to go home and join the queue in Dublin. My disappointment was so visible that this man advised me of a back-door means of getting into the action quickly by joining the IRA in England where, he told me, it was recruiting, and I made my way there on the Liverpool boat the very next day.

I had been given the address of a Sinn Féin contact in London and was told to approach the house carefully since it would be watched from time to time. I arrived late at night and walked by the house a number of times, looking hard for signs that the police were about. I had absolutely no idea how to do this and was relying on my imagination and what I may have seen at the pictures. Eventually, although far from satisfied, I turned into the driveway and knocked on the door. A man called Tom opened it. He was a leading Sinn Féin member in London whom I had already seen speak from platforms. I introduced myself and told him who had sent me. He ushered me into the kitchen and made tea while I told him my business. I gave him a shortened version of why I was there, and showed him evidence of who I was in the shape of a cutting from the *Irish Times* which had carried my letter defending the disruption of the university meeting the previous spring. I had been expecting a grilling but Tom asked me no questions and we simply spoke about the general political situation and Belfast in particular, since I had just come from there. This was standard; there was then an extraordinary tendency to take people on face value. He brought me into his sitting room and introduced me to his family as 'John'. This, too, was typical, and everyone knew that whatever my name was, it certainly wasn't John. It was a Saturday night, but Tom was one of those rare republicans: a non-drinker. Having made sure I was okay for somewhere to stay, he introduced me to his daughter, who, in Brendan Behan's phrase, would have been about my weight, and told me she would be my contact with the England O/C, with whom I was to be put in touch the following day. The very acronym, reversing the usual British designation with which I was familiar from comics and war films, sent a frisson of excitement through me.

That night I could hardly sleep. In the morning I put on my toughest demeanour and headed for Hyde Park, where I was to meet Tom's daughter and get passed on. She arrived on time with a short, fresh-faced man beside her whom I will call Jim. The girl left us and we began to walk. I retraced the story I had given Tom the previous night. I was fairly practised at it now, having told it a few times in Belfast, but Jim pressed me a bit harder than Tom, tracing back into my past, into how I had gotten involved and why I wanted to join the IRA, and warned me of the near certainty of imprisonment or death. He told me he would see me the following Saturday, and that meantime I should get myself a job and start merging into the background. I was not to hang around republicans – which wasn't a problem since I knew none – and was to stay away from Tom except in an emergency. The following day I went out to the agencies and picked up casual work and for the next few weeks I filled in at factories and on delivery trucks. I was staying in a house on the outskirts of London with mainly English students, far from Kilburn, Camden Town and the other Irish enclaves. Perfect cover according to Jim, who himself used to hold open house for English students in his university town home.

On Saturday I met Jim again, this time near King's Cross station. He told me that I had been checked out and cleared to join. I was impressed and had visions of assorted IRA men working through a vast network of contacts in Belfast and in Dublin, right back to my schooldays. There were a couple of things I hoped they hadn't managed to hit on. Jim stayed with me for the afternoon. He was from Tyrone and spoke bitterly about the situation in the North, the mendacity of the Southern government, his hatred of the Officials, and his hopes for England, which was then being reorganised and for which he was preparing an ambitious plan. He was fairly open about the resources he had, and about what was being worked on, and told me I would be travelling to the Midlands the next day for training.

On Sunday I caught a train to a Midlands city and made my way to a housing estate on the outskirts. There I knocked on the door and introduced myself to Mick. Mick was from Meath and was an impressively large man with steady hands and a casual manner. After a friendly grilling – during which he dropped names right, left and centre, so making it clear to me that he was an important IRA man – he got out his little bag of tricks and spent the next couple of hours showing me how to strip a Walther P38 and guiding me through the basic bits and pieces of bombing equipment that he had. He later took me out to a nearby wood and let me fire the weapon. He stressed that it was a weapon, not a gun, and that the latter was a civilian word never to be used by soldiers like ourselves. The thrill of cocking and then firing the weapon, finger held hard against the trigger guard as I had been shown between the couple of shots he allowed me, was fantastic; the weight of the weapon, the crack of the gunshot, the smell and taste of cordite, the power and sudden violence that emanated from what was in fact a small pistol – unforgettable.

Back in the house, my excitement palpable after the outing, my new mentor asked me if I had been sworn in. I hadn't and he straightaway rectified this oversight on Jim's part – though it would have been difficult for the latter to conduct the ceremony, given that our only contact had been in public places – and swore me in then and there. I raised my right hand and repeated the words of the Army declaration after him: 'I, Kieran Conway, hereby promise that I will promote the aims and objects of Óglaigh na hÉireann to the best of my knowledge and ability and that I will obey all orders issued to me by the Army authority and by my superior officers.'

I was in. There was no lecture, no other introduction, nothing else to it. He just said, 'You're an IRA man now.' I all but trembled with pride at this unshareable knowledge, the formal culmination of everything I had hoped and wished for over the past twelve months. I had made it and now my chosen destiny was about to unfold before me. I had lost interest in sport sometime previously, just one more opiate of the people, and now determined to stop listening to popular music as well. Oh, and no more dope. It was time to give up on childish things.

***

Soon afterwards, I was introduced to Pat Ward, a rangy Donegal man in his mid-20s, from a small-farming background. He was Jim's right-hand man and had been a member of the Communist Party in Britain before going to Derry in 1969, where he participated in the rioting, becoming a republican and subsequently joining the IRA. He was bright and exceptionally well read for someone with little by way of formal education, something that can be attributed in part to his period with the communists. I had found a soul mate, my first true comrade, and had long theoretical discussions with him about Marxism and anarchism, as well as the Irish situation. Pat was a provocative thinker and I was never quite sure to what extent he had his tongue in his cheek when suggesting post-revolutionary changes, such as a mandatory return to pre-Christian paganism and the Brehon laws. He was clear-sighted, decisive and utterly fearless on operations, and his confidence made him an easy man to follow. His health suffered as a result of a series of hunger strikes he later undertook in Portlaoise Prison and he died prematurely in 1988.

The England IRA unit had been broken up in mid-August when Scotland Yard raided an engineering training session and arrested a number of men, including the then O/C and, crucially, Jim Monaghan from Dublin – head of the Dublin active service unit before the split and one of the IRA's leading engineers – who had been sent over to do the training. Accordingly, I was joining at a time when England was in upheaval and Jim was looking for willing hands.

By now living back in Russell Square, I socialised in nearby Camden Town, where Pat lived in various squats, and where another of our unit had a spectacularly loud and torrid relationship with a Connemara girl who, in an act of linguistic sectarianism, broke the Munster Gaelic long-playing records from which he was trying to learn the language. In the first couple of months, Pat and this other man would disappear from time to time, and though I knew better than to ask where they had been, I was aware that a senior British officer was being specifically targeted. Jim's initial injunction to stay away from other republicans had meanwhile very quickly gone by the board and, aside from drinking in the Camden Town bars, we would occasionally venture over to Kilburn to see other volunteers, or down to Streatham in south London where the remnants of the old England unit were based. Security was appalling and I often ended up drinking with well-known Sinn Féin members and the relatives of IRA prisoners in south London pubs where republican ballads were blasted out. Jim himself breached security, turning up to Sinn Féin meetings a couple of times with Pat and me in intimidatory tow to demand funding for the unit.

I got a job with a marine underwriters in the City, where I went each day to tap in accounts figures and meet with *Daily Telegraph* readers, among them a special constable with whom I exchanged prescient banter, who told me he had joined up with a view to shortcutting his way into MI5. Though working-class London could be a different matter, in the heart of the City I encountered no anti-Irishness at all, rather a sense of bemusement as to what was going on in the North, and I continued to like the English.

In Belfast, the IRA had gone on a limited offensive after Easter, with McKee authorising selective sabotage operations and the first of the incendiary attacks on city centre shops. In early July an army recruiting office there was wrecked in an explosion and, in quick succession over the following days, a hotel and a clothing company were bombed, before a blast at a Northern Bank branch resulted in the first instance of widespread civilian injuries from flying glass. I was in Belfast at the time and had walked by the bank a little bit earlier, and could easily have been caught in the explosion.

Following Danny O'Hagan's death, the bombing intensified, with attacks in Armagh, Lurgan, Newcastle, Newry and Magherafelt, as well as in Belfast. On 11 August matters became a lot more serious when two RUC men were killed in south Armagh after they opened the door of a booby-trapped car. Though the British army was the intended target, this did show a new willingness to kill and, though no one ever claimed it, there is no doubt that the IRA was responsible. In November, General Farrar-Hockley warned that the British army was gearing up to face a prolonged IRA campaign. Rioting was taking place almost daily; in Ardoyne the first nail bombs had been thrown, causing the tabloid press to react with horror, and by the close of the year, the bombing of utilities in border areas and beyond were regular occurrences.

Shortly after Christmas I was sent home for training with another seven or eight England volunteers. Having travelled separately, we met up in Parnell Square and were moved from there to a nearby house where Seán MacStiofáin turned up to look us over. He was then chief of staff and cut a formidable figure, though his English-accented Dublinese was peculiar. Also there was Paddy Ryan, one of

MacStiofáin's right-hand men and the then director of training. Paddy was a Limerick man long domiciled in Dublin, where he worked as a milkman, and three or four of us piled into his car. We rendezvoused with the others at one of the pubs along the Naas Road and were soon on our way to the Midlands, where the camp was supposed to take place. There was some last-minute problem there, so Paddy drove us through the night to a farm somewhere on the Limerick–Tipperary border where – after heated discussion with a clearly reluctant farmer sympathiser – we finally parked. The others arrived soon afterwards, along with two training officers, Pat McKenna from Dublin, who was in charge, and Robby Donnelly from Derry. Neither are their real names.

McKenna was a pre-1969 IRA man who, along with Jim Monaghan and others such as Seán Treacy, was key to the Provisionals' success in getting going, providing a youthful Southern component for training and general back-up. McKenna, so I heard, had been out trawlering when the split in the Army took place, and was greeted on his return by the sight of both MacStiofáin and Goulding standing well apart on the pier in Howth waiting for him. His decision to go with MacStiofáin was important and, as a vocal socialist, he easily gave the lie to the notion of the Provisionals as counter-revolutionary right-wingers. But my admiration for McKenna was then in the future as he lined us up in the farmyard and put us through our paces like any British sergeant major, barking commands in Irish and curling his lip with contempt at our clumsy efforts at coming to attention or standing at ease. Colm D., in particular, shook with hatred as McKenna had a withering go at his unsoldierly appearance, and I bristled in resentful solidarity with Colm. I liked McKenna even less when I gathered that he was refusing to take a stint at 'stag' or sentry duty at night, on the grounds that, as the man in charge, he needed his sleep. McKenna's apparently anti-egalitarian attitudes and insistence on this modicum of drilling were out of line with my own expectations of brotherly relations within a revolutionary army, so much so that I challenged him about it. His explanations were standard need-for-discipline stuff, but the fact that he was prepared to discuss them with me went some distance towards mollifying me and, by the end of the week – though still dubious as to the value of parade ground discipline – I admired him hugely. As to drilling, what we learned was muted enough, confined as it was to showing us how to fall in before, and out after, a specific training session or IRA meeting, and I quickly got used to it that summer when I was sent to the border and never questioned it again. We were supposed to be soldiers, albeit revolutionary soldiers, and all that being ordered to fall in and out really did was underline the switch into, and later out of, formal mode – though regular army-style drilling and marching would later become an issue in the prisons.

Robby was completely different to McKenna; a mild and friendly Derry man, he was there for the explosives part of our training. With the exception of the then on-the-run Seán Keenan – son of the IRA leader of the same name and also from Derry – we were England-based volunteers and the training was, so we were told, designed with that in mind. We were divided into two-man battle teams and trained in the use of short arms and explosives, both interspersed with tactical talks from Pat McKenna and fieldcraft sessions in the countryside after dark. As I remember it, there was a Luger, a Walther P38 and a number of ancient revolvers – old Webleys and Colts of the sort you might have seen in a western – which we learned to strip and clean to the point of monotony. The explosives lectures were more elaborate, with a heavy emphasis on safety and dire warnings as to what could occur otherwise. At this stage three volunteers – together with the two young daughters of one of them – had died in Derry in an accidental explosion, and another volunteer, Michael Kane, had been killed in a premature explosion while on an operation in Belfast in September 1970. Others had been injured, some of them seriously, in various accidents with explosives.

We were introduced to both commercial and electrical detonators, to fuse wire and alarm clocks, so we could make up either kind of basic timed device. The simplest bomb requires no more than a few sticks of gelignite taped together with a detonator and length of fuse inserted in one of them, which would be ignited by a volunteer at the chosen location. The person planting the bomb would then have a couple of minutes to make himself scarce, while hoping that no civilian chanced to be walking by when the charge exploded. Cheap clocks were combined with batteries and electrical detonators when greater delays were required. One wire was attached to the minute hand, the paint having first been scraped off to expose the metal, and the other to a tack inserted into the face of the clock. When the hand then reached the tack, the circuit was completed and the charge exploded. Clocks had to be checked with great care, and a number of volunteers were killed carrying these devices, which should never be carried primed but too often were. I had already been through the rudiments in England and, though not mechanically inclined, had no difficulty understanding what was required in safely assembling the basic charges.

One crude but simple timing device involved a wooden clothes peg with drawing pins as contacts. Soldering wire would be wrapped around the ends of the peg to keep the contacts apart, and the spring would gradually overcome the solder until the pins met and the circuit was completed. Obviously, different pegs and different wire would produce very different delays, as we learned by experimentation, and this method was one to be used only when relatively indifferent to timing. The same clothes peg, this time with a wooden dowel separating the contacts, was also used – with the dowel attached to a trip wire made of fishing line in the most basic of booby traps – where the circuit was completed when the dowel was yanked out. Conventional landmines, based on line of sight, would be set off using electrical detonators attached to bell wire, with the circuit completed by pressing on a bell button or other domestic switch. We were also shown how to make the then standard incendiary, in which sulphuric acid was sealed within a candle wax container, produced by melting the wax onto a small test tube which, when it dried, was then placed within a condom, at that time still illegal in the South. The idea was that when the candle wax was broken by the person planting the device, the acid would burn, more or less slowly, through the condom and ignite an incendiary mix of sugar and sodium chlorate, the latter then still available over the counter as a weedkiller.

Robby also led us through the wider range of shaped charges, booby-trap devices and alternate timers – much of the information being drawn from British and US army field manuals – and showed us how to put together nail bombs, which had just appeared in the North. These were easy to make and required no more than a stick of gelignite wrapped in a strip of corrugated cardboard, into which nails were then slotted and secured with electrical tape. The device was completed by using something like the non-leaded end of a pencil to make a hole in the stick of gelignite, into which the detonator – attached to a short piece of fuse designed to give a seven- to ten-second delay – would later be inserted. The commercial fuse wire we used, which burned at a rate of 30 seconds to the foot, came in coils and might have suffered a degree of damp from poor storage, so, accordingly, different pieces from the coil were cut and carefully timed for consistency.

Many devices failed for want of this simple test, with the fuse simply fizzling out some time after being lit. You also had to be careful to measure the distance to the high explosive at the base of the detonator, both to ensure that the fuse wire did not come into direct contact with it and possibly set it off, while also leaving a short enough gap for the burn from the fuse to leap across. This was done by using a piece of paper or blade of grass which could be safely dropped into the open detonator to get the correct measure. Safety matches, rather than the red-topped 'friendly' ones, were taped to the open end of the fuse, accommodated by its being cut at a slant to expose the powder, and the fuse was then placed in the detonator, leaving the appropriate space as previously measured. Finally, the detonator was crimped to the fuse using a pliers or whatever other suitable tool might be to hand, often a penknife. Robby told a cautionary tale of a volunteer in west Tyrone who lost half his jaw, having stupidly crimped the detonator with his teeth in an act of showmanship, and we were under no illusion as to the comparative power of this tiny device, the size of a thin pen cover, having seen a number exploded in training. The final step was to insert the firing mechanism, the detonator plus fuse, into its already created space in the stick of gelignite, and secure it with electrical tape.

On the camp we had gelignite, plaster gelatine and a small amount of plastic explosive, which Pat McKenna confidently told us was the explosive substance we would be working with in the future. In fact, the opposite happened and once the sources of commercial gelignite had dried up towards the end of that year, the IRA campaign would rely more or less exclusively on home-made explosives until the Libyan arms shipments of the mid-1980s.

I found sentry duty especially difficult because of the responsibility I felt being placed on my barely adequate shoulders. We had staggered shifts and most nights I was woken by the volunteer coming off duty. I quietly crawled out of my sleeping bag and into the January night to briefly confer before taking over the weapon and standing – eyes straining against the darkness, every nerve on fire – staring at shadows and listening for breaks in the country silence: an approaching car, a rustle in the undergrowth or the quiet tread of approaching men. General Army Order No. 8 dictated that under no circumstances were Free State troops or Gardaí to be fired on and the idea was that, in the event of a raid, an orderly evacuation of the camp would take place along a prearranged route, taking the equipment with us if possible. We were instructed to wake McKenna in the event of any suspicions at all, but naturally I was just as worried about causing a false alarm. To add to my problems, McKenna had told us a story about how a camp had recently been raided, supposedly by the UVF, but in fact as part of a misguided training exercise. The volunteers had been dragged out of their sleeping bags and put up against the wall where one of them had had something resembling a breakdown and had gone to pieces. Though the pretence was quickly abandoned, this unfortunate, shamed and terrified, had decided he wasn't up to remaining in the IRA. I was almost as afraid that McKenna would set some sort of test for me that I would fail as I was of the Free Staters or UVF arriving in force.

The camp ended, as good camps did, with a shoot-off in a quarry some distance away. There we each got the rare opportunity – ammunition being in permanent short supply – of firing a live round or two from the various shorts and we also set off a series of mini-explosions. We were given the Luger and the P38 to bring back to England, along with a small explosives kit, and, for reasons that I cannot now recall, I took custody of the material and carried it in a duffle bag everywhere I went for the next month or so. Although I had been teamed up with Pat Ward on the camp, he had gone back to Donegal for a few weeks, while Jim, who was married with small children, was also absent.

Far from hitting the ground running, the next few weeks were cruelly boring. I had lost my base in Russell Square and moved into what were conventional digs in Kilburn, where I slept in a room with two or three young Irish labourers and took my duffel bag off to the City job each morning where it sat under my desk. In the evenings I avoided social-ising by spending time in Dirty Dick's – the famous London pub near Liverpool Street station – on my way home from work, duffel bag eter-nally to hand. As soon as I could manage it, I moved to a tiny bed-sit in Shepherd's Bush, which was a huge improvement in that at least it was possible to hide the bag there, basic concealment techniques having been something else we were shown at the camp.

Chapter 4

When Jim turned up again, his instructions had changed. The so-far desultory surveillance we had been doing on various public buildings and barracks across London – with an ambitious assassination and bombing campaign in mind – was being put on hold and, instead, we were to be involved for now in fund-raising. Armed robbery has a long and respectable revolutionary pedigree, even within the IRA, and I had no difficulty with it at all, not even when I was told the IRA would disown us if were caught, though in retrospect this was an unwise use of England-based volunteers.

By now I had realised that the volunteers in England were of two kinds. There were glorified Sinn Féiners whose roots had come to lie in England and who had jobs, flats and girlfriends or wives to protect, and a small number of us mad and dangerous more nomadic types with no ties whatsoever and nothing to lose. We got used to being let down, especially by drivers, to hearing the weak excuses of those who were now alarmed at what they may have let themselves in for, and to the bleak, unfriendly looks of their women as we sat in kitchens and living rooms where we were no longer welcome. I knew there were more volunteers coming in and, I suppose, to compensate for the type of operation we were being asked to undertake, we were told that we would be sent home for good in a particular order. The volunteer with the Connemara girlfriend had since decided against a future in the IRA and, having given up my job in the City, I had leapfrogged into the vacant place as Pat Ward's assistant and one of Jim's few full-time reliables. I was told that Pat was to go after the first batch of operations and me after the second, with the others to follow.

In and around Camden Town I met various Greek Cypriots who had fought in EOKA against the British, and one of the Saor Éire men then being sought for the Garda Fallon killing. On one occasion, we went out for a wages snatch which proved abortive and arrived at the second getaway car only to find a couple of Saor Éire men there. We assumed that they were planning to rob us in turn and avoided them thereafter. This part of London Ireland was peopled by an extraordinary mix of idealists, hard men, mavericks, chancers and informers, and there was a great deal of serious drinking, drug use and low-level crime. The IRA operation in England was premised on our being self-financing, and so I worked on and off on building sites and in factories, sometimes with Pat, sometimes on my own, seeing first-hand the way in which the Irish brutalised their fellow countrymen. I encountered the lump system a couple of times, myself and Pat a pair of sub-humans to be gratuitously picked or rejected from a bunch of men collected at a bus stop and taken off in a van for a day's work, getting paid cash in hand in a pub at the end of the day where you were expected to ensure that the drink flowed for your day's benefactor.

By late January 1971 riots, British army raids and IRA attacks were all but routine in Belfast, and, shortly afterwards, the army declared itself to be at 'battle' with the Provisionals and named Billy McKee, Proinsias MacAirt and others as its leaders in Belfast. In early February a volunteer, Jim Saunders, and a civilian, Bernard Watt, were shot dead in Ardoyne, the latter in another controversial shooting where the British press loyally repeated the line that Watt was a petrol bomber. The *Guardian* correspondent Simon Winchester defended his reporting of the army version as fact with the following syllogism: the army was not legally permitted to shoot rioters unless they were committing one of a number of specified offences; the army had shot Bernard Watt; therefore Bernard Watt must have been committing one of the specified offences.

On the same night Robert Curtis became the first British soldier to be killed in action when he was shot dead during a gun battle with IRA members in the New Lodge Road area. These deaths naturally received considerable publicity in London, particularly when television footage and newspaper photos from Jim Saunders' funeral showed a British soldier delivering a respectful military salute from the turret of his armoured car as the cortege went by complete with uniformed IRA guard of honour, and it was impossible not to get caught up in the unnerving feeling that things had been decisively stepped up. This was underlined soon afterwards when five civilians were killed when their Land Rover hit a tripwire on Brougher Mountain in County Tyrone, triggering a landmine. The men had been on their way to inspect a BBC transmitter on a route regularly travelled by the intended target, the British army, and died in precisely the type of operation that I had been trained for just weeks previously. Next came the killing of a second British soldier, this time in Ardoyne, quickly followed by the double killing of two RUC men, including a Special Branch detective inspector, also in Ardoyne. Ten days later came news of the roadside execution of three Scottish soldiers – two of them brothers aged seventeen and eighteen – who had gone drinking with the wrong people. Though denied by the IRA, whose denial I believed, these killings showed definitively that some dreadful corner had been turned.

While visiting the northwest of England where we were preparing a robbery, Pat and I accompanied Jim on a typical recruiting mission. From someone who knew someone in Sinn Féin had come the address of yet another would-be IRA man and, after updating ourselves on the forthcoming operation, we drove to Manchester where we knocked on the door of the parents of Michael Gaughan, a 21-year-old from Mayo. After the shortest of job interviews, Michael came away with us, his life transformed in that instant of decision. He died on hunger strike in Parkhurst Prison three years later, the first IRA hunger striker to die in the latest round of the conflict.

The robbery came off a couple of weeks later. We stayed overnight with the man who had set it up, an incredible number of tiny children running about our feet, his wife a bag of nerves. The next day we were let down by whoever was to be the driver on the job and, not for the last time, I saw an IRA unit forced to press someone else into service fast, with Jim himself driving a hastily borrowed getaway car.[4] On arrival, Pat and I pulled our jumpers up over our noses and entered the

---

[4] Short-notice drivers were always in demand. Many years later, the joke in Belfast was that men either denied they could drive at all, or had the good sense never to learn.

building, waving our short arms in the direction of an indignant, far-from-terrified wages clerk, who I truly feared would do something that would cause us to have to shoot him. He relented when Pat gave him a whack on the arm with a baton but continued to bristle resentfully. We made off with the few thousand pounds that were being prepared for wages, and after Jim withdrew a certain amount to keep England going, Pat and I got a train for Liverpool and then the Dublin boat. I had been on the boats before, but this time, for security reasons, we got a berth. While Pat slept noisily below me, I tossed and turned on the upper bunk, worried that he'd let fly at me with the short he had under his pillow. In Dublin we met up with MacStiofáin and Leo Martin, who had recently been named as one of the top Provisionals in Belfast. We handed over the money, which, as I recall, went straight into Leo's pocket for Belfast, and he and MacStiofáin questioned us in a friendly way about how things were in England.

We were to go to a second camp for which the travel arrangements were much as before. This time we did establish base in the Midlands, at the Heath near Portlaoise – Seán Treacy's home area. Although the bulk of the training was conducted by a Dublin volunteer who did not make an impression on me, Treacy – a member of the first Provisional Army Council – would turn up from time to time to run a session and I was utterly taken with him. Treacy, who had seen active service as a teenager in the 1956–62 campaign, taught moral lessons too and asked me one day what I would do in the event of a raid, if faced with the choice between saving myself or the weapons from capture. Weaponry was in very short supply at the time and I assumed the correct answer was to save the weapons and said so. He told me I was wrong and that while new weapons could always be obtained, I was irreplaceable and I should never forget it. This was an important moment which radically sharpened my own sense of worth to the Army and was a lesson I in turn used on training camps when I later came to run them myself.

The weaponry available was far more interesting this time and included a Belgian FN rifle – practically identical to the British self-loading rifle (SLR) then in use – a Lee Enfield .303, a US Garand, and a number of submachine guns, including a British army Sterling, the early World War II Sten it displaced, German and US machine guns, and the legendary Thompson, complete with dubious drum maga-zine. We learned to strip and assemble the weapons blindfolded, the Thompson with its handful of moving parts and huge rounds of .45 ammunition proving a particular hit with me, though, again, Treacy persuaded me that just about any rifle was preferable to a submachine gun in just about every situation.

Following a change of direction, presumably provoked by the Brougher Mountain disaster, it had been decided that explosives train-ing would be confined to specialists, and accordingly we received no engineering training this time. Instead, we concentrated on weapons and extensive fieldcraft, urban guerrilla warfare, street fighting, house clearing and so on. The battle-team concept survived and Pat and I did our stint of sentry duty together, using the time to improve our skills, though we both knew he was staying in Ireland and I was going back to England. Many of the sessions involved planning various ambushes and other operations – training that later proved pretty useful on the border but which I found of limited value when I was sent into Derry towards the end of the year.

Back in England, I was put in charge of a team that included Michael Gaughan, under Jim's ultimate control. Our instructions were straight-forward and we immediately started looking out for robberies from an intelligence base that was utterly blank. In hindsight, there were better ways of going about our task and we should have used the wider network of Sinn Féin members and sympathisers to set up raids prop-erly. But impatient for results, and lacking even a modicum of inside information, we were pressed remorselessly in the direction of the high street banks, it being obvious that nothing much was needed other than to get in there and take what money we could. The trouble was that, by now, we were being heavily monitored by the Special Branch. We knew we were being watched, though none of us had any idea of the scale of it until after the unit had been broken up and those arrested were shown photographs of themselves socialising in bars and walking with their girlfriends in various parks. On my twenty-first birthday we abandoned a robbery in Camden Town, calmly walking on and past the bank when we spotted the surveillance standing about waiting for us. Taking anti-surveillance measures even in a big city like London sounds easier than it actually is and, again not for the last time, increasing frustration resulted in an appropriate level of caution spilling first into paranoia and later into recklessness as everyone and everything became a possible watcher. Thus, having planned to rob another bank some time after the aborted operation in Camden Town and following a spate of similar abandoned operations, I was convinced that one member of the unit was running scared and determined that this time we were going ahead. On the morning of the planned raid, when this volunteer was sent out to steal a getaway car and came back reporting surveillance, I refused to accept it and frogmarched him back to the public car park where I stood over him while he hotwired the selected car.

The drill was for me to enter first and make for the counter, while Michael covered the handful of customers in the bank and a third member of the unit stood with a shotgun at the door. I would grab whatever cash was thrown to me by the tellers and then we would make our way out, piling into the getaway car and screeching off like something out of a bad movie, as the driver squealed around corners and banged off the occasional kerb.

Soon after one such episode, I was dropped off at a tube station, as planned, with the bulk of the cash, and made my way to King's Cross and from there to the house in the Midlands. I stayed the night there, moving out first thing the next morning and hitching a succession of lifts to Liverpool. I heard later that the police raided the house soon after I had left and have assumed that my unconventional mode of travel must have assisted me. At any rate, I caught the boat to Dublin without incident, although I could see plainclothesmen watching the passengers embark, and the next day again made my way to the Sinn Féin offices in Kevin Street where I unloaded the cash. I was home and looking forward immensely to whatever the Army had in mind for me. I had a quick debrief with Paddy Ryan, who told me I needed a break, gave me a tenner and said I should make myself scarce for a couple of weeks.

***

My parents had moved to Wexford town while I was away and I decided to go down to see them. By now my father had a fair idea of what I was at, but he assumed my involvement was on the fringes and certainly didn't take me or my republicanism seriously.[5] He was, though, resigned to the fact that I had dropped out of college and made no more than a perfunctory suggestion that I might get it together to go back the following autumn. I had been in Wexford just a couple of days when I went to a nearby pub to read the paper and stumbled on the news that Michael Gaughan and three others had appeared in a London court amidst a massive security operation, charged with bank robbery. I was effectively on the run and went back up to Dublin the following day and sought out Paddy Ryan to tell him so. This was fortuitous as it meant something actually had to be done with me. As I would find out later, Pat Ward had been sent to south Donegal, where he was asked to sell the republican paper, *An Phoblacht*, and, finding himself surplus to requirements, had simply gone home to Burtonport. Given the number of IRA volunteers then seeking full-time work, there is little doubt that this would have been my fate as well, at least in the short term. Instead, they were stuck with me, and after spending a few mind-numbing days holed up, literally, in Paddy's Walkinstown home – where Paddy would give me ten fags a day and the paper to read – I was fit to be tied. Finally, MacStiofáin himself came to see me and asked how I would feel about going into the training department. I was delirious at the prospect of getting to go anywhere at all and told him so. The first move was to attend another, seriously special, training camp, this time in the west of Ireland, where my own training was to be completed to a standard high enough to allow me to run camps myself.

On the way there, I spent a night billeted in Ruairí Ó Brádaigh's house in Roscommon. Though Ruairí was the then, and for long thereafter, president of Sinn Féin and a member of the Army Council, I wasn't as awestruck by him as I was by MacStiofáin and some of the others with a purely military profile within the movement. I also thought of him as the main progenitor of the watery socialism that was

---

[5] One of his favourite taunts was that 'We'd still be swinging from the trees if it wasn't for the British' – a line that would enrage me. Decades later I use it on my own son, though to lesser effect.

then Sinn Féin policy, but I was well aware of his record in the Army in the 1956–62 campaign, during part of which he had been chief of staff, and certainly I was respectful and attentive. In fact, Ruairí was among the more likeable of our then leaders and spent hours talking to me, drawing out my own views and giving me some insight into the personalities and thinking among the then leadership. Although there was no loose talk as such, there was a remarkable equality between leadership and volunteer in those early days, something that was killed off in the later 1970s.

The next morning I was picked up by a man I later discovered was a senior figure in the Belfast Brigade, and a young woman whom I would realise only when her picture appeared in the papers three years later, when she was being force-fed while on hunger strike, was Dolours Price. The pair were responsible for ensuring that the twenty or so Belfast volunteers I was about to be trained with made it to the various pick-up points and by nightfall I was on my uncomfortable way in the back of a crowded transit van with a bunch of Belfastmen, the last batch to be dropped at the final rendezvous. The camp was being run by the 1st Battalion, centred on Andersonstown, which seemed to have set up its own contact in west Mayo close to the mountains.

The training officer, Paul Marlowe, was a tall, lean, super-fit ex-British soldier who had served in both the Parachute Regiment and the Special Air Service, and the training reflected this. It was designed for a classic rural guerrilla war and, aside from transforming our fitness levels in the course of the week, it was hard to see its relevance for Belfast. We were taught the elements of map reading, use of a compass and how to crudely navigate by the stars. The fieldcraft we learned was much more advanced than previously and we were even shown how to abseil. These were skills that might have had some relevance in the border areas, but had none at all for what was unfolding in Belfast. The thinking seems to have been that the campaign in the city would be unsustainable when internment was introduced, as no one doubted it would be, and that the volunteers would reassemble in the border region from where the standard IRA rural campaign would be launched. If this was simply 1st Battalion rather than Belfast Brigade or leadership thinking, it was to have unintended consequences a year later when the British occupied the no-go areas during Operation Motorman, and the bulk of the 1st Battalion staff took off across the border only to find themselves treated as deserters rather than praised for their tactical acumen. Among other things, there was a concentration on the use of the standard British army self-loading rifle, on the assumption that the bulk of future IRA weaponry would be captured in the field. Marlowe also liberally borrowed tactics from Che Guevara's *Guerrilla Warfare*, such as singling out the point man or radio operator in ambushes *pour encourager les autres*.

This camp was the first I attended without running water or toilets and, although we had a farmer's outhouse to bed down in, conditions were spartan. I had slept on people's floors all over London and Dublin, but now, fully clothed in my sleeping bag, like Sartre's character in *Iron in the Soul*, I fancied I could feel the hardness of the concrete seeping into my body, making me strong. Marlowe wouldn't allow us to brush our teeth, pointing out that the smell of toothpaste was capable of being picked up downwind, and also refused us permission to smoke save at prearranged times, to add to the realism of the training. We had a Lee Enfield rifle that had been adapted to fire .22 ammunition, and this realism was underscored by his cheerful use of live ammunition, with us all suffering the nervy experience of hearing and feeling bullets whizzing by far too close as he taught us how to keep our heads down. At night he entertained us with his own SAS war stories from Borneo and Aden and I for one developed a healthy respect for both it and the better British army regiments. In the course of the week we were visited by a Japanese photojournalist who stayed for a couple of days and told us we were tougher than the Viet Cong – something that was praise indeed, even if we took it with a pinch of salt.

There was a considerable amount of gunfire at the camp and, despite our remote location, this attracted the attention of the authorities, and a spotter plane began to criss-cross the mountain. Marlowe ordered that the camp be broken up a day or two prematurely and although the area was said to have been cordoned off, we had no difficulty slipping through whatever lines there were, having first buried the arms in a temporary dump, and everyone got off the mountain and eventually back to Belfast safely. I would meet a number of the volunteers again in Long Kesh and elsewhere. One, Marty Forsythe, was killed in action within a couple of months, and Paul Marlowe himself died as the result of what seems to have been a premature explosion while on an operation in 1976.

Having come off the mountain, I was billeted for a few days in nearby Newport with Peter Rogers, who had been injured while abseiling on the camp and had been brought off some time previously. While there, I had my first encounter with the Special Branch when the house was raided. We both simply gave false names and refused to otherwise account for our movements. The detectives went away. Peter was an attractive character who was subsequently involved in the escape from the *Maidstone* prison ship. His IRA career took a tragic turn when, having married a local woman and settled in Wexford, he was responsible for the death of a local detective in 1980 and spent the next twenty years in Portlaoise Prison, time that became even harder to do when he fell out with the IRA leadership in the jail.

From Newport I was transported to Letterkenny by means that changed little in the succeeding years. What would happen was that you were passed from area to area – for example, from west Mayo to south Mayo, to north Mayo, through parts of Sligo and then various segments of Donegal – with the local unit or perhaps a single contact taking charge of you at one end of the area and seeing you safely through to the other. Contacts might be missed or lifts not materialise, but while you could find yourself spending a day or two in a safe house waiting for a pick-up, the system worked well and increased in sophistication as time went on. On this occasion, I went through three or four exchanges before being brought from Sligo to Bundoran. On the very first stop, somewhere in the wilds of west Mayo, I sat by a fireside and listened to an old man reminisce about the Tan War, the Civil War, Fianna Fáil and street fights with the Blueshirts in the 1930s, while his two sisters, covered from head to toe in black, worked quietly around him, one of them then joining us in silence at the fire, a clay pipe firmly stuck in her mouth in an Ireland that seemed not to have changed an iota in a hundred years. Billets and pick-up points varied widely and you could find yourself one night in the big house of a prosperous businessman being treated like royalty, and the next on a barely functioning small farm where conditions were primitive and your ageing host for the night might spend time comparing you unfavourably with the men who had stayed with him twenty or thirty years earlier.

In Bundoran I spent a couple of days waiting in Joe O'Neill's pub. Joe was well organised for visitors, with a billet-like set of bunk beds, and I met Seán Keenan from my first camp there, passing down the line in the opposite direction to myself. From Bundoran I was dropped in Ballyshannon; the bridge there was the only entry point on the southern side of the border to the rest of Donegal and would later be heavily policed. From Ballyshannon I was driven to Donegal town and from there passed on to Ballybofey and eventually Letterkenny. This was my final destination and after a couple of comfortable days billeted in Pat Dawson's house, then the titular O/C of Donegal, I was given a minimal briefing and driven to a newly established camp in the wilds of Donegal, close to the Carrigart home of Pat Doherty – later to be a senior IRA and Sinn Féin figure. There I took charge of a number of camps for volunteers from Derry city in the weeks just before and after internment. Replicating what I had learned myself, I divided the time into training the ten or so volunteers in explosives (which had mysteriously reappeared on the training menu) and weapons, with some discussion of tactics and then fieldcraft in the nearby hills after dark.

Of course, being on a camp and having responsibility for one are not the same and I quickly came to regret taking a comradely turn on sentry duty as I found myself also being woken up, sometimes more than once a night, by jumpy volunteers who thought they had seen or heard something. There were a couple of false alarms when the camp was reasonably calmly evacuated before we paused on a nearby hill and saw those approaching car lights go off in some other direction. I had to keep up to a dozen men in line, many of them older than me and some of them hard chaws, and there were a couple of dodgy enough instances. I sent one man home for repeated indiscipline, the most difficult bit of which was affecting to be quite confident he would sit there quietly twiddling his thumbs until the next day when the transport arrived to take him off the camp. On another occasion a local stumbled across a couple of the volunteers outside and was 'arrested' by them. I then had to make a call on whether I could believe his promise to keep his mouth shut and let him go or hold him for the day or so it would take to close down the camp properly. I let him go.

One day shortly after the conclusion of a camp, while I was waiting to be taken off for a couple of days, a carload of men arrived and out spilled Seán Treacy and Pat McKenna. They were part of a new unit under headquarters' control which had been given operational responsibility for the stretch of border from Derry in the north to Swanlinbar in the south, and apparently I had made sufficient mark on them in the course of the camps to be invited to join them. Better again, they had discovered that Pat Ward was sitting in Burtonport doing nothing and had no trouble persuading him to come away with them, while we were also soon joined by Robby Donnelly. Though there would still be training duties, I would now share these with Pat, and this began a period of intense activity in which I moved up and down the border and took part in regular operations, punctuated by the taking of further camps in Donegal and Leitrim. At the time, Treacy had the use of a dark-green Cortina and I thought us the finest beings on the planet as we travelled the length and breadth of our area, preparing and mounting operations, picking up intelligence, moving material, test-firing newly acquired weapons and so on.

At the Donegal town end of Barnesmore Gap one day, Treacy flashed a car travelling in the other direction. We rendezvoused at a nearby pub and I met Dave O'Connell for the first time. It wasn't until a year or two later that he became known to the public, and indeed within the movement, as Dáithí, and I always continued to address him as Dave. He was a legendary figure from the 1950s' campaign having, amongst much else, participated in the famous Brookeborough raid on New Year's Day 1957, during which Seán South and Feargal O'Hanlon were killed, and he was later himself hit six times in an RUC ambush. Dave had serious charisma and at the outset I was in awe of him. Though he would become very much the public face of the IRA, and many assumed he was chief of staff after the later arrest of MacStiofáin, he was never to hold that rank. He exercised such power as he might have had internally, first through his role as chairman of the Army Council – a function that was denied to both the chief of staff and the president of Sinn Féin on the basis that they report to the Council – and secondly, and very much secondarily, through his profile in Sinn Féin. Together with Ruairí Ó Brádaigh, Dave was responsible for whatever political strategy the Provisionals might have been credited with during the early 1970s.

At that time Dave had taken leave from his teaching post in nearby Ballyshannon and lived on the outskirts of Bundoran. One of my tasks, as the youngest of the volunteers about, would be to babysit his children on the occasional Saturday night to enable himself and his wife Deirdre to get out, a task I resented but quietly performed. I met Maria McGuire some weeks later in almost identical circumstances and again we repaired to the nearest pub. Dave patronised Maria hugely, acknowledging with discreet winks to us that her real wish was to operate with an active service unit as we were doing, rather than engage in boring political work. Maria was a middle-class Dubliner just like myself (though they had forgotten I was one), whom Seán Ó Brádaigh, then Sinn Féin's director of publicity, had recruited for the party, and she had been all too quickly passed on to Ruairí and Dave. Dave subsequently took her to Amsterdam as cover on an arms purchase operation where, unfortunately for him, in addition to losing the arms, he had a fling with her which became public knowledge. The fact that the mission failed, coupled with Maria's 'defection' less than a year later and the revelation that they had been having an affair, did Dave long-term damage within the movement, giving some of the prissier volunteers an additional reason to dislike him.

There were already some reasons. As the joint architect, along with Ruairí, of our political position, Dave was responsible for the social and economic policies then being devised, which fell well short of the revolutionary change I for one envisaged, not to mention the idea of creating regional assemblies in Ireland such as Dáil Uladh, a nine-county parliament, in which the unionists would have a bare, but working, majority. It seemed entirely insane to me that we could argue, and fight, for the destruction of the Stormont parliament only to propose giving the whip-hand straight back to the unionists in the event of our success. That this particular policy was so hard sold in the border areas, and among volunteers like myself, has caused me to wonder how the hell it went down in places like Belfast, which had been under the unionist cosh since partition. In my own case Seán Treacy persuaded me that it deserved adoption as a clever revolutionary stratagem which called into question the existence of the hated 26-county Free State.

In the summer of 1971 the reality was that the vast majority of IRA members were so taken up with 'military' matters and 'politics' was so reviled – not least on account of where it had taken the previous leadership – that those with any interest were simply let run with it. A policy of 'Brits Out' may have seemed simple-minded but that was where things were, and it seemed to me that there was little point in devising detailed positions in advance of the revolutionary, transforming change that was the prerequisite for the implementation of any change at all. The leadership thought differently; it felt the need to both 'respectabilise' itself with the media by being more than 'just' the spokespeople for nationalist gunmen, while at the same time distancing itself from the principal authors of that libel, our rivals in the Official IRA. So pressing was this requirement that, it seems, the various policy stances taken by the movement were adopted whole from possible positions discarded during the period of reassessment that took place in the late 1960s by those who had become the Officials.[6]

Not that we were then a left-wing movement. For sure, there were Reds like myself and Pat, but there were also plenty of right-wingers about. In some of the better-ordained billets, you could sense the message that we were the boys who would do the business, expelling the British while keeping the country safe from the communists in the Official IRA, and I occasionally found myself being patronised by small businessmen and medium-sized farmers whose guests we were and whom it seemed unmannerly to contradict. Sometimes, though, you got the genuine article and I can remember Pat Ward and I slack-jawed

---

[6] Known, derisively, as Sticks and Stickybacks, on account of the gum with which they affixed paper Easter Lilies to their lapels to commemorate the Rising, they retaliated by calling us Provos and Provies as well as Pinheads, because Provisional Sinn Féin had been forced by the speed of events to use pins to secure those bits of Easter paper. The latter appellation had the additional attraction of suggesting a lack of intellectual bottom in our political position. Fortunately, it would fail to stick.

after talking to two visitors from Noraid, the IRA's US support group, who were virulently anti-communist and saw absolutely no contradiction between their support for both the IRA in Ireland and the US effort in Vietnam, where they had served, while giving us a few tactical tips from the Viet Cong repertoire, including the suggestion that we smear excreta on the shrapnel intended for use in landmines to contaminate any wounds we might cause.

Chapter 5

As IRA activity increased in early 1971, Chichester-Clark demanded the military occupation of the nationalist areas. When Heath denied him this, Chichester-Clark resigned; the purpose of his resignation to bring home to 'the people' the reality that Westminster had tied his hands. British plans for direct rule had been reformulated, their perception of the threat of the loyalists unilaterally declaring independence having receded, and they were ready to introduce it immediately if William Craig – the Home Affairs Minister sacked back in 1968 – were to be elected as Clark's successor. The plans were simply shelved again when Brian Faulkner succeeded to the leadership, beating Craig by an impressive twenty-six to four, and making his own priority plain when he said the immediate problem was law and order.

McKee and MacAirt were arrested in mid-April, framed by Scotland Yard detectives for possession of a short arm, leaving Joe Cahill to take over as Belfast Brigade commander. By now the bombing campaign was well underway, with night-time bombs in Belfast city centre producing surprisingly few casualties. Though Billy Reid, a New Lodge Road volunteer, was shot dead during a gun battle with troops in May, the IRA was generally getting the better of these exchanges, with numerous cases of soldiers being wounded in gun and bomb attacks. In May, the Officials shot dead a soldier in the Markets – which was, together with the Lower Falls, their strongest area – and towards the end of the month a caller to Springfield Road RUC barracks casually threw in a suitcase which exploded seconds later, killing a paratrooper sergeant.

Everyone knew internment was coming, and though countless words have since been spent decrying the decision, it is hard to see how the British army could have held any sort of line without it. Throughout the first half of 1971, the IRA had become visibly stronger. Spectacular operations were taking place in Belfast where a hijacked double-decker careered down the Springfield Road, spraying machine gunfire at the barracks and its observation posts as it went, and the now daily IRA gun and bomb attacks were becoming ever more audacious. In mid-July the IRA in Belfast daringly rescued Gerry Fitzgerald, a volunteer who was lying wounded under armed guard in the Royal Victoria Hospital, and, the following day, an IRA unit, perhaps fifteen strong, destroyed the *Daily Mirror* plant on the outskirts of the city. Both commercial and strategic targets were being hit and indeed it emerged years later that attacks on the electricity distribution system during 1970 and 1971 came close to producing a state of emergency. Unfortunately these more or less ceased following internment, almost certainly because of the arrest of the IRA officer behind them. Meanwhile, the bombs were getting bigger and better, and, already, a battle of wits between IRA engineers and British army bomb disposal experts was underway, with anti-handling devices occasionally incorporated into the bombs being left out.

The campaign of arson attacks on city centre shops, using cigarette-packet-sized incendiaries, was causing considerable damage and disruption. More conventional bombing was meanwhile increasing month on month, sometimes with spectacular results, as when the IRA bombed the Esso depot in Belfast harbour, or the forensic science laboratory in the city centre, destroying much painstakingly collected evidence against its own members in the process. Commercial bombing was politically risky owing to the near inevitability of civilian casualties, but Belfast in particular was absolutely wedded to it and I was to be on the losing side of many arguments against it down the years. The theory was that bombing made governing the North costly in economic terms while also showing up the inability of the British government to prevent it. In addition, the bombs stretched the British army, tying down troops in the centre of Belfast and other towns across the North, denying the army the ability to concentrate its patrols in the nationalist areas, forcing it into guarding various stationary points where they presented targets for us, and generally taking the war out of the nationalist areas. The problem with the argument against this was the bombing campaign's blinding effectiveness, though I am not sure how much real thought the leadership ever gave to it. GHQ (which runs the IRA on the basis of policies decided by the Army Council) was dominated by those who had been in the IRA in the 1956–62 period, when Belfast had been left alone. They were more used to the standard, rural guerrilla tactics that had been employed in that campaign and the training right up to the time I went into jail reflected this. I suspect that the extension of MacStiofáin's 'sabotage' campaign to commercial targets was adopted almost accidentally – because of the dominance of 1940s' men like McKee, Seamus Twomey and Joe Cahill in the Belfast leadership who remembered the English bombing campaign – and was then taken up elsewhere owing to its perceived success in Belfast.[7] Throughout 1971, IRA training included (with the exception of the period noted earlier) training in explosives, but it was oriented to anti-personnel use and a classic behind-the-lines sabotage campaign aimed at disrupting communications and the power supply. While those who went through IRA training back then knew how to bring down an electricity pylon or cut a railway line, none of us were ever told how to go about bombing a city centre shop – shop-lifting as one Belfast wit subsequently termed it. In any event, the bombing campaign pre-internment was remarkable for the absence of civilian casualties and this did not become an issue until 1972.

Internment came as no surprise and we were ready for it in the South as well. No special intelligence was required to know it was coming and nor do I remember being given any specific warning in relation to 9 August, when, partly as a result of the great many false alarms, some volunteers had taken a chance and stayed in their homes, where they were caught. What did come as a surprise – certainly to me – was the scale of the reaction to it, not only on the streets, but also from the government in the South, and the Social Democratic and Labour Party (SDLP) and wider nationalist constituency in the North.

The level of the conflict was to be transformed by internment, markedly so in Belfast and Derry, while also spreading into areas previously

---

[7] There is also the factor that Belfast nationalists did not see the city centre as belonging to them, though I have no idea if this contributed to the adoption of the tactic.

quiet and now made hostile by the dawn raids. There was intense fighting in Belfast between the IRA and the British army – which sometimes became three-way, the loyalists having joined in behind the British – and mass evacuations in the mixed streets off the Springfield Road. Thirteen people died on the first day of internment and, by the end of the week, twenty-four were dead, among them two British soldiers and two IRA men. Another man, the first UDR (Ulster Defence Regiment) member to be killed by the IRA, was shot dead while on patrol at Clady on the Donegal border. The rest of the dead were civilians, all but two of them shot dead by the British army, and at least half of them killed in circumstances as murderous as those on Bloody Sunday the following year. The most obviously savage were those that took place in Ballymurphy, where soldiers from the Parachute Regiment's 2nd Battalion shot ten people dead, including a priest administering to a wounded man and a 50-year-old mother of eight, and perhaps intra-regimental rivalry contributed something to those killings that would be carried out less than six months later by 1st Battalion paratroopers in Derry.

British claims that the internment operation had been a success seemed questionable in circumstances where gun battles raged, and then ridiculous when the IRA scored a propaganda coup, apparently the brainchild of Gerry Adams, by organising a press conference in Ballymurphy at which Joe Cahill told the assembled media the IRA was intact and fighting. Though he conceded that ammunition was becoming tight, Cahill denied that the IRA had suffered serious losses and in particular rubbished British claims that soldiers had killed twenty to thirty IRA men. Cahill said our casualties were two dead and eight wounded and that only thirty volunteers had been lost to internment, of whom just two were battalion or brigade officers. The fighting quietened towards the weekend with Derry and the barricaded nationalist areas of Belfast now more or less reconstituted as no-go areas, entered by the British army cautiously, by surprise, and then only in considerable force.

Few volunteers died while directly engaging the British. In Ardoyne the local O/C, Paddy McAdorey, died in the fighting there on internment day, and Seamus Simpson was shot dead while throwing blast bombs in Andersonstown a couple of days later. Eamonn Lafferty, adjutant of the Derry Command, whom I knew well from the camps, was the only other direct IRA fatality in this period. He was killed in a gun battle in Creggan on 18 August; on the following day, sixteen-year-old James O'Hagan, who had been on one of my camps, also died – apparently in an accidental discharge. Insanely, it was decided to run a guard of honour of volunteers from across the border for Eamonn's funeral and a carload of us were stopped by the newly formed UDR, the first member of which had been killed just a week earlier in our operational area. Fortunately, we were allowed proceed but Billy Kelly, then a member of our GHQ staff, who had arrived to take charge of the colour party, baulked when he saw the state of me – I was just off a camp – and I ended up simply walking in the funeral procession, past Eamonn McCann, who stood in a doorway, seeming to me then the eternal observer, all revolutionary talk and no action.

Complaints that internment was one-sided were also a little misplaced; after all, we were the ones who, with some assistance from the Officials, were firing at soldiers and RUC men and, in our case, bombing the hell out of Belfast especially. The British claimed to have arrested some 350 of the 450 listed as IRA members, but the trouble was that their lists were old and inaccurate. Though it has been said that fewer than 100 of those arrested were IRA members, that would not have been a bad result and the impact of internment was anyway cumulative as hundreds of men – some of whom broke under inter-rogation – were arrested and interned over the following months. Another mistake was the interning of the wider, radical political oppo-sition, in the shape of People's Democracy leaders like Michael Farrell and others, who had no links whatsoever to the IRA, simply on the basis that they would otherwise be available to make political trouble for the Stormont government at home and abroad.

The reaction to internment, both nationally and internationally, put any thoughts Jack Lynch may have entertained of interning in the South out of the question – he had threatened it earlier. Lynch sent his foreign minister to London and in a secret phone call protested to Edward Heath, who told him, not for the last time, to keep his nose out of Britain's business. Lynch then delivered a number of ill-tempered state-ments, provoking equally bad-tempered responses from the British, and at a meeting with Heath in early September sought a statement from the British indicating that they saw unification as a desirable long-term solution. This was almost laughable in circumstances where Heath was offering at most, and then only following an end to violence, a mechanism for guaranteeing minority rights with some as yet undefined element of 'participation' in government for nationalists. The difficulty with the latter was that the British agreed with Faulkner that it was out of the question to allow persons opposed to the very existence of the Northern state to take part in its governance, and though Faulkner was forced into three-way talks later that month, he did so with the agreement of the British that the border would not be an issue.

Soon after internment, the British were in further difficulty when stories of brutality came out of Crumlin Road prison. In Belfast, prisoners were made to run barefoot through a field of broken glass, and then through a gauntlet of baton-wielding soldiers, some of them with guard dogs. Everywhere men were savagely beaten, both during and after their arrests and in the course of interrogation, with some being thrown blindfolded out of helicopters which, unknown to them, were hovering just feet above the ground. Worse, it emerged that 'special techniques' were being used in interrogation and that a small number of key activists, selected on a geographical basis (a number of whom were indeed key activists), had been subjected to techniques of sensory deprivation, some familiar from the Cold War, burnished by the British in campaigns from Palestine through Kenya, Malaya, Cyprus, Borneo and Aden. The techniques were taught at purpose-built centres in Britain and the interrogations carried out by Special Branch men, supervised by army intelligence, at a location which remained unknown until some years later. They included hooding, prolonged standing in the search position, sleep and food deprivation, and the generation of white noise, in a carefully calculated combination designed to disorientate and confuse the victims. Many of the men reported that they suffered hallucinations, and Francie McGuigan was so disorientated that he could not spell his own name. All of them lost serious weight and such was the state of McGuigan and the Belfast cohort that when they finally arrived in Crumlin Road the governor told him that he would now be treated as a human being by men who were themselves human beings.

An inquiry into the stories coming out of the interrogation centres – forced on the British and carried out by Sir Edmund Compton – was established at the end of August to 'investigate allegations … of physical brutality'. Boycotted by the internees, his inquiry was confined to those arrested on internment day and in fact it 'investigated' only 40 cases, as opposed to the hundreds that were going through the system. Compton's findings were laughable. Exercises the detainees had been forced to do, were, he found, designed to counteract the cold, though they may have been 'thoughtlessly prolonged' beyond what was necessary. The hooding, white noise and maintenance of the search position – for days on end – was either for the detainees' own protection, to stop other IRA men identifying them, or, alternately, to prevent them from communicating with each other. Various black eyes, signs of bruising and other injuries were 'assumed' to have been caused accidentally. Indeed, even as Compton was sitting, two other men 'disappeared' into the hands of the Special Branch where they were subjected to techniques very similar to the ones used on those who became known as the Hooded Men. Forced to add these two cases to his inquiry, Compton dismissed the suggestion by one of the men that a gun had been put into his mouth and blanks fired, saying that this could not possibly be so since the regulations for the holding centre required 'visitors' to give up their arms on entry.

Compton laid out his problem thus: 'We consider that brutality is an inhuman or savage form of cruelty and that cruelty implies a disposition to inflict suffering, coupled with indifference to, or pleasure in, the victim's pain.' While conceding there had been 'instances of ill treatment', he found that none of the men had 'suffered physical brutality as we understand the term'. As to just what this 'understanding' was, Compton reasoned that, because the people administering the torture or ill-treatment did not intend to inflict pain, it followed that no one had suffered brutality, a torturer's charter which may have been first used during the Inquisition. Defended by the British as little more than 'robust', when not being flatly denied and dismissed as republican propaganda, the European Commission would later decide otherwise and find Britain guilty of inhuman and degrading treatment and of torture; though when the issue came before the European Court of

Human Rights in 1978 the 'torture' finding was deleted in an important, to the British, stroke of legal finessing.

***

Curiously, there was no indigenous IRA in the border areas, or at least none on our stretch of the border, and indeed little organisation at all outside the cities and small pockets of west Tyrone and Fermanagh. For ourselves, we were travelling gunmen, an IRA unit at large with the authority to do whatever we wished over what was an enormous area. Of course we needed intelligence from inside the North, as well as billets and so forth, but there seemed to be a fear among Northern nationalists as to what they were letting themselves in for, and when we got across the border we tended to stay in outhouses, which gave the farmer plausible deniability in the event of our being caught. There were various fixed points, places where the British army was based, where nothing was required but to take a look, and I spent a couple of afternoons walking a Cumann na mBan volunteer through the hills that overlooked one such position, stopping for a realistic-enough looking 'court' here and there, while we sought out suitable firing points. I returned there at night with others a number of times looking for a hit, but we drew a blank each time.

Outings of that sort were typical. Much of the time IRA activity was deeply frustrating with only a fraction of what was planned and prepared for actually coming off. It was not unusual for a volunteer to be dug in on a hill waiting to detonate a landmine for weeks, only for no target to show and the operation to be abandoned and the mine lifted. Pat Ward and I spent about a week so, one of us breaking cover to go down the hill just before dawn each day to disconnect the detonator and take the wire back up to the firing point, fervently praying that no mobile patrol would happen on the scene during our five minutes or so of exposure. We would then re-cross the border as daylight broke, rest up, and return that night to reconnect the detonator and run the wires back, never sure that the operation hadn't been compromised in the meantime. It was nerve-pulling work, perhaps the worst part of which was trying to make sure you didn't press the button on an innocent target.

Other operations were aborted because the British army turned out in unexpected force or sometimes in heavier than anticipated vehicles – say the armoured Ferrets sometimes in use rather than Land Rovers. In retrospect, we were overly cautious, certainly compared with what I saw in later years in rural areas and was about to see in Derry. One huge operation was planned for a stretch of main road near the Cavan–Fermanagh border, for which another unit arrived over from Dundalk complete with an old bazooka. Our weapons that night included .303s, FNs, SLRs and US Garands – the US military rifle used during World War II – as well as a couple of Bren guns and a landmine. The 25 or so of us were expecting a couple of lorry-loads of passing troops and this particular operation would have resulted in massive British casualties had it come off. No one turned up and the operation was not repeated.

Organisationally, things kept shifting and for a time we were subsumed into a headquarters active service unit which would supposedly be capable of operating anywhere. In fact, this creation lasted for just one aborted operation and was killed off in the chaos that followed internment. The plan was for us to take over the RUC barracks in a town across the border, in the kind of operation typical of the War of Independence and last mounted during the 1950s' campaign. Billy Kelly from the New Lodge Road in Belfast, then GHQ director of operations, was in overall charge, with Paddy McDaid (not his real name), yet another ex-Para, this time from Ardoyne, as his No. 2. Both men were on the run from the North but it soon became clear to me that Kelly's nerves were shot. McDaid, for his part, was unflappable and a born soldier – though one with a doubtful sense of humour. Shortly after we assembled in the same Carrigart base that was used for the camps, Kelly decided to address us and quite properly began by ordering us to fall in. The formality of the occasion was then ruined when, halfway through the briefing, McDaid materialised behind him with a bucket of water which he proceeded to empty over his commander, leaving the latter wet, humiliated and speechless in front of his new charges. This bit of horseplay fetched an instinctive response from Seán Treacy, who turned to me and said grimly that if McDaid had done that to him, he would have shot him, which I thought revelatory of Treacy's true attitude towards our own future commander.

Initially we were told no more than that an ad hoc unit was being put together for a special operation. In addition to ourselves, there was a handful from the Falls Road, some of whom I would meet again in Crumlin Road, and an engineer from the 3rd Battalion, based in the New Lodge Road/Ardoyne area, which was Kelly and McDaid's home area, making us about a dozen strong. MacStiofáin came to admire us on the camp site and we were all kept incommunicado from the time the operation was outlined. The plan was for another man (who went on to have a successful professional career) and a female volunteer to seek assistance at the barracks on some spurious basis, whereupon we would storm it when the door was opened. The purpose of the operation was to clean out the arsenal of weaponry that had been assembled there during the recently concluded gun amnesty. We had the layout of the inside of the barracks and were assigned specific tasks. Our instructions were to release the uniformed RUC men, having first made them strip to their underwear, and then blow up the building. A section under Seán Treacy had responsibility for the couple of Special Branch men we were expected to find and I'm not sure what was planned for them.

We moved in small groups to Frank Morris's house in Convoy, County Donegal, under cover of darkness in the early hours on the day of the operation, the intention being that we would remain there until it was time to move out again after dark. Morris was an old-time IRA man, and the last man to have been flogged by the Stormont regime. At one point he expressed his distaste for his successors – us – by noting that in his time volunteers would have been on their knees saying the Rosary this close to an operation, rather than laughing and joking. If he had heard the discussion between a couple of the Belfast men about his teenage daughter, who had brought us in tea and sandwiches, he'd have been even more disappointed in us. Night came after a truly long day and we eventually piled into a transit van and a couple of cars and headed for the target. I was in the back of the van with Pat Ward and others and was armed with a Thompson. Pat and I had responsibility for a room where we expected to have to deal with between two and six RUC men.

Tension was high and because of the long build-up, the scale of the operation and the fact that we were confined like sitting ducks in the dark of the van, I was very nervous. Perhaps my nervousness was shared because, having crossed into the North and come close to the barracks, a flap commenced which resulted in Kelly – who was in the passenger seat – screaming, 'What will we do? What will we do?' Pat McKenna immediately took charge, saying 'Get the fuck out of here', and the driver duly followed the only available instruction. So ended that GHQ active service unit's sole operation. I was told later that unusual activity had been spotted in and around the barracks and that the operation may have been compromised, but maybe Kelly just lost his nerve. I took away a valuable lesson regarding leadership and, having lost respect for Kelly, was a good deal more wary about trusting an IRA man in the future simply because of his exalted rank.

***

Internment had followed almost immediately on the GHQ operation that never was. Kelly disappeared briefly, having been moved on to something else, while Paddy McDaid was left in charge of a newly constituted North-West Command. This was to run the entire border area in which we had been operating – down as far as Belturbet where the Mid-Ulster Command, centred on Monaghan, took over – and included much of Fermanagh as well as west Tyrone and Derry city. Naturally, we all had to have titles and a Donegal man became adjutant while Seán Treacy, Pat McKenna and Robby took up the other positions as Vice-O/C, operations officer and quartermaster. I was made training officer and Pat Ward became engineering officer. In fact, we remained the same travelling active service unit we had been all along, picking up local help as we moved around, with, occasionally, volunteers from Mayo, Clare, Dublin and even Cork added to our number for specific operations. Though Paddy McDaid was floating here and there, the reality was that this had always been, and now remained, Treacy's unit.

One day, shortly after internment, a dozen or so IRA men from Ardoyne arrived in Letterkenny looking for McDaid, who had arranged some training for them but had typically forgotten to tell anyone else. The IRA men were fed and fêted in McGlinchey's Grill where they slept on camp beds before we moved them out to Carrigart just before daylight. Bernard McGlinchey, the Fianna Fáil senator whose Golden Grill backed onto the house of Pat Dawson, was at that time linked to the Blaney wing of Fianna Fáil – he would drop Blaney a couple of years later for what were seen as reasons of political expediency. Back at the time of internment, he was typical enough in sucking up to IRA men and was friendly with Kelly and McDaid, both of whom did some drinking with him. After a series of gun lectures close to the camp site, we had a shoot-out where everyone was limited to two or three rounds from the Thompson, a rifle shot or two and a couple more from our various shorts. The man in charge of them rightly remarked that they'd be given a better rattle on the streets back home, and that was the case. We simply couldn't afford to be using valuable ammunition for training purposes. Still, when they headed off, the men seemed pleased enough and I would meet up with a number of them again in Crumlin Road prison or in Long Kesh.

A few days later somebody decided that Pat and I should acquire still further training. I think the idea then was to put us on the camps full-time, but at any rate we were dispatched again to Treacy's territory near Portlaoise. This was supposed to be an advanced or 'officers' camp', but it didn't really live up to its billing, perhaps because of the chaos then engulfing the North, though there were volunteers there from Armagh and Tyrone. Conditions were far from rigorous and we were even able to move in a TV to watch Seán MacStiofáin being interviewed on RTE in the programme that led to the directive under Section 31 of the Broadcasting Act which would keep IRA and Sinn Féin spokespeople off the airwaves for the next quarter of a century. The real excitement that night, however, was provided, not by MacStiofáin's interview, but by Treacy's arrival armed with a Sten gun and orders to close down the camp immediately. Apparently he had been stopped at a roadblock and the Gardaí, finding the Sten in the car, offered to simply take it and let him continue. Treacy refused to give up the weapon and, after a period spent in the local Garda station, he was released by a senior officer, complete with machine gun. Though this sort of incident was presumably unknown to the Minister for Justice, Desmond O'Malley, it was typical of the times. Indeed, a couple of weeks before internment, a Donegal jury had acquitted a Derry man on charges of possessing arms, notwithstanding his accepting responsibility for them in open court. The parting shot of the judge was 'I'm glad that's your verdict, gentlemen, and not mine', whereupon jurors and accused retired to discuss the matter further in the local pub.

On the way out of the Midlands, Pat and I linked up with Paddy McDaid, who for some reason brought us to MacStiofáin's house in Navan late at night. We were ushered into his sitting room where I got the distinct impression that MacStiofáin, in contrast to Ó Brádaigh or O'Connell, did not want the pair of us about. It was perhaps understandable because we must have been in a disgusting state, but we were anyway rapidly moved out of the house and on to a local farmer's hay barn for the night. Pat Ward, unlike me no respecter of rank, was suitably caustic at MacStiofáin's lack of hospitality, but my own hero worship of our chief of staff was hardly dented by the slight. We were then let loose in Dublin for a couple of days where I looked up old friends and got rattling drunk, feeling strongly that this would be the last time I would see Dublin for quite a while.

On our return Pat and I were, as we thought, briefly separated, Pat going into Fermanagh while I was sent back up to north Donegal for another camp. By now a lot of stories were coming out of Derry in the aftermath of internment, which had seen the local leadership all but destroyed. The then quartermaster, whose role required him to spend time on the southern side of the border, was bad-mouthing the people who had taken over and had found the ears of some of the charlatans around Letterkenny. In due course the complaints came to the attention of Paddy McDaid and I was called to a meeting with Paddy and the Derry QM at which I heard Martin McGuinness's name for the first time. The QM made various complaints of inexperience and recklessness against McGuinness and others – as if it could possibly have been otherwise – and the upshot of all of this was that Paddy decided to send me into Derry as GHQ representative, with vague instructions to sort out whatever it was that needed sorting out.

Chapter 6

In early October, I moved into Derry by taxi under notional cover from Robby's sister, who collected me in Letterkenny. The taxi was stopped at a British army checkpoint and fortuitously waved on. Fortuitous because, as would happen all too often over the years, at the very last moment I had been asked to take something in with me – in this case a box of electrical detonators which I handed over on arrival. Martin McGuinness was at this time adjutant or second in command in Derry, having taken over from Eamonn Lafferty, but everyone knew he was really in charge. He was a natural leader who needed no rank to impose his quiet will and he came to prominence in Derry, and later throughout the IRA, on his own and from within, quite unlike myself whose various positions were effectively gifted to me by others.

The first night there I asked to see a unit in action and watched from the upper window of a house on the edge of the Bogside as a three- or four-man unit rattled away at a passing army foot patrol before moving position and rattling again. One local hero was nicknamed 'Scatter' – reputedly from the warning shout he'd let out before his unit let fly – and while it was like nothing in the training manuals, as long as the British army were too nervous to attempt to come in behind them it worked perfectly.

Within a day or two I had gone native, concluding not only that there was not a thing wrong with the personnel or command structure in Derry, but also that I wanted very much to stay there. While I was still trying to figure out just how to swing this, Robby surprisingly turned up in town and the two of us simply hung on there. Three or four days in, Robby said regarding Martin, 'He's something else, isn't he?', and I never had the slightest doubt who the main man in Derry was, whatever the formal position. Martin was not the sort you'd tell a dirty joke to and, though his prissiness was immediately apparent to me, I had no problem with it, being pretty prissy myself.

I knew quite a few of the Derry volunteers from the camps and became attached to an ad hoc unit which operated at brigade or command level – though nobody in there thought or spoke in such grandiose terms – and the Derry Brigade did not at that stage formally exist. While there were regular planned operations, much of the activity was opportunistic and depended on our and other units reacting to patrols turning up in particular places. There were targets everywhere and it was much more exciting and physically far less demanding than operating on the border, with its tough living conditions, exposure to the elements, long hours and days of waiting, and attendant route marches through difficult terrain, often with heavy equipment such as landmines.

At that time there was a unit based in the Bogside/Brandywell area and another covering the Creggan estate – the notional dividing line being the Lone Moor Road. We were free to move between the two and used a number of rental cars, which were quietly supplied to us and regularly changed. At night the units watched for and reacted to raids and incursions, patrolling their streets and checking in with the various vigilante groups who guarded the barricades that ringed the area. There were dozens of false alarms. Apart from my first couple of nights in Derry, when I was billeted alone, I was usually with McGuinness and Colm Keenan. Both were going out with sisters of Cyril Canning, who was arrested during my time in Derry, and we would often show up at the Cannings' house in the Brandywell for something to eat. If we were out at night, we would pick up freshly baked baps at the back door of a local bakery before visiting one of the volunteers' homes for breakfast. Raiding at mealtimes would later become an effective way for the army to net wanted IRA men, but they hadn't at this stage cottoned on to it, and so I was regularly fussed over by Martin's mother, Peggy, Robby's sisters, and the Canning daughters, among them Bernie, Martin's girlfriend and future wife. A particular favourite of mine was Roisín Keenan, Colm's sister and then the chair of the Derry Women's Action Committee, and a significant republican figure in her own right.

I have never subscribed to the theory that internment was good for the IRA, or that British and RUC intelligence was as deficient as has been subsequently claimed. Derry had been particularly hard hit and had lost most of its then staff, young as they were, to be replaced by leaders who were even younger. McGuinness himself was twenty-one, while Eamonn Lafferty had been just nineteen when he was killed in action and Colm Keenan was not yet twenty when he was shot dead by soldiers the following March.

There were a handful of older men. The nominal O/C was in his late twenties, while the finance officer was also older than the rest of us. The then O/C simply gave the units their heads and I saw little enough of him while I was there. One of my first encounters with the F/O meanwhile concerned the £5 sub volunteers were being given, which I argued was wrong. This, in its way, goes to show how out of touch I was with the day-to-day reality of working-class lives. The sub was started following internment, to compensate volunteers for the fact that they could no longer pick up the dole, the risk of arrest and internment being obvious. Though in their late teens and early twenties, many of the volunteers had families who depended on the sub and eventually I accepted the money on the basis that it would be used to buy petrol and occasionally food for those houses that we used and were billeted in. I'd never had my own money since coming home from England and considered myself and the others to be the financial responsibility of the Army. It simply didn't strike me that my own supply of cigarettes and even the occasional couple of pints probably came close enough to the £5 mark. The notion that anyone should profit from IRA membership, no matter how insignificant the amount, was unthinkable. This was a moral absolute and in Donegal a volunteer had been shot in the leg for secreting a £10 note in his sock following a robbery and was lucky not to have been executed. Kneecapping, as it became known, did not feature in the early days. In Derry a civilian was so punished, for reasons I cannot now remember, by being shot in the calf with a .22 automatic while an ambulance – which we had already called – stood waiting around the corner to take him away.

The weaponry in use in Derry was what I was used to from the camps. We were regularly armed in case of raids and I had a Colt .45

for a period, followed by a Smith & Wesson .38. I had a firm preference for revolvers, having imbibed early on from Treacy the lesson that automatics were prone to jamming. However, the ammunition for the .45s – which was often a refill – was not always reliable and you were better off with one of the smaller revolvers. I believe we had an FN or two, some sub-machine guns – Thompsons and a Sten certainly – a wide range of short arms, and a Garand, over which I exercised a degree of proprietorship while I was there. The standard weapon was the M1 carbine, as used by US forces towards the end of World War II and in Korea; the Armalite had yet to appear in Derry, though the first to arrive were being used in Belfast by the time of my arrest. The most effective weapon we had was a Lee Enfield .303 with telescopic sights, which had been properly calibrated across the border for accuracy. A number of British soldiers were shot dead with this in single-shot snipes, and others wounded both then and later. The rifle became known as Jude, following a house raid in which an old woman cursed the soldiers, invoking St Jude who she said would surely punish them for their actions. That night a soldier was indeed shot dead and the army then came looking for Jude, believing it was the name of the sniper.

McGuinness kept a beady eye on our behaviour and insisted that we were polite when mounting roadblocks and in our other interactions with the population, in an unconscious nod to the teachings of Mao and Che Guevara. Everyone knew who was in the IRA. We were never masked except for set pieces like roadblocks, where we might encounter people from outside the area, and then the extent of the masking was to pull handkerchiefs up over our noses. The *Derry Journal* was read with meticulous care on Tuesdays and Fridays and, a few weeks into my stay, McGuinness arranged for a firing party, consisting of myself, himself, Robby and Seán Keenan, to be photographed at Eamonn Lafferty's grave on what would have been his twentieth birthday, as a British army helicopter hovered high overhead. The chopper was a daily presence above us and a target against which few of our weapons were even potentially effective, though that never stopped us blazing away at it to chase it off. The picture of the firing party appeared on the front page of the *Derry Journal* and, together with a statement from the

Derry Command claiming responsibility for various operations, did us no harm at all.

In Derry, as elsewhere, we were competing with the Official IRA, who were operating in more or less the same way as we were, but by now less effectively. They just weren't as good, I think because their collective experience and greater maturity made them more cautious. The main distinction between us was the bombing campaign and, although Derry was a nationalist town, the people didn't seem to mind us blowing its commercial centre to pieces. Thus, once a week, we would make up a few ten-pounders, which would be transported to various shop doorways by volunteers accompanied by girls (as every female under about thirty was called in those days) for cover. No one got caught or hurt while I was there and the IRA in Derry was, in time, to garner a reputation for its careful avoidance of civilian casualties.

This was not necessarily apparent back then. The *Derry Journal* attacked us for our 'madcap course', and accused us of engaging in 'reckless activities' and 'disgracing a noble cause'. We were 'rioters and wreckers [who] could plunge this part of Ireland into a deluge of blood'. They rowed in hard behind the condemnation of the Catholic bishops, which for a republican was never a difficulty as the bishops had been condemning republicans since the time of Wolfe Tone. Even sympathetic neutrals like Bernadette Devlin were unable to rise beyond a patronising 'understanding' of our 'frustration and despair'. In reality, there was nothing remotely despairing or frustrated in our make-up. Well aware of the history of post-war British withdrawals from the colonies, the experiences of the French in Algeria and the impending American defeat in Vietnam, we were hyper-conscious of the body count and had no doubt about the impact it was having in Britain itself. A thirty-sixth dead soldier would bring us level with the number which, in our eyes, had triggered the pull-out from Aden, and this was a milestone we would pass in my own time in Derry. In short, we had all the certainty of youth and were completely comfortable in what we were doing, bursting with confidence and contemptuous of our critics.

***

British casualties continued to mount following internment and by the time I was arrested, in mid-November 1971, a further 23 soldiers had been killed. While IRA activity was spreading throughout the Six Counties, Belfast was still the centre of the fighting, with soldiers being killed and wounded there almost daily. In Ardoyne the resident regiment, the Green Howards, lost three more men, bringing its losses over its four-month tour of duty – which coincided with internment – to five, with many more wounded. The local kids rubbed it in with a cruel ditty based on the nursery rhyme *Ten Green Bottles*. Two soldiers died in the 1st Battalion area and two each were killed in the Falls and Ballymurphy, both then part of the 2nd Battalion area. Meanwhile three soldiers were killed in separate gun attacks in Derry and two more died when sandbagged observation posts attached to Rosemount RUC barracks in the city were bombed. Soldiers were also killed near Crossmaglen and in Newry, Lisburn, Coalisland, south Fermanagh and Lurgan – where two off-duty soldiers were shot dead. The UDR and RUC were also targets, and in the same period a UDR man was killed in south Fermanagh and RUC men died in Strabane and Toomebridge. The RUC also lost five men in three attacks in north Belfast and a further two in Andersonstown. During this twelve-week period, sixty-seven people died, almost half of them members of the security forces.

The manner in which these casualties were inflicted, a couple of them by the Officials, tells its own story. Soldiers were killed in both conventional ambushes, in which dozens of shots might be fired from a number of different positions and a few blast bombs thrown before the attackers withdrew, and by snipers in single-shot attacks, leaving it all but impossible to tell the direction from which the fire had come. Sometimes the British would be deliberately confused with distracting cover fire directed at them from elsewhere following a snipe, allowing the sniper to withdraw in comparative safety from a possibly exposed position. Soldiers were shot at on both foot and mobile patrol; lured into ambush positions by stone throwers; and fired on while guarding bomb disposal teams, setting up perimeters for search parties, dismounting from vehicles, and leaving or entering observation posts, barracks and other fixed positions.

At Castlerobin Orange Hall near Lisburn in September 1971, a Royal Army Ordnance Corps officer became the first bomb disposal expert to die when the device he was attempting to defuse exploded, having been fitted with an anti-handling device. The anti-handlers, which were becoming widely used to discourage the foolhardy from removing bombs from premises, were christened Castlerobins by the bomb disposal unit and obviously gave them something additional to think about. Within weeks the British had captured one intact and were able to work out a means of defusing it, but further surprises lay in store. The bomb disposal unit was led at this time by Major George Styles, who was quite a showman as well as being a caricature Colonel Blimp who referred continually to Murphy's Law and the 'Paddy Factor' when expounding on Irish bomb-makers. His view was that international communism had started and was fomenting the trouble, and, unable to accept that the mere Irish might produce some competent gunmen, he also believed the IRA had foreign mercenaries contracted to do their sniping. Styles personally defused the first Castlerobin left in the Europa Hotel in Belfast in late October after a seven-hour session, and though the IRA returned again just days later with another one, it too was defused, this time following a marathon nine hours, carried on TV and carefully watched by us in Derry and elsewhere. The Europa Hotel, incidentally, set in a prime city centre location and accommodating many journalists, became a regular target and was to be attacked some thirty times over the course of the war, winning it the dubious soubriquet of most bombed hotel in Europe and perhaps the world.

Styles felt this early success represented a major setback for us but the truth was that we were nearly always in a no-lose situation. Bombing is quintessentially photogenic and what now occurred was pure theatre, with an almost daily drama played out on television, complete with footage of bombs exploding, or of the bomb disposal unit approaching a suspect car or device and perhaps managing to defuse it after a contest lasting for hours. Crowds gathered to watch from behind the cordon, and if it was a nationalist crowd they might cheer wildly when the bomb exploded, sending a plume of black smoke into the Belfast sky. Styles also made the mistake of publicly alerting us to some of the methodology involved in his work. Later experts behaved more cannily and made sure to erect screens to prevent the cameras from catching what was going on. In any event, we instantly learned one lesson from the Europa and, just two days later, the anti-handler planted at the Celebrity Club – the operation in which Marty Forsythe was shot dead and his companion captured – exploded as the expert was about to approach it, having been fitted with a simple timer as well. Styles fully appreciated the escape and recognised in his book, *Bombs Have No Pity*, that they were 'really on the end of the plank' and were 'pushing our luck too far'. They now knew for sure they no longer had time on their side when beginning their walk.

During these months the IRA played to its strengths and carefully avoided the lengthy conventional engagements that might have suited the British. Civilians, instead, continued to provide the bulk of the casualties. In Derry, fourteen-year-old Annette McGavigan was shot dead by the British army in early September, as was William McGreanery just a week later. In November, Kathleen Thompson, a middle-aged housewife and mother of six, was shot and killed while standing in her own back garden, probably for having had the temerity to try to warn her neighbours of a British army incursion by banging a dustbin lid. McGuinness took me with him to visit her wake in her Creggan home, and I can remember being struck by the genuine respect with which he was greeted by people old enough to be his parents.

Typically, the British claimed to be inflicting multiple hits in the daily exchanges in Belfast, Derry and elsewhere. In Derry hundreds of phantom gunmen were identified, shot, seen to fall and then 'dragged away by the crowd'. It can certainly be deceptive, in that the first thing someone will do on realising he is being shot at will be to seek to disappear, and we too were inclined to claim hits that never were and to then insist that the British were covering up the extent of their dead, by ignoring orphans, for example, or by attributing casualties to unreported car accidents in Germany. It is an interesting insight into the moral depravity each side thought the other capable of.

Respectable Ireland, the SDLP and our other nationalist critics were simply failing to follow the logic of their own pronouncements. The British army routinely lied when individual soldiers made the shooting errors that, in retrospect, were inevitable when under gun and bomb attack in built-up areas. And they lied again to cover up those acts of gross indiscipline or, worse, deliberate murder which occurred. The incidents of wilful censorship were numerous, but while they may have been believed in Britain, few believed them in Ireland, and no one at all believed them in the nationalist areas from which the IRA drew its support. For me, the mendacity of the British then and later made them hateful. Even then, the British tabloids were carrying lurid planted tales of North Korean snipers being present in Derry because they couldn't accept that their much-vaunted army was getting kicked around by a bunch of Irish hooligan gunmen.

It seemed to me that the whole of Free Derry was in revolt and I encountered nothing but care and support from the people we moved amongst – the mothers, fathers, sisters and brothers of my comrades. I can recall the continuous warnings from the women on the streets – their injunctions to be careful – the dark loveliness of the Derry girls, the solidity and raw courage of the volunteers, and of just how young we all were. My attitude to my own death was the Sartrean one; it was an event only for others. I viewed it with equanimity, with the certainty of post hoc approval, and a generosity towards the world that astonishes me now.

On the night of my capture, Colm Keenan and I had spent part of the evening in a Bishop Street pub watching a documentary on Che Guevara. Going for a drink was a rare event and this was only my second evening in a Derry pub, the Bogside Inn having previously been declared out of bounds for volunteers. There had been times, apparently, when you would have found the bulk of the volunteers there on a Saturday night, but McGuinness had decided drinking was bad for the collective image. He had himself given up alcohol entirely by then. Colm and I were going back up to the main standby house in the Brandywell area, where we gathered each night to plan for the next day and perhaps get a lift to that night's billet. On the way we met a woman looking for her IRA son. We hadn't seen him and ignored her warning that the nearby army base was crawling with soldiers. Stories of the army being out were coming in at a rate of a dozen a night and we felt we had our own much more reliable warning system. If there were any significant movement, the vigilantes would spot it and sound the alert.

Unfortunately, on this occasion the woman was right; the vigilantes were absent for some reason and we simply moved on to the standby house. We entered through the back door, greeted the volunteers already there and settled down for the wait. The finance officer came in and gave one of us a couple of quid after some hard bargaining. We were all exhausted and some of the men had their eyes closed. One of the volunteers was cleaning a Colt .45 automatic and had carefully laid out the various pieces on the arm of the armchair. Someone asked if anyone had seen the son of the distraught woman. Suddenly there was a thunderous bang on the front door and I saw figures flitting by the window. We gasped in collective shock before one of the volunteers decided it was a volunteer messing and went charging for the door to remonstrate. He came flying back as the soldiers came through it and the ten or so of us then in the room began to dive through the back door, down the short yard and sharp right up the alley. Out of habit from the camps – where the training officer was expected to supervise the evacuation – I brought up the rear and was hammered with a baton as I emerged last into the alley.

Chapter 7

My interrogation was not at all what I expected. Primed not just by the then emerging tales of brutality from Girdwood and Holywood barracks, but by films and books involving the French Resistance, the tortures inflicted on generations of Irish patriots and, more distantly, by the lives of the saints I had read as a young schoolboy, I expected and was ready for the worst. After all, soldiers were being wounded and killed in Derry and it was plain enough from the circumstances of my capture that I might know something about this. It seemed to me not at all unreasonable that I would be ill-treated and, while I didn't expect electric shock treatment or to have my fingernails ripped out, I definitely anticipated being physically abused and beaten. This never happened and I think I may have been the beneficiary of both the absence of the Special Branch and a temporary lull in such activity – in Derry at any rate – following the publication earlier that same day of the Compton Report.

I had a rough enough time on my way to the RUC barracks on Strand Road. The army operation was a failure inasmuch as the soldiers who had arrived at the back of the house were seconds late and so missed up to a dozen volunteers, among them Martin McGuinness and the bulk of the then command staff in Derry. At least some of these were fortunate not to have been shot dead as they ran exposed through the back alley. The soldiers were naturally hyped up and I was propelled in front of a sergeant on the way to the Mex Garage with my right arm up against my back. The sergeant held his Browning automatic to my head each time we paused to cross open ground and I was told that if anyone opened fire on them, I would be the first to get it. When we reached the Mex, I was handed over to a couple of squaddies who forced me up against a wet sandbag and quietly encouraged me to make a run for it. Thrown into the back of an army Pig for the trip to the Strand Road barracks, I was face-down on the ground between a half-dozen soldiers and got a few rifle butts and kicks in the ribs, but they'd been warned by someone who I knew from his accent was an officer that it was desirable that I reach the RUC in one piece.

At the time I had no idea that 50 pounds of gelignite and the remnants of the Colt .45 one of the men had been cleaning had been found in the house. So focused was I on the ordeal I was anticipating that it never struck me that the most likely outcome of my capture was not internment but an immediate move to England to face armed robbery charges. This was something I didn't appreciate until Roisín Keenan came to see me in Crumlin Road and told me that the Derry Women's Action Committee had gone to complain to the army about the arrest of an innocent man and been told I was wanted for bank robbery in England. Fortunately for me, the interviews were conducted by ordinary detectives, rather than members of the Special Branch, and followed the still standard police format in which questions are put and answers – in my case, silences – recorded. No name of significance was put to me, no billets were mentioned, no operations; in fact, not a question was asked which hinted at prior intelligence or alarmed me in the slightest and I spent the better part of a day looking past the questioner at my spot on the wall, my resolve to remain unbroken pretty much untested. I wasn't even asked about my time in England, while the height of their efforts to suborn me came when one detective offered to let me have my cigarettes back if I answered a few questions. The only unpleasantness came off camera, so to speak, when a detective began to make indecent suggestions about some named Derry women in what is a routine interrogation tactic designed to provoke and humiliate. Sleep was difficult in my dirty clothes and a greasy blanket on the standard wooden board – which can still be seen in police cells in the South – but came eventually. On the Thursday morning, I was taken on the short journey to court where, after a brief appearance – during which I declined to stand for the magistrate and refused to recognise the court – I was remanded to Belfast Prison amid a smattering of applause from Roisín Keenan, Robby's sisters and others from the Derry Women's Action Committee.

We travelled by road to Belfast and, as we drove through the northern suburbs and up the Crumlin Road to the heavily fortified prison, it did strike me that I could become an incidental casualty of an IRA ambush. After all, how was anyone to know it was me, an IRA man, in the car with a bunch of plainclothesmen? As we drove through the prison's main gates, I met the eyes of a soldier on sentry duty through the slits in his sandbagged post. I had banged away at similar posts from a distance a couple of times and was intrigued to see one close up. I was taken into reception where the prison signed for me and my clothes and few belongings were accounted for – the latter disappearing into a brown envelope which I wouldn't see again for three years. I had the compulsory bath, complete with carbolic soap, and was given prison-issue clothing, consisting of ill-fitting long underwear, brown 'hairy' trousers and jacket, a blue-and-white striped shirt and badly fitting boots. When my clothes were being checked in, the middle-aged screw in reception gave me a quizzical look when I described the ragged underpants I was handing in as white. 'Don't worry, son', he said. 'I know what it's like to be on active service.' I took these as kind words.

Crumlin Road was the standard Victorian prison with four wings, A to D, radiating out from an inner circle. On the first night I was banged up in a cell in the basement area of D Wing, the section of the prison which doubled as a reception and isolation/punishment area. The cell was what I expected: standard width and length, iron bed with bad springs, horsehair mattress and pillow, sheets and grey blankets, iron door complete with peephole, chamber pot in the corner, a table and chair with a basin and jug of water, and a bedside locker with traditional Bible which, having nothing else, I was glad to browse. A heating pipe ran the width of the cell and the strikingly solid walls were split-painted institutional grey and green. I paced the cell a bit, was given a plastic mug of sweet tea and a large, hard Belfast bun, and then lay on the bed and thought untroubled thoughts. The following morning I was moved briefly into a cell with a man from the Falls Road, who told me proudly that he was in for thieving, before we were moved up together to see the prison governor. The screw accompanying us greeted my compatriot by name and, having ascertained what he was back for, noted 'at least you're not one of those mad bombers', giving me a bleak look. At the entrance to the governor's office I ignored the chief officer's 'left–right, left–right' and, striking what I thought was an appropriately defiant stance, was formally received into B Wing by Assistant Governor Gibson.

At this time B Wing housed all the pre-trial or remand prisoners and was heavy with republicans – there were perhaps 80 to 100 of us. Sentenced prisoners were kept in A Wing, while young prisoners and those serving short sentences were in D Wing. C Wing held internees on their way to Long Kesh, which had been opened as an internment camp in mid-September. There was only a handful of sentenced IRA prisoners in A Wing, under the command of the already legendary ex-O/C of Belfast, Billy McKee. The B Wing routine had us up at 7 a.m., down for breakfast and then back to the cells until 10. We had two hours' exercise in the B Wing yard at 10 a.m. and again at 2 p.m. and evening association in the dining area between 5 and 7 p.m. before being locked up for the night, with lights out at 10 p.m. We walked around the yard in small groups and, for some reason buried deep in prison history, in an anti-clockwise direction. Some prisoners kicked a ball around but the football pitch was closed off at the time because an escape of remand prisoners had taken place during a match on the day of my arrest when a dozen players had scaled the wall and vanished into Ardoyne. We were doubled up on bunks in the cells. My first cell mate was Larry O'Neill from Antrim, who had been given a very hard time in custody after the RUC and British army had found a substantial arms dump on his land.

On entering the prison, I had answered standard questions such as name and date of birth. I'd told the screw I had no religion and, though he made the predictable crack about whether I was a Catholic or a Protestant atheist, I certainly knew who to walk with when the screws came calling 'RCs for a bath'. In addition to Officials and loyalists, there were of course ordinary prisoners in B Wing, quite a lot of them, and we often had to put up with screaming, shouting and banging on cell doors and water pipes at night from people who were obviously unwell and should never have been imprisoned. We had chamber pots in which to relieve ourselves during lock-up hours but it was considered bad form to defecate in what was shared accommodation and the various exercise yards adjoining the prison wings were regularly littered with so-called mystery parcels, wrappings of faeces thrown out of the cells at night by prisoners who were ill or otherwise caught short, whom the screws had refused to let out to use the toilets.

I had been admitted to B Wing and shown to my cell during the exercise period and so was brought immediately from there to the yard. We had to pass through a number of gates on the way and I saw how basic prison security operated: you were passed through gate after gate and from screw to screw in a way that ensured that the prisoner was never in a position to force the opening of the gate ahead, behind which the screw with the key safely stood. 'One off, to you, sir.' I entered the yard through yet another locked door and stood there, ignored, looking around. All the prisoners bar me and one other were in their own clothes. I spoke to the other man in brown remand uniform and asked him what he was in for. 'Explosives', he said, to which I replied 'Good on you', not then realising he was a UVF man from Lurgan. There was only a handful of loyalists (Orangies, Huns, Bluenoses) on remand and they kept a low profile and were left alone by the republicans.

In the yard, I sought out the IRA O/C, something which was complicated by the presence of the Officials. Billy Kennedy was O/C of the remand prisoners at the time and I was perfunctorily debriefed by his adjutant, Tony Bradley, a Falls Road man to whom I would become close, the debrief even shallower than my interrogation. The remand unit at that time visibly lacked unity. The O/C was apparently appointed by Billy McKee, who naturally picked someone he knew personally and this inevitably favoured the Falls Road, or 2nd Battalion, men. The O/C then, just as naturally, fashioned his staff after his own image, so that the 2nd Battalion men were running the show, negotiating with the prison staff and so on. This was not to the liking of, in particular, those from the 3rd Battalion – Ardoyne, New Lodge Road, the Markets and Short Strand – where the post-internment fighting was particularly intense. However, it was obviously difficult for Billy Kennedy to make appointments from among people of whom he knew nothing. The result initially was that there were different, in Belfast parlance, cliques, based loosely on the three Belfast battalions, with a further clique composed of those from outside Belfast known simply as 'the country men'. The cliques shared parcels and, as it turned out, escape plans, and this would eventually produce a unified staff on which I would come to serve as the accidental representative of the country men.

For the moment I was fortunate in that a couple of the Andersonstown men I had been at Marlowe's camp with were also in the prison. One of them greeted me as 'Dub', which stuck for a bit and was not the worst of monikers. Shortly afterwards a number of the Ardoyne men who had been on the Donegal training shoot-out turned up on remand and, over time, I would meet up again with many of those with whom I had crossed paths at the camps and otherwise on the outside. Joe Cahill's sister came in to visit me that first afternoon, bringing me a set of civilian clothes as well as a food parcel and tobacco. Billy Kelly's mother also came in with an enormous box of fruit, and then the Derry Prisoners' Dependants' Fund took over and I received visits from various young Derry women for the rest of my time inside.

Prison, in the circumstances I found myself in, was not difficult. There was a general assumption that things were coming to a head politically and that we were not long for the place. Either that or we would escape. Escape was always being planned for, with some plans clearly better than others. There was a time in which an embarrassingly large number of us were sawing away at the bars in the cell windows at night with hacksaw blades smuggled through in the lining of cardboard boxes. We filled the cut with a mixture of soap and dust that supposedly defeated detection when the screws came tapping on the bars with their batons, and concealed the blades in newspapers placed under the chamber pot in the corner – with a view to collecting drips of urine – guessing correctly that the yellow-stained, crisping newspaper looked sufficiently disgusting to discourage a proper search. British army searchlights criss-crossed the yard below, occasionally scanning the prison walls, and you would watch the beam's approach, ceasing work and ducking down at the correct time, just as in the movies. Somehow, we lacked the time or cohesion to complete the job but left many half-sawn bars in B Wing when we were moved on some weeks later.

This was a chaotic period, with arrests, particularly in the Belfast area, running at a furious rate, and the command structure of brigade, battalion and company staffs was under enormous pressure, with key positions continually having to be filled, in some cases by people who were patently not up to the job. The chaos had its mirror image on the inside, with those who had had seniority outside perhaps being required to account to people they had previously commanded. Things were not as bad for us as for the internees since all of us on remand had been caught red-handed with weapons or explosives – rather than in raids on billets or while moving about unarmed – thereby giving us a marked bias towards the rank and file. The absence at the outset of a cohesive remand staff meant, among other things, that there was no proper debriefing, far less a system of reporting back to those outside. This also led to a level of mistrust because it was difficult to know who was who or, indeed, if there were informers amongst us. There were breakdowns in the normal standards of military discipline here and there throughout Belfast. For instance, when the Ardoyne men came in, the then company adjutant openly and wittily boasted about how he had avoided an even worse beating when arrested by paratroopers by blaming a recent attack on the O/C, who had been arrested with him. This was a fine, big man who had been involved in serious operations and I assumed he was joking, but by the time he was returned for trial some months later, books of evidence were being studied within the prison and his weakness on being arrested was subsequently treated very seriously.

In prison you have time on your hands and I did a lot of reading. Junk novels were being passed around but I was hungry as never before to read serious stuff and harassed friends with access to the bookshops of Dublin for reading material. Books by Bobby Seale and Frantz Fanon, more Bertrand Russell, as well as Pelican books on Mao, Che Guevara, Stalin, Lenin, and Irish and Third World history came in and were passed around. Just as on the outside, most of those I spoke with were egalitarian socialists rather than Marxists, who believed we were fighting for a republic that would culminate in the institution of the maxim 'To each according to his needs', and a society in which all would work to the best of their ability and all would be looked after.

With the respect of one's peers replacing material reward, insofar as money would continue to hold relevance at all, everyone would receive the same and be free, Russell-like, to spend their discretionary income on books or cigars as each might choose.

We passed the time and did something useful for the cause, colouring handkerchiefs with felt pens onto which we first traced republican motifs such as Mise Éire, the new Provisional symbol of the Phoenix rising out of the flames of Belfast in August 1969, and the 1916 heroes. These were produced both as personal gifts and for the prisoners' dependants' funds. They were often autographed by groups of prisoners from different areas and were reported to be fetching up to £50 in parts of the South and hundreds of dollars in the United States. Later, we graduated to wooden wall plaques painted with poster paints and then varnished, and, later again, when following sentencing we got access to rudimentary workshops, those among us with the will and talent produced sometimes beautifully crafted harps, Celtic crosses and other items hand-carved from wood, as well as leather key rings, wallets, purses, belts and handbags.

The days flew by, divided into the segments of prison routine, among them mealtimes. A fastidious eater despite some experience of institutions, I was fine with breakfast and tea, but was unable to stomach the main meals and would spend the next three years eating sandwiches. It was rumoured that the screws were putting something into the tea that would make us both compliant and impotent, but we drank it all the same. Among the highlights of prison life were the visits, which at that time were conducted at a room-long table where we were separated from our neighbour by wood panelling and from our visitors by wire grilles, which made it difficult to properly see one another. An additional highlight was the weekly court appearance before my return for trial, first in Derry and then in Belfast magistrates court, on the return journey from which some young Houdini slipped his handcuffs on successive weeks, to the consternation of both his fellow prisoners and the screws.

***

Day and night we could hear the gunfire from Ardoyne, New Lodge and farther afield, as well as the crump of the bombs going off in the city centre. At the end of November, twenty explosions occurred in the space of just thirty hours throughout the North in what was the first coordinated bombing strike. We had radios in the cells and were avid listeners to the hourly news reports of shootings, bombings and political developments.

One of the worst atrocities of the entire conflict occurred in early December when the UVF bombed McGurk's bar in the New Lodge Road area, killing fifteen civilians, including two children. Though the authorities tried to blame the massacre on an IRA accident, an 'own goal' in the dreadful parlance of the time – a story carried without demur by the British press – in prison we knew well that a loyalist murder campaign was getting underway. A Shankill Road furniture shop was bombed a week later, with four Protestant fatalities, including two small children, in an attack that we blamed on the British but which is now widely believed to have been an IRA message to the loyalists that pub bombings would be repaid in kind. I felt in particular for the Belfast men, given the special intensity of the conflict in the city and the edge the UVF added to things. Every shot and sudden bang in the distance was a mystery that might presage personal havoc for one of my comrades.

In September, eighteen-month-old Angela Gallagher had been killed by a ricocheting bullet in Belfast, a stark reminder of the dangers of urban guerrilla warfare. Ruairí Ó Brádaigh was walked into an unfortunate press comment when he referred to the death of the infant as precisely that – 'one of the hazards of guerrilla war' – though the, to the authorities welcome, sound bite was ripped from its context. Shortly after internment, a man had died and 35 people had been injured, some of them appallingly, when caught in an explosion at the offices of the Electricity Board in Belfast. It was the first time we had directly caused a civilian fatality in a commercial bombing and was the result of an inadequate warning. This was simply not good enough, either then or later, but for every botched IRA operation, the British would respond with an atrocity of their own, which allowed us to quietly put the error behind us.

In mid-December a group of us were moved from court in Belfast to Armagh prison, where we stayed until early January. Though Armagh offered open visits where you could sit across a table from your visitor, the conditions were otherwise worse and the IRA leadership in the prison decided that we would go on hunger strike on Christmas Day. It was one of those self-defeating protests, a gesture that made no difference to our situation and I lay on the bed in the cell I shared with Jim McCrystal from Lurgan, feeling foolish rather than heroic but certain at least that I would face no further Christmas in captivity.

I was glad to get back to Crumlin Road where, amid the move and the bickering, Jim Davison from the Markets had taken over as O/C in B Wing. Jimmy was then in his mid-20s and was a tall, fair-haired man with great physical presence who had held no rank on the outside but exuded natural authority and common sense. Tony Bradley became his adjutant and things were tightened up, with regular parades at which orders were handed out. On my return I became involved in an escape plan with a couple of Tyrone men who had managed to smuggle two small revolvers into the prison. We were permitted to buy our own cereal in the prison shop and I was holding the shorts in my cell, concealed in a cornflakes box. Whether the plan was betrayed or otherwise discovered, a surprise cell search of the entire wing was conducted one morning while we were at breakfast. We had to undergo personal searches on the way back from the canteen and I held the box aloft while the screws frisked me, certain we had gotten away with it. Half an hour later a more targeted search of my cell and a couple of others took place and the guns were discovered. The authorities made no effort to remove me from the prison for questioning, perhaps suggesting they knew all they needed to know, and about a month later I was charged with possession of the two guns.

The immediate consequence – aside from my alarm that I might be taken out to one of the interrogation centres – was that the O/C, naturally enough, wanted to know what the hell was going on. This effectively resulted in my co-option onto the wing staff and less than a week later I was told that a group of us would be going out through the front gate disguised as screws, having first taken over a section of the prison. To that end, those selected were given haircuts and, in the long-haired seventies, I was later easily able to spot my prospective co-escapers. For reasons I don't now remember, this plan, like many others, ultimately came to nothing, but it mattered little given our state of permanent expectation. Internees Martin Meehan, even then a legend, Dutch Doherty and Hugh McCann went over the wall from C Wing in early December, and the inevitably nicknamed Magnificent Seven swam ashore from the *Maidstone* prison ship in mid-January and disappeared into the Markets area before surfacing within the week at a press conference in Dublin, among them Peter Rogers, my companion from Paul Marlowe's Mayo camp.

On 30 January 1972 an anti-internment rally took place in Derry where – as everyone knows – paratroopers brought in from Belfast went on a killing spree, leaving thirteen demonstrators, all male and most of them very young, dead. A fourteenth died some time later from his wounds and a further twelve were wounded by gunfire. The dead and wounded were initially dismissed by the British as gunmen and bombers, some of whom they claimed were on the wanted list. As the reports came in and the number of the dead increased, I lay in my cell mentally trying to put names to the numbers, quite certain the toll would include practically every IRA man I had known in Derry and not suspecting for an instant that the British army might have been unleashed against the civilian population in the way it was.

With the sheer scale of this slaughter, the last vestiges of nationalist participation in Northern public life evaporated. In the South, Jack Lynch was forced to call a day of national mourning and to send ministers north for the funerals, while at Westminster Bernadette Devlin physically attacked Home Secretary Reginald Maudling when she crossed the floor of the House and clouted him in what was the only decent human response then open to her. The day of the funerals was marked by us with another futile hunger strike, while in Dublin the British embassy was torched by IRA men in front of a crowd estimated at 30,000. Bloody Sunday, as it instantly became known, had its impact in Britain too, where Harold Wilson, then in opposition, said there was 'no solution without a United Ireland with proper safeguards' for those who would constitute the new minority. The British Foreign Secretary also pitched in, advising, privately, of the Foreign Office preference for

Irish unity. They at least knew well the opprobrium the British were receiving throughout the rest of the world.

In April, the Widgery Tribunal excused the paratroopers' actions, something that was no surprise to us. British mendacity was by now expected and Widgery was neither the first, nor the last, senior judicial figure in Britain to disgrace himself when dealing with Irish issues. A second inquiry under Lord Saville a quarter of a century later was finally published in 2010 after a twelve-year investigation. The report was naturally welcomed for its exoneration of the victims, but there was plenty there for the British too, in Saville's parallel exoneration of the two governments, British and Unionist, together with the upper echelons of the army; his finding was that the killings were the work of a paratrooper colonel and a few rogue soldiers and were premeditated by neither the government nor high command, nor subsequently covered up by anyone at all.

Chapter 8

In mid-February we were given C Wing when the internees were moved out to Long Kesh. Conditions improved dramatically thanks to Gibson, the governor in charge of our wing, who was completely reasonable, giving us almost everything we asked for, subject to there being no security implications. We had boilers on the ground floor landing for tea or instant coffee, an additional television in the recreation area dispelled all argument about what to watch, the open visits previously available to the internees were now ours, and we had virtually full association throughout the day. Free association turned out to be a Trojan horse, allowing us the time together to organise, plot and plan. Things were tightened up internally and what had been a disparate collection of republican prisoners began to resemble a unit, with an escape committee, regular staff meetings and parades of the unit, at which directions were handed down and grievances properly dealt with. We had internal control of the wing, and among the arcane but thorough discussions I remember, one that stands out was the debate over whether or not our POW status would be better underlined if we voluntarily slammed our cell doors closed at night rather than allow the screws to lock us in.

Our most ambitious escape attempt took place when, cued to the music that introduced the television programme *Dr Who*, C Wing was seized by IRA prisoners, screws disappearing into alcoves, cells and doorways as they were taken from behind. We were to disappear in ten-strong groups over a blind spot on the exercise yard wall and then into the night, assisted by 3rd Battalion volunteers who were ready with rope ladders on the far side. I was among the first group to go but, unfortunately, as we entered the C Wing yard the alarm went up and we quickly chose retreat back into the wing over the alternative of affording the sentries a turkey shoot. Attempts to escape continued but that was our best effort and, as the authorities learned from their mistakes, escaping became more difficult.

With a preponderance of very young men – the vast majority in their late teens or early twenties – there was inevitably a certain amount of horseplay and practical joking. Though I knew nothing of this one at the time, and would have tried to stop it if I had, new prisoners were likely to be encouraged to attend a makeshift confessional in a darkened cell where another prisoner sat behind a screen posing as the priest. He would show a special interest in the sexual transgressions of his victim, loudly repeating the whispered acknowledgments and demanding further detail, to the huge amusement of those listening nearby and the subsequent mortification of the poor fellow who had fallen for it. Sometimes the joke was designed to backfire on the joker; following his re-arrest, Martin Meehan, playing the father confessor, had to be pulled off his 'victim', who had been put up to 'confessing' that he had been sleeping with Meehan's wife. In addition to this, beds were rigged to collapse when sat upon and remade with half-sheets so the victim found himself unable to get in. Water, sometimes buckets of it, was occasionally thrown over other prisoners, perhaps when the victim was engrossed in a toilet cubicle, though a lid was kept on this. Sharp Belfast slagging, not at all kind, was routine, and one soon became able to take it and dish it back out. Some of the 'mixing' was a bit cruel. Months later, after we had won political status, a number of newly sentenced men from south Down were told on admission to A Wing that they were in luck because there was an escape planned for that very evening. They were given boot polish and told to black up their faces and come running out of their cells and down the stairs at a certain time, which the unfortunates duly did, to the great amusement of those observing, screws as well as prisoners.

Shortly before the move to C Wing, I had been tried on the Derry charges in Belfast, moving back and forth from the prison to the courthouse through the narrow tunnel that linked the two under the Crumlin Road. This was before the introduction of the non-jury Diplock courts and the jury, to my astonishment, was unable to agree a verdict and I was put back to be tried again. Judge O'Donnell, a well-known Catholic, presided at my first trial. There were rumours at the time that he would resign over Bloody Sunday and I heard in later years that, unlike other members of the judiciary at the time, he was not an IRA target. He quite properly directed the jury to ignore my refusal to recognise his court and then put to them as a possible defence that my presence in the back yard from which the evidence had me emerge could have been for a variety of purposes. I could, for instance, have been held there against my will. While this was hardly likely, given my stance, it was enough to split the jury and indeed an even better outcome was being predicted by one of the screws, who offered to place money on my acquittal with a colleague of his. At any rate, a Derry jury with a different judge had no difficulty in reaching a unanimous verdict to convict a couple of months later, though, fortunately for me, the conviction was for simple possession only and I was found not guilty of possession with intent to endanger life, which would have led to a longer sentence.

By now I was reconciled with my parents. Soon after my arrest, my father had come up to visit me. Approaching the grille, he, who had never used bad language in my presence, asked me – no doubt for effect – what the fuck I thought I was playing at refusing to recognise the court. I told him that if that was his attitude, he could take himself off, and turned to leave. My father immediately folded, though I did have a little battle to prevent him from going to see Ruairí Ó Brádaigh to seek an exemption for me.

The cornflakes box incident put paid to any notions my father may have had along those lines and he became resigned. He visited Derry where he met Roisín Keenan and later told me he was shocked at the housing conditions he had found there. My father was a local authority engineer who had been responsible in his time for social housing and knew what he was talking about. He became, I thought, quietly supportive and, to my knowledge, opposed local authority workers in Wexford – where he was the town engineer – being asked to paint out IRA slogans on roads and bridges, arguing that in the circumstances this was a task for someone else. I am sure he reflected on his time in Malaya where, in common with much of the colonial service, he was a police reservist during the so-called Emergency when the British fought, and defeated, the Malayan communist guerrillas in the early 1950s. My father, who had a private pilot's licence, dropped the wages into local rubber plantations and though I remember little enough, I do recall being with him at the firing range once, where he let off a few shots, and of our house being broken into and his gun stolen. Once, too, when an engineer was accidentally killed, an apology had been issued by the guerrilla leader, Chin Peng, which would have been similar to those now coming from the IRA.

My father wasn't the only one to urge me to take my chances with the British justice system. Sometime in February I was called for an unexpected legal visit and found myself facing a representative from the Crown Prosecutor, who tried to persuade me to recognise the court. The visit lasted perhaps fifteen seconds before I walked out. The Quinn brothers, John and Jimmy, caught *in flagrante* on a street with rifles in their hands, had received five-year sentences having refused to recognise the court, while a non-volunteer sympathiser convicted of having a firearm hidden in his back garden got ten, despite his bank of barristers. There was no rhyme or reason to the sentences being handed down and, back then, none of us gave a damn what we got as we didn't for an instant believe we'd have to serve it. In any case, you were going to be interned immediately if you happened to be acquitted, making recognising the court a thoroughly useless exercise.

***

By the close of 1971 there had been over 1,000 explosions in the North, three-quarters of them following internment. The New Year would bring a significant increase both in British casualties and bombings, which were now going off at the rate of three or four a day. Belfast and Derry were regularly being hit by multiple bombings at government offices and commercial buildings, giving both city centres the appearance of war zones. The British army continued to put out what were self-defeating statements, claiming, for example, on 19 January that a very precise 99 IRA men had been arrested since the year opened, of whom no less than 40 were officers. One week later fourteen bombs exploded across the North, suggesting there was no shortage of IRA members, or officers come to that. Set-piece battles were also taking place on the border, where a unit under Martin Meehan was involved in a two-hour gun battle with troops in south Armagh, in the course of which thousands of rounds were fired. The retreating Meehan conducted an impromptu press conference on the southern side of the border in which he claimed to have given the British 'a pasting' and added 'you could nearly hear them squealing in Belfast'.

Though Bloody Sunday had ended the lingering doubts and moral qualms of many, as the IRA fought on the inevitable casualties Ruairí Ó Brádaigh had referred to reinstated people's concerns, souring the mood and letting the moderates back in. In late February the Officials messed up a perfect opportunity to inflict significant military casualties when a car bomb assault on the Parachute Regiment's headquarters in Aldershot backfired, leaving an army chaplain, five cleaning women and a gardener dead. The Officials went into denial, stupidly claiming that its own intelligence had it that a dozen officers had also been killed in the blast but had 'miraculously disappeared'. For us, the bombing campaign, to which Belfast would show such devotion over the years, meant an accident was always waiting to happen and in early March a Saturday afternoon explosion at the Abercorn restaurant killed two young Catholic (as it happened) women and wounded dozens of others, some appallingly. Though the IRA denied the bombing, no one really believed it – though at the time I did.[8]

While it was not inconceivable that the loyalists were guilty, our prime suspects were the British, something that was not entirely beyond the bounds. The British had psychological warfare and black operations capacity from the outset, having used both elsewhere in the retreat from empire, and the occasional bit of murder designed to sow confusion or reflect badly on the insurgents would have been nothing new. Its principal intellectual, Brigadier Frank Kitson, commanded the brigade that operated in Belfast up to April 1972. Though the youngest brigadier in the British army, Kitson had been handed the biggest

---

[8] Throughout the conflict republicans made great play of always telling the truth. In fact, we lied whenever we thought we could get away with it, though it would be some years before I realised this.

job and treated the North as a laboratory, believing that trouble in 'mainland' Britain from indigenous revolutionaries was a real prospect down the line. He had previously served in Kenya, Malaya and Cyprus, and his *Low Intensity Operations*, which came out in 1971, was the field manual for much that occurred, particularly in terms of intelligence gathering, psychological operations and propaganda. Kitson also hinted at the later formation of pseudo-gangs, though he sensibly omitted any details on them in his book, or indeed of the interrogation methods that might be used.

In March 1972 a report from a commission headed by Lord Parker gave the green light to 'vigorous interrogation'. Parker said he believed the army's claim that hooding, standing in position, and the production of 'white noise' were designed to ensure that the detainees could not communicate with each other, making him either a credulous fool or a liar. Lord Gardiner salvaged something for Britain's reputation in a minority report where he said bluntly that the techniques were illegal under English law and 'not morally justifiable'. Though the British government accepted Parker, they implemented Gardiner, but while the use of sensory deprivation in its August 1971 form may have been ended, this made little difference to the Special Branch who, in the words of the late John McGuffin – a well-known Belfast anarchist and the author of works on both internment and torture – had anyway 'always preferred the less sophisticated methods of boot and fist'.

From around the time of my own arrest, the British were employing 'robust' interrogation not just for intelligence purposes but also to beat signed confessions out of suspects, which could then be used to convict them before the courts. Most of the prisoners with me in Crumlin Road had been badly beaten while in custody. 'Techniques', if they can be called that, included slapping, kicking and beating with fists, batons and boots, the squeezing of testicles, blindfolding, the firing of blanks and in some cases the administering of injections allegedly containing truth serum, and the use of electric shock. Those badly treated in my own wing included Larry O'Neill, Bobby Lavery, Micky Walsh, Tony Bradley, Dickie O'Neill, Rocky Morgan, Dingus Magee, sixteen-year-old Paul Kane, Luger Maguire and Joe Rafferty. Dickie was one of a number whom the screws refused to admit to the wing until he had been seen by a doctor, to avoid any subsequent suggestion from the army or RUC that he had received his injuries while in the custody of the prison, while Joe Rafferty had to be hospitalised for his injuries immediately following his appearance in court. Geordie Burt, who had been shot and wounded, was beaten by troops while in hospital. Dingus and others were repeatedly kicked awake, humiliated and made sing 'The Sash' and 'God Save the Queen'. Maxie McDermott said a broom handle or other wooden implement had been shoved up his anus. Brothers John and Jimmy Quinn got almost identical treatment in Springfield Road barracks. Jimmy had his head stuck in a coal bunker and later down a toilet bowl, which was then flushed, perhaps to allow him to clean up, though perhaps not since John was given the same treatment minus a trip to the coal bunker. Both had guns forced into their mouths and the triggers pulled. All these and others were documented by Fathers Denis Faul and Raymond Murray and by the Association of Legal Justice in Belfast, and many of the reports included incontrovertible medical evidence. Incidentally, the complaints of ill-treatment, even torture, didn't come from us. Back then, we fully accepted, indeed expected it, though we became adept at whingeing about it with the best of them as time marched on.

***

There had been republican peace proposals almost from the outset and soon after the Abercorn bombing in early March 1972 the IRA declared a three-day ceasefire to be extended if the British agreed to their demands. There was no response from the British, who used the opportunity to continue house raids and arrests, but while the Officials mounted a handful of operations, Provisional IRA guns stayed silent and the leadership showed that it exercised complete control over its units. During the short ceasefire, Harold Wilson had exploratory talks with the IRA in Dublin under cover of meetings he had arranged with government ministers and opposition parties, something that naturally outraged the parliamentarians so used when Wilson went public with it a week later. Wilson had been interviewed on RTE shortly before the meeting and went out of his way to flatter us, describing the IRA as a disciplined, tight-knit organisation that would certainly be capable of honouring a truce, sentiments that infuriated the unionists. The talks with Wilson concluded as the 72 hours ended and hostilities resumed with a large car bomb in Belfast and the shooting dead by the British army in Derry of IRA volunteers Colm Keenan and Eugene McGillan. Both of them were unarmed and the blood-soaked cigarette Colm had been smoking when he was shot was still clutched between his fingers when his body was carried into a nearby house.

By now it was clear that the British could no longer continue to prop up Stormont in the face of the offensive – military and political – they were undergoing. Battered by world opinion, they knew that giving the unionists the lead had brought nothing but disaster and now determined on an initiative that might gain the approval of nationalists, the Southern state and indeed the rest of the world: taking back control of security. A week after Colm's death, Heath told Brian Faulkner, in a move that seems to have surprised nobody but Faulkner himself, that Stormont was to lose control of security, thus precipitating direct rule and the arrival in Belfast at the end of March of the first Secretary of State for Northern Ireland, William Whitelaw.

The abolition of Stormont had been a key IRA demand and no one was in any doubt that we had brought about its demise. For us, MacStiofáin 'completely and totally rejected' the British proposals, while Ruairí described them as an 'advance' and called for a 'cool appraisal' of the situation – something that apparently fetched him a bollocking from MacStiofáin. The Officials, to the surprise of many of their volunteers, condemned direct rule as a backward step. While it brought huge external pressure on the IRA leadership to call a cease-fire, the pressures on the Officials were from within the organisation as well as from without, and, following another 'unpopular' killing, that of a Derry-born British soldier home on leave, they declared a unilateral ceasefire towards the end of May.

We had our own difficulties. Shortly before direct rule, MacStiofáin was slightly injured when a parcel bomb posted to his address exploded while he and another volunteer were preparing to defuse it. MacStiofáin made the mistake of appearing in public with an eyepatch covering his relatively minor injury, so giving the media the opportunity to christen him 'General Die-On' in a nod to the famous Israeli general Moshe Dayan. MacStiofáin, unfortunately, did look ridiculous and, though I was reluctant to admit it and certainly kept my mouth shut, it was embarrassing. Much worse, on the same day there was an explosion in Donegall Street in Belfast city centre which killed six men; a seventh died later. Again we excused ourselves, blaming the authorities for deliberately ignoring bomb warnings while they in turn said the warnings had been contradictory, but the pressures on the leadership to react to the new situation now increased.

***

Jim Davison had by then moved on following sentencing and Tony Bradley was again O/C. I was his adjutant and heir apparent and, after Tony was sentenced, I duly became O/C. I appointed Paddy Fitzsimons, a tough boxer from the New Lodge Road, as my adjutant. Paddy had been one of those subjected to electric shock treatment at Girdwood barracks and, rather than see the matter aired publicly in court, the authorities later withdrew the charges against him. During this time Gibson, our wing governor, convened a few meetings attended by ourselves and representatives from the Officials and the loyalists, at which we were quizzed about our political positions. The Officials and loyalists had surprisingly little to say for themselves and we dominated these sessions. We reported at length to McKee and I assume the results were also winging their way to civil servants in the Northern Ireland Office. Direct rule had created uncertainty among the screws as well, who were now sucking up to us and at great pains to underline their non-political role as equal opportunity gaolers.

***

In May the people of the South disappointed us by voting heavily in favour of EEC membership, opposition to which was then the touchstone of anti-imperialist sentiment. I rationalised this away – as I would every future election result – on the basis that the people could not be expected to vote for war and, more dubiously, by way of the usual revolutionary argument that the people were unfortunate dupes, blinded by propaganda and incapable of acting in their own true interests. Parliamentary democracy was a rigged game, operating within parameters that we rejected. We were neither part of this game nor, indeed, democrats at all, either then or later – notwithstanding the revisionism of the 1990s.

With a brief pause after Bloody Sunday, the Southern state had gone on the offensive against the IRA. But while many men were brought before the courts, most cases were being dismissed or struck out, and it seemed that the judiciary had little appetite for the role of fall guys for the government. Now, against the backdrop of direct rule and bombing disasters, and emboldened by its referendum success, the government quickly introduced Special Criminal Courts. These sat without a jury and in the 1940s and again in 1961 had been staffed by Irish army officers. This time the judiciary, interestingly, agreed to sit on them. Joe Cahill, Ruairí Ó Brádaigh and his brother Seán were immediately arrested while the rest of the leadership went on the run. All three were charged with IRA membership and, as had been planned, duly commenced hunger strikes at the same time as we were on hunger strike for political status in Crumlin Road. The cases against them were to collapse within weeks. In Cahill's case, the Special Court itself threw out incitement charges, suggesting that the courts were not yet quite ready to start slamming up freedom fighters.

Outside, civilians, British soldiers and IRA volunteers continued to lose their lives. More than half of the IRA casualties in Belfast in 1972 were victims of explosions; in the early months, fifteen volunteers died in four separate episodes while assembling or moving explosives. A number of these deaths are controversial and there can be no certainty as to whether the explosions occurred as a result of faulty equipment, handling errors or deliberate sabotage by the British, for this had become a dirty war.

Between the beginning of 1972 and the coming into force of the truce at midnight on 26 June, sixty-four security force members were killed: forty-four British soldiers, nine RUC and eleven UDR members. Most of the last were shot off-duty, though this was a description we took exception to, arguing that IRA members were at risk of death or capture at any time of the day or night and that the same should apply to the UDR, who, especially in the religiously mixed rural areas, were always watching and learning and never off duty. The majority of the fatalities occurred in the cities, but by now other areas were becoming more active and soldiers also died in south and north Armagh, Fermanagh, south Derry and east Tyrone. In the rural areas, a pattern of landmines and large-scale gun attacks, particularly in south Armagh, was now being established. This area, and east Tyrone to a slightly lesser extent, remained absolutely solid in the years that followed, while the other rural areas were variously strong or weak depending on the presence there of perhaps just one or two strong personalities who would galvanise the rest.

Chapter 9

As the sources of gelignite dried up towards the end of 1971, we had begun using various home-made mixes, and while the precise origins of the car bomb are uncertain, the fact that far greater quantities of explosives were required to achieve the same result – together with the increasing difficulty of 'walking' bombs into town or city centres – resulted in this, in retrospect, very obvious means of conveyance being adopted by units throughout the North. The weapon was difficult to battle and became even more so in 1973 when proxy bombs made their first appearance. These were conveyed to their targets by unwilling drivers, and occasionally by drivers who could plausibly claim to have been unwilling. Bombing attacks were regularly combined with hoax bombs, all of which had to be checked out individually, and every one of which presented a challenge to the bomb disposal experts, who had to look out for trip wires, pressure plates and other hazards on their walk to the target.

The contest with the bomb disposal teams went on, with IRA engineers incorporating increasingly complex anti-disturbance mechanisms into their bombs. The British responded, most notably with the Wheelbarrow, a remotely controlled vehicle used to perform many of the dangerous moves the expert would previously have had to carry out personally. But while their defences increased in effectiveness over the years, we always held the initiative and in 1972 the British suffered serious casualties in what was a tiny unit. Two more bomb disposal men died in Belfast shortly after their commander, Major Styles, left in February, a move that was anyway necessitated by the propaganda disaster the British army would have faced if we had managed to kill him. His successor, Major Calladene, was killed in the Falls Road area in March, and by the end of the year eight bomb disposal experts had been killed while attempting to defuse IRA bombs.

Meanwhile, the loyalists had been preparing for doomsday. With direct rule looming, William Craig had launched his Ulster Vanguard movement at a rally in Lisburn where, having 'inspected' the serried ranks of Ulster Defence Association (UDA) men, he pronounced unionism 'determined, ladies and gentlemen, to preserve our British traditions and way of life. And God help those who get in our way for we mean business.' The following Saturday, Craig arrived at a rally in an open car flanked by a twelve-strong, uniformed motor cycle escort. He was introduced to the crowd as 'The Leader' and took a quasi-fascist salute, either oblivious to, or consciously aiming at, comparisons with Hitler and Mussolini. Asked if the impending loyalist 'action' might mean the killing of all Catholics in Belfast, he said 'It might not go as far as that. But it could go as far as killing.' At the final rally in Belfast, on 18 March, he warned that 'We must build up the dossier on those men and women who are a menace to this country, because one of these days, if and when the politicians fail us, it may be our job to liqui-date the enemy.' In the event, despite shutting down the Six Counties for two days when direct rule came in, and continuing to say that the British government would not take over without a fight, Craig failed to carry through on his threat, thus adding to the republican conviction that, ultimately, the loyalists were all wind and bluster.

It is hardly a coincidence that the indiscriminate killings of Catholics began around this time, though the RUC, with the shameful conniv-ance of the media, would persist in characterising these murders as 'random' and 'motiveless'. Broadly random they may have been, in that they were premised on the slogan 'any Taig will do', but that the motive was to terrorise the Catholic population was never in doubt. This was no more than the traditional unionist response to perceived national-ist uppitiness and began in earnest with the shooting dead of Bernard Rice on the outskirts of Ardoyne in early February 1972. At the end of the month two Catholic men were badly wounded in separate shoot-ings. There was much more to come, particularly in north Belfast. In March a nineteen-year-old living in a mixed area was shot dead when standing at his front door. Another man was killed in mid-April when he went over to assist the occupants of a car seeking directions, while Gerard Donnelly became the first of many Catholic taxi drivers to die, having volunteered to drive his murderous fare to Ardoyne. When his killers asked to be taken to a nationalist area, they could be certain they would be assigned a Catholic driver, and this was to become one very dangerous way to earn a living. There were other ways in which one's religion might become apparent and in early May a young sailor home on leave was stabbed to death in a Belfast laneway. It is believed he was identified as a Catholic because he was wearing a cross and chain. Later that month, Gerard McCusker was killed by a loyalist assassination squad. In what was to become a feature of such killings, his badly bruised body bore clear marks of torture: both his wrists were broken and his hair had been pulled out by the roots. The RUC tried to blame the IRA. Three days later the body of a drinks representative was found shot dead in a beauty spot to which he had been forced to drive after being abducted from the pub on the Shankill he had been attending on business. His killers first sat with him and drank his samples. Ten more Catholics, one of them a seventeen-year-old girl, were to be shot dead by the UDA/UVF before the IRA truce commenced on 26 June.

Meanwhile, following a loyalist bomb attack on Kelly's Bar in Ballymurphy in which one man was fatally injured, and a subsequent three-way gun battle in which six people died, the local UDA established a temporary no-go area to put pressure on the British to move into the Bogside and Creggan. They dismantled the barricades after the weekend but promised that they would continue to erect them until the British moved on Derry. Instead, the British decided to deal with this head-on, and when barricades went up the following weekend in east Belfast, paratroopers were sent in to clear them, with the inevitable firing of shots and allegations of brutality. The UDA responded to this setback by erecting more substantial barricades in the Shankill Road area and, faced with the prospect of an all-out confrontation, the British swiftly folded, entering into negotiations to 'talk down' the barricades and effectively recognising the UDA leadership.

By May, so, while the IRA and the British army were going at it hammer and tongs, a loyalist assassination campaign was also underway and the UDA had successfully seen off the army in a direct test of wills. In the same month I was tried and sentenced in rapid succession on the prison guns and Derry charges and found myself in the A Wing Annexe just as the hunger strike for political status was beginning.

***

Curiously, the wearing of prison clothing had not been an issue in Crumlin Road at the time of my arrival. We had been given no instructions on the outside as to how to behave on entering prison, though we were well briefed on remaining silent during interrogation and on the requirement that we refuse to recognise the court. In consequence, I had no hesitation in donning the uniform I was handed in reception, if little real choice given the filthy state of the clothes I had arrived in, and as those on remand were sentenced, they put on prison uniform without any difficulty. In the hothouse that was the remand wing, some of us read and argued and learned much of which we'd been ignorant before our imprisonment. Despite having, so I fancied, steeped myself in left-wing and republican literature, I did not make the connections between republican history and our then situation until I was on remand. Assisted no doubt by the conditions that faced us on conviction – two visits per month, wearing prison clothing, eating prison food and working for something like four shillings a week in the tailor shop or laundry – we started to canvass the idea of fighting for political status. We began to first hint at it to Billy McKee in our regular communiqués, or 'comms', and, when this received no response, boldly suggested that the wearing of prison uniform was not necessarily in keeping with the republican prison tradition. In reality, the tradition was pretty complex and typically depended on the strength, and sometimes the weakness, of the movement outside.

McKee himself was quite a pragmatist. Although a man with a deserved reputation for being highly principled, he chose his principles with care and would prove far too smart to strike for political status, being perfectly content with the substance. At first he ignored us, and then at some point felt it necessary to remind us that he knew a thing or two about republican history, having been jailed in both the 1940s and 1950s. Slowly political status came onto the agenda and,

shortly before I was sentenced, we received instructions that coop-
eration with the prison authorities was being withdrawn and a work
strike commenced among the sentenced prisoners surrounding what
became known as the five demands. The important ones were the
right to wear our own clothes and the right to free association; we also
sought improved visits and letters and the admission of food parcels
from outside. McKee's pragmatism had rubbed off on me, so much
so that during one meeting with Gibson I said I understood that the
European Common Market had a rule forbidding any member state
from having political prisoners and that, accordingly, as long as we had
our own clothes and free association, we would – I thought – be happy
for the British to name the arrangements as they pleased.

Having been shown some mercy by Judge McGonigal – a Catholic
ex-Special Air Service member with a fearsome sentencing record –
who treated my refusal to recognise his court as the act of an impudent
pup and sentenced me to just three years on the Crumlin Road guns
charges in early May, I had been sent back to B Wing. For a week or so
I was one of just a handful of short-term republican prisoners there,
where the work strike meant we were locked up for 21 hours out of
the 24. McKee ratcheted things up in A Wing when he instructed the
republican prisoners that they were no longer to double up in cells,
long-term prisoners being notionally entitled to single cells. This was
achieved by simply placing a book in the hinge between cell and door
and slamming the latter, thus separating it from the cell – an extraordinary vulnerability. Some days later I picked up the grey, long-term
uniform on my return from court in Derry where the jury had found
me guilty of possessing the explosives and Colt .45 pieces and the judge
had given me the four-year sentence that qualified me as a long-termer.
By now McKee and four others, chosen for their geographical spread,
were on hunger strike and were to be followed by five others on the
following Monday and by another five on each successive Monday.

Because of the refusal to double up, A Wing was full and those most
recently sentenced were being housed in a part of the prison that was
called the A Wing Annexe. Tony Bradley was the Annexe O/C and
held a meeting just after my arrival to seek volunteers for the hunger
strike. Those chosen were to start the third and fourth weeks, McKee

having decided by now that twenty strikers would be enough. Some 90 per cent of us volunteered to strike and the under-21s were furious when they were told that McKee had directed they not be considered on account of their youth. Tony peremptorily excluded a number of volunteers who were in ill health and the rest of the names went to A Wing, and I believe outside, for final selection. Both Tony and I were chosen, in part I believe, because McKee was of the view that people should lead by example and we had been O/Cs in C Wing, and in part I'm sure because he thought we would prove reliable. Although I had an additional advantage being the only Dubliner, indeed the only Southerner, on the list, I was extremely proud to have been chosen and would have been devastated had I been overlooked.

All these years later I remember little enough of the strike itself. I can recall the powerful cravings, a new intensity in the sense of smell which allowed me to find food a corridor away, and the dreams I had about it. During waking hours I read, talked, moved around slowly and tried not to think about food. It was not unlike trying to break a bad nicotine habit in that the craving continually intruded, making concentration on anything else difficult. Hunger striking was wholly novel and we had no idea how our bodies would deteriorate. We had heard rumours that our teeth would fall out, but these did not seem to be borne out by the news coming from the trailblazers in A Wing. Though it was difficult, there was no way anyone would fold and give in. It was simply unthinkable and in the course of three separate hunger strikes during my time in Crumlin Road and Long Kesh, just one striker out of some 60 men decided that he could not stay the course. As for its voluntary nature, our taking of names in open parade was not a good idea and in the two subsequent strikes names were submitted privately. Despite this, the volunteer rate remained extremely high and men seemed anxious, no less than they had been outside, to do whatever they could to advance our common cause.

Against the backdrop of the impending IRA–British army truce in the summer of 1972, the hunger strike progressed to the point where McKee and MacAirt were receiving the appropriate answers, though confirmation came only at the end and then in the context of events outside. McKee and the first cohort spent 35 days without food. At the close, he was rumoured to be on his death bed and indeed riots took place when reports swept Belfast that McKee had died. Bobby Campbell had earlier been moved to the Mater Hospital from where he escaped with some assistance, and I believe the apparent deterioration in his condition that led to the move had been carefully manipulated. My group of strikers did twenty-three days and I lost something over two stone, and though it seemed a mighty thing at the time, it has since been put into the shade by what came later in 1980 and 1981, culminating in the death of Bobby Sands and nine others. There had been strong reports the night before the strike ended that the deal was done, but apparently the relevant officials clocked off at 5 p.m., so that the news was not communicated to us until the following morning. For a long time, I resented this piece of pettiness or, more likely, simple laziness by the machine. That said, victory was indeed sweet. I awoke the following morning to be greeted by warm milk and shortly after this by scrambled egg and other delights like custard. Food never tasted better and, like children, we ignored the medical advice given to us and suffered the consequences in the shape of wind and stomach cramps, as we indulged those of our food fantasies it was possible to indulge within a prison.

Just as the hunger strike was getting underway, the loyalists had joined the work protest. There were far fewer of them in prison at this stage and, while they were smart enough not to go on hunger strike, they benefited fully from the efforts of others. I had little or no respect for them then or later and considered the UVF leader, Gusty Spence, in particular, a grandiose poseur. McKee certainly had no time for him. One story – possibly apocryphal – had it that prior to political status, Spence had sent his 'aide de camp' to McKee's cell to propose a meeting. The aide came marching up the wing, knocked on McKee's cell and found him shaving. Snapping to attention and saluting, he addressed him as General McKee and announced that General Spence had sent him to request that a meeting take place at 1600 hours, or whatever. McKee, barely pausing to break stroke from his shave, told him to 'inform General Spence that Field Marshal McKee is indisposed'.

The big gain from the strike was free association, made meaningful by the accompanying right not to do prison work. The wearing of our own clothes was merely the symbol of our political status, but this symbolism was rooted in history and had, and would retain, its own imperatives. The additional visits and letters and our access to food parcels from outside were no more than the material pay-off. Above all, there was the recognition of our command structure. Though nowhere spelled out, this was the essence of political status and allowed us to be treated by the prison administration as an organisational equal. Thus, there was no contact whatsoever between republican prisoner and prison officer; everything was mediated through the command. McKee and other members of his staff had regular meetings with the appropriate level of governor and we replicated their structure with Landing O/Cs dealing with their equivalent prison officer rank and so on. Meanwhile, we had, as it were, all the time in the world and did our best to put it to good use.

A few days after the successful conclusion of the hunger strike, we were moved to A Wing where we voluntarily doubled up. I shared a cell with Tony Bradley, who had acquired the nickname 'The Cat' in humorous reference to qualities he claimed to share with the Chelsea goalkeeper Peter Bonetti. Tony was a Nana Mouskouri fan and I got to hear quite a deal from the Greek chanteuse during our time together. McKee re-formed his staff, which had included Proinsias MacAirt as his No. 2 and Tony O'Kane as adjutant, and brought in Jim Davison, Tony Bradley and myself. Later, the unit – notionally the 4th Battalion of the Belfast Brigade – was subdivided further into companies and sections, just as on the outside.

The level of discipline was, I thought, no more than was necessary for sustaining reasonable order among 120-plus men. If anything, McKee erred on the side of leniency and had the wisdom, most of the time, to allow people the space to recover themselves. He had personally seen it all before and was determined to avoid the disintegration of unit morale that had sometimes featured in the past. For a start, he was insistent that there would be no lazing about, or 'wasting' as it was in Belfast parlance. McKee told a story about a volunteer back in the 1950s who was forcibly removed from his bed and washed by his fellow prisoners, having refused to leave it for some weeks. It was, he said, the easiest thing in the world for someone to just take to his bed and turn his face to the wall, and this was not going to be allowed. Forced up every morning, we made our beds and tidied our cells while the landings and toilets were cleaned on a rota basis. Every day was a full day of classes, lectures and endless activity.

Relations with the governor and screws were superb and conditions as good as they could possibly be in a prison. You were allowed to have a certain amount of cash in an account which could be used to buy things like cheese or tins of sardines in the prison shop. There had been a couple of occasions on remand when cigarettes sent to me from the South were returned to the sender because there was insufficient money in my account to pay the customs duty, but now I was simply given credit and the cigarettes came in.

On the open visits you could get tea or coffee for a small charge, which gave you the brief illusion that you were entertaining your guests. The screws were supposed to keep you under observation at all times and ensure there was minimal physical contact but many of them were decent men who would wander off, so giving the prisoner the opportunity to kiss his wife or girlfriend and, unfortunately, exploit the same screw's kindness by smuggling in communications or contraband.

As well as cigarettes, we were permitted toiletries, fruit, cheese, biscuits, Northern breads like soda or wheaten farls and potato bread, a cooked chicken, and up to a pound of cooked meat, which came generally in the shape of sausages, bacon, strips of steak and so on wrapped in tinfoil, which could be reheated on hotplates we had in the canteen. The various cliques shared the contents of their parcels and one of the prisoners acquired the nickname Tear-the-Beef from the relish with which he would attack a parcel's contents. In the context of the hardships people thought we were suffering in prison, I'm embarrassed to admit that I ate so much cooked chicken in my few years there that I went off it altogether.

That summer was almost idyllic as we exchanged books and music tapes, swapped life experiences and held rolling debates in each other's cells. It was the first time for many to meet people from another background; Belfast men meeting rural Tyrone men, even Falls Road men getting to know volunteers from the middle-class parts of Andersonstown. It was the summer of the Bobby Fischer–Boris Spassky world chess finals and A Wing became part of the craze, with players and spectators gathered in the canteen and games spilling over into the cells after lock-up. Tony and I often played into the early hours, begging the screw who looked through our cell peephole to leave the lights on for just another short while. When my old school friend Dave Connolly came to visit me from Dublin, he whipped out a portable chess set and we spent as much of the visit exchanging pieces as we did swapping news. Foul-tasting vodka was smuggled in from the outside, contained in balloons and later to be decanted into plastic tea mugs. Tony Bradley acquired some yeast with which we were able to make just about drinkable hooch and I can remember spending at least one Sunday evening getting pleasantly plastered in our cell. McKee banned alcohol after an incident in which a couple of Antrim men were so drunk at our weekly film that they asked the screws to call them a taxi, though typically he turned a blind eye towards a couple of the older men who continued to make it.

One of the more interesting IRA men in Crumlin Road was Davey Morley from Newry. He had been a drill sergeant in the British army and was now given the job of teaching us how to march. On the first day of drill, the entire unit was untidily paraded around the yard in ranks of three. Unfortunately, Davison, Bradley and I found something hilarious in the whole business and were briefly unable to control our giggling. Morley could certainly have ignored it but, being well used to dealing with trainee officers, abstracted the three of us and marched us separately around the yard in front of the rest of the unit for some ten to fifteen minutes as an example, as McKee stood there stony-faced. McKee's only response was to take his staff off marching duty so that we stood at the top of the parade flanking him while the others marched, which may or may not have been a good idea. In any case, Morley had laid down a marker which he would follow up six months later when we were moved to Long Kesh.

This was the summer of the Munich Olympics and the killing of a group of Israeli athletes by Palestinian guerrillas briefly threatened our internal unity. I was one of a clique, which included Brendan Holland and Denis Donaldson (shot dead as an informer many years later), who were both left-wing and pro-Palestinian, and a couple of the Armagh city men complained about us to McKee, citing in particular General Army Order No. 4 (since abolished) which forbade membership of the Communist Party. By this time I was well used to seeing off this type of argument, quoting from Fintan Lalor, James Connolly and indeed Patrick Pearse himself in favour of 'socialism', and arguing that the order in question applied only to reformist, pro-Soviet organisations, such as the Officials, who were far to the right of us genuine revolutionaries. McKee, at any rate, rebuffed the delegation and I never had the slightest difficulty with him on theoretical grounds, though his republicanism was rooted in the 1940s and he was no admirer of Saor Éire and the other left-wing republican organisations of the 1930s.

The Israeli–Arab conflict was one of the few issues that divided the camp, with a vociferous pro-Israeli minority among us who would not hear an anti-Israeli view. At one stage in 1972, when we were being described as mad bombers in the media, Ardoyne man Terence 'Cleeky' Clarke decided to literally don the mantle and stood up in Belfast Magistrates' Court to shout 'Up the Mad Bombers!', having first refused to recognise the court. Cleeky's intervention was widely reported and left me – solemn and proper – mortified, though I lightened up as the years went by and took to the Belfast humour. Cleeky was one of these Israeli supporters and there were raging rows at times of tension and particularly during the Black September attacks in 1972 and again in Long Kesh during the 1973 Yom Kippur War. The Israeli guerrilla/terrorist campaign against the British in 1939–48 and the methods of Irgun and the Stern Gang, in particular, were admired – especially by the 1950s' broadly anti-ideological generation of republicans – as were the efforts of General Grivas and his right-wing EOKA, who had fought the British in Cyprus. Middle East politics aside, we were more or less at one, and the later military revolt in Portugal and consequent changes in Angola and Mozambique were unanimously supported, as were the other liberation struggles in Africa and Latin America, every advance of which was greeted by us with approval and a vicarious pride.

Chapter 10

The summer of 1972 was truly historic, bringing as it did the truce, its breakdown, the continuing rise of the UDA, the Bloody Friday bombings and Operation Motorman. The republican refusal to respond to the imposition of direct rule had produced a fledgling peace movement which contributed to the existing pressures on the leadership, particularly on Seán MacStiofáin, who was depicted as living with his wife and family in easy distance from the violence.

In response to intermediaries, the IRA held a press conference in Free Derry in early June. This was attended by MacStiofáin and O'Connell (on behalf of the leadership), and Seamus Twomey and Martin McGuinness (the then O/Cs in Belfast and Derry respectively) to offer peace talks, thereby – it was hoped – putting the political pressure back on the British. The offer this time was for a suspension of operations for a seven-day period, provided Whitelaw agreed to meet the peace plan first announced in March. Though Whitelaw turned this down within hours, behind-the-scene contacts resulted in a secret meeting between British representatives, Dave O'Connell, and Gerry Adams. I later heard that Adams had been especially released from internment for that purpose at Dave's insistence.[9] These discussions led to the truce and the first negotiations between the British government and the republican leadership since 1921.

Our proposals were put directly to Whitelaw at a meeting in London attended by the same leaders who had been at the Derry press conference, together with Ivor Bell and Gerry Adams. Adams and Bell were both then part of the Belfast leadership and the fact that no less

---

[9] Dave was not the only one to come to regret giving Adams a leg-up. Years later I was told of a 3rd Battalion meeting which was attended by Adams for a time. When Adams left the room for some reason, McKee pretty much anointed him, telling the volunteers present, 'There goes your future leader.'

than three Belfast Brigade members were present testifies to the then primacy of Belfast within the IRA. The proposals, which were non-negotiable, were for a public recognition by the British government of the right of the Irish people acting as a single unit to decide the future of Ireland, a declaration of intent to withdraw troops from certain areas immediately and to be out of the North altogether by 1 January 1975, and an amnesty for all political prisoners – proposals that Whitelaw undertook to take to Heath and his cabinet.

Back in Belfast UDA barricades were in place, and Catholics who came across them were in serious trouble, getting badly beaten and occasionally shot dead. Six died at the hands of loyalists during the fourteen-day truce. By now the patterns were clear, with drive-by shootings taking place on Catholic streets and outside houses and shops where the killers could be pretty certain the victim would be a Catholic. The killings naturally terrified the Catholic population. Worse than being shot dead, though, was the thought of falling into the hands of the killers, as had many of these young men. To be despatched quickly by gunfire was one thing, but given that the purpose of loyalist terror was to terrorise, there was a sort of logic to their stepping it up to torturing their victims. In a ghoulish instance of loyalist humour, the torture venues were known as 'romper rooms' – the name taken from a children's TV programme of the time. Here, the unfortunate victim would be beaten and tortured in the back room of a pub or other loyalist drinking den, sometimes in front of dozens of spectators, before being taken elsewhere to be shot and dumped.

Loyalist killings, and the failure of the British to deal with them, contributed to the breakdown of the truce, though it was probably beyond saving anyway given the British position on our demands. Like us, the UDA were perhaps then at their most powerful. The British had paid little or no attention to the development of loyalist paramilitarism and now, haunted by the mirage of having to fight on two fronts, allowed them to erect barricades in Belfast and to mount parallel 'joint patrols' with British soldiers within their own areas.

Elements in the British army were also unhappy with the truce and had connived in the setting up of UDA-ruled areas in parts of Belfast from which Catholic families were being systematically expelled.

Families were being rehoused in empty dwellings elsewhere and when the British had to decide who to back in a housing dispute in Lenadoon, they sided with the loyalists, ramming a lorry loaded with Catholic furniture while the UDA cheered them on. A riot ensued, with CS gas and rubber bullets used against the nationalist crowd, and shortly afterwards the IRA opened up fire on live television and the truce was over.

As the truce ended on 9 July, gun battles once again raged throughout Belfast; in Ballymurphy five people were killed in just ten minutes of unprovoked firing by British army marksmen. Again, the soldiers involved were paratroopers and claimed to have shot fourteen gunmen, though when the identities of the dead became known, they tried to blame the loyalists. The dead 'gunmen' were Father Noel Fitzpatrick, the second Catholic priest to be shot dead in Ballymurphy while attempting to minister to the dying; a fourteen-year-old member of the Officials' youth wing; a thirteen-year-old schoolgirl; a sixteen-year-old member of the Fianna, the IRA's youth organisation; and another man thought to have been killed by the same bullet that had earlier passed through Father Fitzpatrick. The ten minutes of unexplained and unjustifiable mayhem became known as the Westrock Massacre; it was the third slaughtering match in Ballymurphy in under a year, and one more shameful episode in the British army's murderous history in Ireland.

The UVF/UDA were also active, and on 11 July one of the vilest atrocities of the conflict occurred when the home of Margaret McClenaghan and her thirteen-year-old mentally handicapped son was invaded by UDA men. A Protestant lodger living with them may have been spared when he manage to prove his Protestantism by producing his Orange sash, though he was taking no chances and escaped through a skylight. Meanwhile Margaret McClenaghan tried to persuade her assailants that she too was Protestant, but the ruse failed when her young son was told by the UDA men to go and fetch his and his mother's prayer books. Having no idea what would occur, he did so and their fate was sealed. Mrs McClenaghan was raped by at least one of the men before her son was shot to death before her eyes. She was also shot and left for dead but survived to give evidence of her ordeal. The killing shocked everyone, particularly because of the sexual assault. The UDA men involved subsequently pleaded guilty, thus minimising the amount of detail aired, and went on to do their time yards from my own cage in Long Kesh.

British soldiers continued to die almost daily following the breakdown of the truce, most of them in Belfast, as an intense series of gun attacks were mounted throughout the city. Also killed were IRA men and civilians shot dead by troops or blown to pieces by IRA bombs, among them a five-month-old child hit by flying glass following a bomb blast in Strabane. Though the IRA claimed to have given an hour's warning, and the baby's pram was more than 100 yards from the explosion, again the damage was done. It remains that he who puts the bomb out must accept responsibility, something that we would finally begin to face up to when bombs exploded across Belfast, killing nine people and injuring a great many others on the day that became known as Bloody Friday. On that day, 21 July 1972, the Belfast Brigade put out 22 bombs, most of them in or close to the city centre, which exploded over a 75-minute period during the afternoon. Two of the bombs killed two soldiers and seven civilians, and caused multiple civilian casualties. The dead included two women and two boys, aged fifteen and fourteen. Television footage of body parts being shovelled into plastic bags was heart-breaking and, despite attempts to blame the authorities for not responding to the warnings quickly enough, there was no doubt – even back then – that the IRA had simply pressed them beyond what they could deal with and, this time, had to accept responsibility for the consequences. Among these was a further weakening in our soft support and the pretext for the British to launch Operation Motorman, designed to put an end to the no-go areas.

***

Motorman was billed as the biggest ground operation by British forces since Suez. With Navy frigates based offshore and serious armour deployed for the first and last time in the North, the British army – now 22,000 strong and reinforced by 15,000 UDR or RUC men – breached the barricades in Derry, Belfast, Newry, Armagh, Lurgan and

Coalisland in the early morning of 31 July in a well-flagged operation. Though Edward Heath apparently contemplated casualties of the order of a thousand, the troops met minimal resistance as the IRA disappeared into the background, though this did not prevent the casual killing by the army of a fifteen-year-old in Derry. An IRA volunteer also died in the city, apparently as the result of an accidental discharge.

In the following days the British occupied the now famous republican ghettoes of Ardoyne, the Falls, Ballymurphy, Andersonstown, the Bogside and Creggan, taking over schools, sports grounds and church halls as temporary posts while they constructed permanent forts.[10] From these they aimed to control the populace, and defeat the IRA, by physically occupying the streets along which men and material moved, polluting, as it were, the water in which the guerrilla fish had to swim. In Derry, known IRA men took temporary refuge across the border in Buncrana, which had come to provide the main logistical base for the Derry Brigade. This was not possible in Belfast, which was many miles from the border, and the 1st Battalion staff caused consternation within the IRA when most of them unilaterally decided to take themselves off across the border. Many fine and experienced operators had their IRA standing and reputations destroyed, as they were promptly labelled deserters and their places filled by younger, less cautious and inevitably less experienced men.

Again, though, a British operation was overshadowed, this time by the planting of three car bombs in the Derry village of Claudy, which resulted in the deaths of nine civilians. Six died immediately and the others over the following days, both Catholics and Protestants, male and female, among them two teenage boys and an eight-year-old girl. The IRA denied the bombings and the by now usual charge was made of British intelligence complicity to detract from what they were doing in Belfast and Derry. MacStiofáin went on television to say so, and, according to his memoir, the local IRA denied the bombing, though the denials must have been less than convincing since an internal court of inquiry was established to investigate it. Though this apparently cleared the local unit, it now seems certain that it was an IRA operation

---

[10] Deep into 'Indian' territory, these were given exotic names including Fort Apache, Fort Jericho and Silver City.

where casualties resulted yet again from an inadequate warning; on this occasion the chosen phone box was out of order because of previous bomb damage to the local telephone exchange. Apparently no one had thought of checking it beforehand. As with the Bloody Friday dead, the converted remained unshakeable. At best, these dreadful casualties had been knowingly caused by the British as part of their black propaganda campaign; at worst, our volunteers had done their utmost to deliver the mandatory warning but had been frustrated by circumstances beyond their control. Meanwhile, the final excusing factor was that none of this would be happening were the British not occupying part of Ireland, and, so, ultimately responsible for everything that happened, for our actions no less than their own.

Inside Crumlin Road, these developments were discussed and endlessly analysed. The truce had its long-term consequences in that O'Connell, who made some efforts to resurrect it, came to be portrayed as weak and credulous, while Gerry Adams and Ivor Bell achieved a standing that would reverberate through Long Kesh in due course and later through the IRA proper. Though McKee, too, was strongly of the view that the truce could, and should, be put together again, the IRA outside – in the shape of Belfast in particular – wanted to fight and the British were not ready to stop. The growing strength of the loyalists and then the Bloody Friday bombings made Operation Motorman inevitable, and so the North collapsed back into conflict for another few years. Post-Motorman, the British and the IRA settled in for a war of attrition, albeit on a changed basis, with the city barricades down and the rural areas becoming more active. The discussions that took place in 1974–75, and again in the early 1990s, resumed where they had left off earlier; the telling difference, in my view, being that the time was more propitious in the latter period when those who had opposed talks earlier – or claimed they had – had themselves grown into middle age.

Though the IRA initially coped well with Motorman, security force casualties began to radically reduce as the squeeze came on from September, and there was a very obvious shift towards attacks on off-duty UDR and RUC members. Catholic civilians meanwhile continued to be shot, knifed, strangled and beaten to death. Among the dead was Thomas Madden, whose body was found in a north Belfast doorway. He had suffered more than a hundred stab wounds and witnesses heard him begging to be killed. He was a victim of the UDA. The killing was described by the RUC as both motiveless and 'the most sadistic yet'. Not to be outdone, another loyalist artist, this time from the UVF, went to work with his knife on the bodies of two Catholics abducted in north Belfast later in the month before shooting both men dead. Philip Faye, a 21-year-old barman, was shot dead by an east Belfast UDA unit. One of its members, Albert Baker, was a British army deserter who subsequently claimed British intelligence was up to its neck in sectarian murders.

Protestant men were dying too, and though the targeting of Protestant civilians was contrary to IRA policy, it was not difficult for a local unit to claim that its victims were members of the UDA/UVF. Complicating matters was the presence alongside us of not just the Officials but also defence organisations, such as the Catholic Ex-Servicemen's Association and, in areas like Ardoyne and Short Strand, local Catholic Defence Leagues. I have since heard that the latter were responsible for some Protestant deaths. There's no doubt, however, that some IRA units were either given limited instructions to retaliate or took it upon themselves to do so. Following the attack on Kelly's bar, a pub in the Protestant Sandy Row was hit by a no warning bomb, in which seventeen civilians – including three young girls – were injured and, later again, four Protestant workers leaving their factory were wounded by gunfire. During the truce period, six Protestant civilians were killed by either the IRA or local defence organisations, and, in September, a Protestant man was shot dead by the IRA while standing at a street corner in north Belfast. One of the two teenagers subsequently convicted told the RUC he had orders to shoot two Orangemen. Such episodes were both morally wrong and politically stupid and played into the hands of the British, who were ever-anxious to portray what was going on as a sectarian war in which they were the peacemakers.

Many civilians died in clouded circumstances, such as Edmund Woolsey, who was killed in south Armagh in mid-September when he went to recover his car, stolen earlier in Dundalk. He was advised by the RUC that the army had checked the car and that it was safe to approach it. This was an operation that was blamed on, and denied by, the IRA. It has since emerged that the Officials, of whom Woolsey was a supporter, suspected Kenneth Littlejohn – an Englishman with a criminal record and links to British intelligence – of having engineered the incident with a view to killing Official IRA members, something that underlines a difficulty in the easy attribution of killings to republicans, and even in certain instances to the loyalists.

Some time in early 1972, the British had established the Mobile or Military Reaction or Reconnaissance Force (the title underlying the MRF acronym is disputed, but unimportant), which operated undercover in plainclothes and was involved in the murder of Catholics and suspected republicans. The initial sighting, so to speak, came in April 1972 when a plainclothes unit fired on two brothers in Ballymurphy as they ran from armed civilians whom they thought were loyalists bent on murder. Both men were badly wounded and when the soldiers reached them, they radioed for a uniformed patrol, the commander of which berated them for having shot the wrong men. It seems that the intended targets were Jim Bryson and Tommy Toland, IRA men who had escaped from the *Maidstone* in January and were by then back in Ballymurphy. There is evidence from at least one of the participants in these shootings that undercover soldiers had lists of names which included a number of individuals who were to be shot on sight.

Two other men, Patrick McVeigh and Daniel Rooney, were shot dead in separate incidents by undercover troops using weapons that were not army issue, but these were not the only instances of plainclothes soldiers firing on nationalist civilians. By very definition, it is impossible to know which killings to attribute to them and which to loyalists, or indeed to some combination of these forces – as would be demonstrably the case in later years. The MRF, or its predecessor, has since been accused of involvement in killings going back to the bombing of McGurk's bar and before.

There also remain suspicions of British involvement in the two bombs that exploded in Dublin on 1 December 1972 while anti-IRA legislation was being debated in parliament, killing two men and wounding numerous others. Minutes before the first bomb exploded, a warning was called in to a Belfast news desk by a man said to have spoken with an English accent, while both bomb cars had been hired in Belfast, again by men with English accents. Fine Gael had previously decided to vote against the bill, the sole dissenting voices being its leader Liam Cosgrave and border TD Paddy Donegan, but its opposition was withdrawn as the first reports came in and the legislation was swiftly passed. The timing was exquisite, there being not one thing more, short of his introducing internment himself, that Lynch could then have done for the British.

While army intelligence and the RUC Special Branch had been targeted throughout the campaign, the most effective operation against them came in October 1972 with the destruction of an undercover unit which had been using business fronts in Belfast. One of these, the Four Square Laundry, operated a van with video and camera facilities in a hidden roof space and collected clothing in republican areas which was then tested for explosives and firearms residue. It had long been known that informers, either concealed within personnel carriers or heavily disguised, were being taken around by ordinary British patrols as spotters, but this operation had gone up a gear in its refinement. Informers could be deployed in the roof space to covertly pinpoint locations and identify target individuals for an accompanying operative. An IRA volunteer, Seamus Wright, having come under suspicion for various reasons, revealed under questioning that he had been in Palace barracks with British minders over the course of the summer and was part of a unit being set up by the British which consisted of a mix of undercover soldiers and Irish civilians. This unit was controlled by the MRF and was a classic pseudo-gang of the type used by the British in Kenya in the 1950s.

Wright's revelations started a chain of investigation that culminated in a coordinated attack on two business premises, as well as on the laundry van. On 2 October, while the van was collecting laundry in the Twinbrook area of Belfast, an active service unit pulled up alongside and a locally born British soldier was shot dead. His female companion was nearby and was later rescued. Though the roof space of the van was raked with gunfire, the British army denied that any other casualties were suffered. Two premises were simultaneously raided by other

IRA units, with, again, contrary messages regarding casualties. Wright and another IRA volunteer, Kevin McKee, were meanwhile abducted and subsequently shot dead, among the first of those who decades later became known as 'the Disappeared' – a group of people shot dead and secretly buried with no public, or indeed private, acknowledgement of their deaths. Appalling as this undoubtedly was, it seems that in the case of these two men, at least, their being 'disappeared' was a misguided effort to spare their families the ignominy of being associated with informers and agents.

***

Life went on in Crumlin Road where, following Motorman, the expectation of an early end to the war evaporated and people settled down to do their time. We lived for the most part vicariously, secondhand, our collective mood going up and down in tandem with the successes and set-backs of our comrades on the outside. Escape plans came and went. The loyalists staged a protest and won segregation from us. We had no contact with them anyway, but it was good to have them off the wing as their sectarian murder campaign was being stepped up. When, soon afterwards, a group of them lobbed bricks over the wall between our exercise yard and theirs, McKee turned a blind eye to a forced incursion into their wing which left those not quick enough to lock themselves into their own cells with sore heads.

It would not have happened had Gusty Spence been there. But in early July Spence had gone out on parole and failed to honour it, having been supposedly 'kidnapped' by his followers. He was not recaptured until November, having in the meantime given media interviews while his comrades 'restrained' him from voluntarily returning to prison. Spence was the cause of our second hunger strike, this time for eighteen days, over the parole issue, which began when someone decided that parole for family funerals was no longer guaranteed. The long-standing tradition was that the authorities had the word of the republican prisoner that he would honour the terms of his parole, and, failing this, our organisational promise that he would be forcibly returned. The threat to the parole arrangements was seen as a most serious attack on our de facto political status, and when negotiations by McKee to restore the status quo failed, a hunger strike was inevitable. Again it was led by McKee, and once more I was proud to be included among the twenty who began the strike – I believe one quit along the way – which was settled successfully on the eighteenth day.

Though I now knew what to expect, it didn't make things any easier and I went through the same grind of hunger cravings and low concentration levels. This time I was doubled up in a cell and found a marked difficulty in sleeping. This produced a sequence, the meaning of which was not to be unearthed until the following year when we were in Long Kesh, and which has stayed with me as a reminder of the solid comradeship of the time. Tony Bradley was my cell mate and night after night his snoring was keeping me awake to the point where I would feel myself eventually forced to make enough noise to wake him. Tony would then prop himself up, roll a cigarette, which he'd offer and I'd refuse, wanting only to sleep, and then try to engage me in conversation. When we were in Cage 9 a year later and others woke him over his snoring, it emerged that, like those who snore everywhere, he had not believed he was snoring and thought I had been using this as an excuse to get his attention and company.

As the first hunger strike had coincided with a similar protest by Joe Cahill, Ruairí Ó Brádaigh and his brother Seán, this one coincided with the much more fraught hunger strike of Seán MacStiofáin, who was arrested in Dublin in late November 1972, when we were about a week into our strike. In greatly charged circumstances, he announced – on being brought before the Special Criminal Court on a membership charge – that he had been on hunger and thirst strike since the time of his arrest and that they would have no defendant to try if they didn't get a move on. I certainly believed him and I'm sure the Southern authorities did too. A thirst strike was upping the ante and was uncharted territory – though Seán McCaughey had died in 1946 after twelve days on thirst strike in Portlaoise Prison, after enduring almost five years in solitary confinement in the most shameful conditions. MacStiofáin's thirst strike was also an unfortunate escalation in that it gave the movement, as well as the government, little time to prepare a response. A week later MacStiofáin was sentenced to six months' imprisonment in controversial circumstances, the evidence against him the seized tape of an interview he had done with RTE, together with the 'opinion' of a policeman that he was an IRA member. He was moved to the Mater Hospital, where he was visited by various luminaries, including both the retired and serving Catholic archbishops of Dublin, who sought to get him to end his strike.

The next day Dublin Brigade volunteers unsuccessfully attempted to rescue MacStíofáin from hospital, an effort for which they paid with heavy sentences and might well have paid with their lives. Following this, he was airlifted to the military hospital at the Curragh where he was 'persuaded' to end his thirst strike on 28 November. MacStíofáin had become a believer in his own image, convinced that the struggle required him and that the country would burn without him. There was no disguising our disappointment with him, and this was compounded by the fact that he remained on a futile hunger strike. That disappointment became embarrassment when it emerged that he was taking glucose and ultimately the IRA leadership ordered him off the strike. While General Army Order No. 7 (which forbids hunger striking without GHQ sanction) has been more honoured in the breach than in the observance, it has always been my understanding that just as the IRA will not order anyone on strike, it will not order them off it either. Though there were breaches with MacStíofáin and others in the 1970s, this was firmed up during the H Block hunger strikes, and since then volunteers looking for cover to come off strikes – and there have been a couple – have been refused it.

Direct rule had divided the nationalist North and the collapse of the truce, Bloody Friday, Motorman and Claudy sharpened that division. In May, the SDLP had issued a call encouraging those Catholics who had withdrawn from public office to return, and it later used the IRA ceasefire and London talks to dilute its own commitment not to engage with the British while internment lasted. Relations between the South and the British had also dramatically improved and by the autumn they were at one in viewing the IRA as the problem. Lynch and the SDLP were now firmly on the offensive against us. At the end of October, the British published a Green Paper, *The Future of Northern Ireland*. With its passage on the Irish Dimension, albeit one constrained by the 'absolute' that the status of Northern Ireland would not be changed without the consent of the people of Northern Ireland, it did much to satisfy Lynch, while he was giving the British just about everything he could.

That Christmas in Crumlin Road represented the height of our togetherness and cohesion. With the wing close to bursting point, we knew it would be our last Christmas together as a unit and we celebrated it with a concert. John 'Bap' Kelly, a natural entertainer, who brought out an album of rebel songs following his release, and was subsequently killed in action, was the organiser and gave a rendition of Kris Kristofferson's 'Me and Bobby McGee', adapted to 'Billy McKee', with brand new lyrics which were hilarious but, unfortunately, are now forgotten. Tommy Mullin, a Dublin volunteer, who was a recent addition from the courts and so an unknown quantity, performed an act in which he very convincingly 'hypnotised' my cell mate, 'The Cat', who made a fool of himself in a succession of well-rehearsed sketches. We, the audience, however, were the real fools and for a day or two afterwards, prisoners could be found complaining bitterly at our short-sightedness in having blown the opportunity to get Tommy to hypnotise the lot of us all the way out of prison.

In terms of the numbers killed, 1972 was the fiercest year of the war, though 1973 would roughly match it, at least in the sheer poundage of explosives put out by the IRA. But notwithstanding the acquisition of rocket launchers towards the end of the year, the experimentation with home-made mortars, and the ubiquity of Armalite, Operation Motorman dramatically changed the dynamics of the struggle and robbed us of the advantages we had previously held. With the British now dug in amongst us, occupying the centres of nationalist areas in Belfast, Derry and other towns, the initiative was now shared more equitably. Support for the IRA also dipped alarmingly. The Green Paper contained an outline of policy that would remain more or less unchanged over the decades ahead. And the nationalist unity that had existed, particularly following Bloody Sunday, was dissipated and allowed to drift away on the back of those civilian casualties we continued to maintain were anathema to us and yet seemed powerless to avoid.

Chapter 11

In early January the long-anticipated move to Long Kesh took place. The British army had been into A Wing a couple of times for searches, disrupting various escape plans and worse, for on one of these occasions McKee had vetoed a plan master-minded by Tony O'Kane to electrocute some of the soldiers by making part of the staircase to the wing live. We knew with the numbers then coming in from the courts that we were living on borrowed time and were at the stage where there was daily speculation as to whether or not we would be moved that night, and we kept a close eye on the weather conditions. One night after lock-up, the inevitable came and we were ferried in a heavily protected convoy down to Long Kesh.

We looked around in the early morning. My first impression, having been kept in a cell for just over a year, was of sheer vastness. We were put in Nissen huts similar to those I had seen in Smedley's canning factory in Spalding, which, like Long Kesh itself, was on an old RAF base. After getting used to life in a standard prison cell, the huts seemed like aircraft hangars. We were 30 to a hut, which measured 120 by 24 feet and in which the noise levels seemed extraordinary. There were three dormitory huts per cage or compound, one of which was divided, leaving a half-hut for table tennis and the like. A fourth hut served as a canteen and meeting place and there was a small garden shed type structure in the middle of the cage which was designed for study but came to be used for handicrafts. A further structure held toilets, showers and wash basins. Electricity points were available in the huts and we looked forward to getting in record players and television sets.

The feeling of spaciousness continued outside the huts, with the wide sky above and the mountains in the distance. We were encaged by

16-foot-high meshed fencing topped with razor wire, and army watch-towers were dotted strategically here and there. The cages measured 70 by 30 yards and, of course, we walked around them anti-clockwise. The other instant impression was that of fresh air, and rather too much of it as the huts were not at this stage adequately weatherproofed. We had to acclimatise to the damp and cold and at the outset many of us came down with colds and flu.

Relations between ourselves and the prison administration were quite different to what they had been in Crumlin Road. Correspondence, both outgoing and incoming, was now strictly censored and I often didn't receive letters I was expecting, or had my own returned to me for 'rewriting'. Parcel limits, more honoured in the breach than the obser-vance in Belfast, were strictly observed and it was apparent that the regime was determined to give us nothing that had not already been nailed down. Our collective mood was not helped by the fact that we began life in the Kesh by refusing visits, in solidarity with the position then being taken by the internees, and, in addition, it took us time to adjust to the internal bustle and the new absence of privacy. Huge credit must go to McKee, in particular, for keeping us in line and bit by bit he wore down the administration, which came to behave more reasonably. I believe they were led in part by their experience with the internees, who were less disciplined than we were and therefore more difficult to deal with as a cohesive unit. Though relations would stead-ily improve before taking an unexplained nosedive in the latter half of 1974, they never again reached the levels of sheer reasonableness that we had witnessed in Crumlin Road.

Within a week or two, we had adapted to the new circumstances. I was in a clique, essentially a parcel-sharing collective, with Bobby Gamble, Tony Bradley and the Quinn brothers, John and Jimmy. All of us had been together since B Wing in 1971 and by now were friends as much as comrades. Other old B Wing comrades were Dickie O'Neill, Gerry Rooney and Jim Davison, and I was also friendly with others who had come in a bit later, like Brendan Holland from Belfast and Seamus Keenan, Colm's brother. Bobby took the Irish language revival seriously and soon became fluent. Inspired by MacAirt, he was among those who founded the Gaeltacht huts where Irish was spoken all the time. But though I made various token efforts over the years I was in jail, I could never warm to the language, the damage done in childhood apparently irrevocable, my lack of interest perhaps bolstered by McKee, who himself couldn't speak a word of Irish and showed no interest in changing that situation.

At the time I was responsible for putting together education and training programmes and we also began a camp paper, *Faoi Ghlas* (roughly 'imprisoned by the foreigner'), which I edited and part wrote. In truth, my editing was confined to typing up the copy on a battered portable with one finger, a dreadful habit that I never would break. Suggestions that the then prison leadership was right-wing and intolerant of left-wing views are simply untrue and extant copies of the paper would show that. I have since read about anti-communist witch hunts and even book-burning and can say that nothing of that sort occurred, at least in my time, for, if it had, my books would have been among the first on the pyre. Military training took the form of lectures and workshops, with written lectures and model weapons hidden in the roof spaces against the periodic searches. Quite accidentally, I discovered that a volunteer from Turf Lodge had an extraordinary knowledge of firearms and ammunition, while the cages also contained a couple of the best engineers in the IRA. There were also significant tactical workshops led by a Falls Road man who was a highly experienced operator.

McKee and MacAirt were a pair of wise old heads. MacAirt was a Gaelgoir, a widely read, deeply cultured and gentle man, who seemed at first sight an unlikely revolutionary but was in fact a clearly discernible Irish republican type. Conciliatory where McKee may have been confrontational, he seemed to me his perfect complement, an alter ego urging caution at the appropriate time and underwriting action when it seemed required. MacAirt, on account of his shock of white hair, became known as Snowy or Sneachta. We knew better than to nickname McKee, though behind his back some of the Falls Road men referred to him as Old Jack. McKee gave talks on the Army's real history, its structure and legal system, of courts of inquiry and courts martial, which would have been used, indeed overused, in peacetime but of which we knew little or nothing. The system was as complex as any, but the impact of the talks was ruined for me when, having been asked what he would do with a volunteer who had been cleared by an inquiry but whom he knew for certain to be guilty, McKee said that he'd have to shoot him anyway. Both men were steeped in republican history, in particular recent history – which they had lived through and helped to frame – and it was fantastic to listen to their views on the characters and events of the 1940s and 1950s. McKee had a low opinion of some past icons and had no time at all for Brendan Behan, though he could be just as scathing when it came to his own contemporaries.

Shortly after MacStiofáin's arrest, I asked McKee who would take over as chief of staff, Cahill being also imprisoned at the time. I suggested Seamus Twomey as a possibility and McKee started to laugh. The idea was plainly too ridiculous for words. He thought Dave O'Connell the only man for the job, but unfortunately Dave had been seriously damaged by the Maria McGuire business, though this was not then apparent to us on the inside. Meanwhile, Twomey would indeed become C/S and grow easily into the job in the way that tends to happen.

Tony O'Kane, who had been McKee's adjutant in A Wing, was a not bad poet who contributed regularly to *Faoi Ghlas* under the pseudonym *An Madra Rua* (the Fox, literally the Red Dog). Tony was an engineer, originally from south Derry, who had been part of the special Belfast Brigade unit that had operated secretly in 1970. He had been with Michael Kane when he was killed in an accidental explosion while on a bombing mission, and Tony had suffered bad injuries himself. He was one of the first republican prisoners and had a low opinion of Gusty Spence in particular and the loyalists more generally, whom he had been observing for the guts of a year in A Wing. Tony had also been part of an IRA bodyguard provided for the MP Gerry Fitt in 1969 and hugely resented the latter's attacks on us in his new role as SDLP leader. One of Tony's poems had us as 'a comrades' camp of men who fight for liberty', a fine line that struck me with great force at the time.

As a staff member, I had some contact with the prison administration. It seemed that a succession of ambitious young Home Office types were spending periods in the Kesh with assistant governor rank as part of their progression and that it had become an essential posting for CV purposes. At any rate the turnover was brisk and they were bright and fast on their feet. A friend had sent me a copy of Maria

McGuire's book, *To Take Arms: A Year with the Provisional IRA*, which was withheld because it was in hardback and only paperbacks were allowed in. I went out to request that the book be let in, stripped of its hardback cover if necessary, and was refused by this young man not much older than myself with an English public school accent. He added that the decision might well be in our own interest as he gathered that Ms McGuire had pretty much spilt the beans on us. I left his Portakabin office feeling bested and vaguely humiliated. I told McKee about the exchange and of course he had the perfect riposte. He would have asked the young governor, mock-worriedly, if he really thought reading the book would damage republican morale, and having received confirmation would – after a suitable pause for troubled thought – have dismissed it as not that likely, noting that the Profumo affair hadn't done the Tories a bit of harm.

Though negotiations in the Kesh were tougher than in Crumlin Road, and the administration less rational, McKee tended to get his reasonable way in the end and things never boiled over as they tended to do in the internment cages. Not that there was no dissent: there was and there would inevitably be more as our numbers and frustrations grew. Shortly after we had moved into A Wing, John Joe Magee – an ex-Royal Marine who had also been in the Special Boat Service and was the prison quartermaster – resigned from McKee's staff for reasons that I never discovered. However, John Joe kept whatever his grievance may have been to himself and caused no difficulties. Dissent was inevitable given differing views about internal discipline and in particular distaste for such regimentation as McKee insisted on – especially the daily drilling. Sleeping, as Nietzsche put it, 'is no mean art; you need to stay awake all day to do it', and McKee insisted that everyone got out of bed in the morning and stayed awake all day. Thus, the watching of daytime television, which in the early 1970s consisted solely of children's programmes, was banned after a number of younger volunteers were noted slumped in front of the TV on successive afternoons. Lights out, similarly, was at a fixed time, after which conversation was discouraged.

Occasionally, political delegations came in to inspect conditions. Paisley himself arrived with a delegation of unionists and, though they spent their time in the loyalist cages, Paisley, who had a reputation as a good constituency MP, met a couple of our volunteers from north Antrim and promised to look into their grievances. McKee and I showed a delegation around Cage 9, among them Paddy Devlin, late of the Northern Ireland Labour Party and by then one of the six SDLP MPs. Devlin, who was nicknamed Topper, had been interned with McKee in the 1940s and approached us with some trepidation, unsure of the reception he would get. Paddy Kennedy of Republican Labour, who had appeared with Joe Cahill at the famous post-internment press conference in Ballymurphy, was also there, as was Bernadette Devlin. Bernadette was a deeply impressive individual and for my money one of the bravest, most charismatic and politically consistent figures to emerge from the Troubles. She was at this time close to the Officials, though she would subsequently join the Irish Republican Socialist Party when it split from the Officials in 1974, and she became close to Sinn Féin in the late 1980s.

Among those who might be termed dissenters, Bobby Campbell stood out. Bobby had escaped from the Mater Hospital during the 1972 hunger strike and had been recaptured some time in 1973, having meanwhile achieved significant rank in the 3rd Battalion area. He was a decent enough man but was one of nature's incurable bigheads, one of those who just had to have his own way, and it was inevitable that he would come into confrontation with the camp staff in due course. By now we also had Martin Meehan, who had an even bigger reputation. Various people tried to use and flatter Martin, but he always stayed within the line, and was loyal to McKee in particular.

Joe McKee, a Falls Road man whom I thought highly of, was disliked by Billy McKee for reasons buried deep in Falls history, though the men were not related. Billy, perhaps appropriately for his age, was a prude and on overhearing Joe tell a dirty story overreacted and paraded the entire cage to publicly tell him he was a disgrace to the movement and his family and that he, Billy McKee, would not have entrusted him with a position as a section leader outside. While Joe, who had been pretty senior at the time of his arrest, could do little but bristle with resentment as he stood to attention before a red-faced Billy, this public dressing down was judged to be wrong by many who viewed it, particularly all those Falls Road men in their teens and early twenties who knew both Joe and his record well.

***

On New Year's Day nineteen-year-old Liz McKee from Andersonstown became the first female detainee when she was served with an interim custody order and taken to Armagh Prison. Brendan Holland's seventeen-year-old sister Trish followed some weeks later and by August there were some ten women internees in Armagh together with sentenced and remand IRA female prisoners. Then, in early February, the first loyalists were detained, later arriving in Cage 14, right beside us. McKee knew a few of them and, much to my surprise, treated them in a fairly friendly fashion. The internment of loyalists resulted in a Protestant strike which, given the skewed nature of employment in the North, might as well have been a general strike. During it, there were attacks on Catholic churches and schools, as well as the by now predictable frustration-born clashes with the official forces of the Crown in which troops shot dead both a UDA and a UVF man. The strike failed to win significant support among unionists generally, who were perhaps alarmed by the violence.

With his majority disappearing, Jack Lynch called a surprise election in the South in early 1973. By now, whatever pro-republican fever there had been in the South following internment and Bloody Sunday had long gone and, in any case, as revolutionaries we were above parliamentary elections, though not entirely disinterested. Despite the clear portends of what was to come from the prospective coalition partners, Fine Gael and Labour, as foreshadowed in the pronouncements of Conor Cruise O'Brien and Garret FitzGerald – whom I considered and continued to consider a fool on the national question – I favoured the election of the coalition, in part because I believed it would be less stable than Fianna Fáil, but more because by then I simply hated Lynch, Brian Lenihan, Des O'Malley and the rest of that crew.

The British government was rolling out its new policy. A referendum – the Border Poll – was held in March 1973 on the question of the union with the United Kingdom, which was boycotted by nationalists and which putatively put the constitutional question to bed for another ten years. The White Paper that was published some days later – the coalition government having meanwhile come to power in the South – proposed a new Assembly at Stormont with a share in power for those Catholics represented by the SDLP, the recognition of an 'Irish dimension' in the shape of a Council of Ireland in return for the South's more wholehearted support in the fight against the IRA, and the acceptance by both it and the SDLP of the constitutional position. Local elections in May, boycotted by Sinn Féin, were followed in June by elections to a Northern Assembly, which again we ignored.

Despite the bomb explosion at the London post office tower in October 1971 and the Officials' botched attack on the Parachute Regiment headquarters following Bloody Sunday, Britain itself had remained immune to the war in the North, save for the occasional troubling news item and the steady return of dead soldiers. This changed on the day of the Border Poll, 8 March 1973, when four car bombs were placed in London. The British had, it seems, already been alerted, though the true extent to which the operation was compromised is unknown and likely to remain so, and ten of the bomb team were arrested before they could board a flight to Dublin some hours before the bombs were due to detonate. A warning was duly phoned in an hour in advance and it remains a mystery why the areas were not cleared. In any event, two of the bombs exploded, injuring some 250 people and indirectly causing the death of one man who suffered a heart attack.

Outside, the war continued. At the end of March a Cypriot-registered ship, the *Claudia*, was boarded off the south-east coast. Joe Cahill and five others were arrested and 250 rifles and a similar amount of short arms, together with anti-tank mines and explosives, were seized, following a tip-off from British intelligence. Despite this loss, the volunteers were now almost universally equipped with Armalites, while a dozen Russian-made rocket launchers, believed to have been supplied by the Palestinian Liberation Organisation, were also in use.

The IRA had settled down; we were no longer suffering as many of the self-inflicted casualties of the previous year in the grotesquely titled 'own goal' explosions, though half of the volunteers who died in 1973 were killed in that way. Most of the IRA men shot dead by the British army in Belfast were either unarmed or no threat when they were killed. In Ardoyne, three volunteers and a number of civilians – among them a seventy-six-year-old woman and a twelve-year-old boy – were killed in the early months of 1973. Some years later a soldier contacted the press about one of the shootings and said he had been ordered to open fire on a group of men because they were all either IRA men or IRA scouts and 'it was too good a chance to miss'. In March, Edward Sharpe was shot dead while standing at his front door. A neighbour, Seán Murphy, in effect lost it and went down to the barracks to remonstrate. He and a local priest, Father Myles, agreed to try to force an investigation and Murphy made a formal statement to the RUC to try to get something going. A couple of weeks later Murphy was himself arrested and taken to Castlereagh, where one of his interrogators turned out to be the detective who had taken his statement of complaint. On the weekend after his release, Murphy and another man were fired on from a passing car and both were wounded. Believing that the paratroopers had been responsible for what were either warning shots or attempted murder, Father Myles decided it was time to call it a day. Everyone in Ardoyne knew what had happened anyway.

Notwithstanding Bloody Friday and Claudy, the bombing campaign had continued, with over 1,200 explosions in the month following Motorman and the Belfast Brigade planting bombs in the city centre within a week of Bloody Friday. Although the number of explosions dropped in 1973, the poundage used increased, and this pattern was repeated again in 1974. Bombing remained intrinsic to the war; sporadic but consistent, the bombs were a constant reminder of the IRA's capacity, every one a further embarrassment for the British, who were seemingly powerless to stop them. Indeed, the IRA was visibly more reliant on commercial bombing during periods of relative weakness; the Belfast Brigade O/C who would do perhaps the most damage to the city would be the one appointed following the arrest of Brendan Hughes in the summer of the following year, when it was credibly claimed that the IRA in Belfast was on its last legs.

Seventy-five members of the security forces were killed in 1973, the bulk of them British soldiers. These numbers were as important to us as to the British, with their never-ending lists of IRA men arrested and explosives and/or weapons seized. The Belfast Brigade was still the dominant force in the early part of the year, killing ten soldiers in gun and rocket attacks, nearly all of them in the 2nd Battalion area. Three more died in a city centre flat, having been lured there for a party while off-duty in a classic 'honeypot' sting, for which we received considerable criticism from the Church and media. General Frank King, who took over as British commander in early 1973, believed (as did we) that the key to beating the IRA was to defeat them in Belfast, and diverted troops and other resources to the city. He had some success; from April onwards there was a marked reduction in operations there, and in July the leadership was badly hit with the arrests of Gerry Adams, Brendan Hughes and Tom Cahill in the Lower Falls, and of other key men throughout the city, following a major intelligence operation.

Other areas were picking up the slack and, in east Tyrone, soldiers died in bomb and landmine attacks and five were killed there in May when the car they were returning to after a night out in Omagh exploded. This operation, too, received considerable criticism, but we were impervious to it, certainly where British army casualties were concerned. Others, including four paratroopers, were killed in booby-trap and landmine attacks in south Armagh. Brigadier Peter Morton, who was then the company commander in the area, wrote a book, *Emergency Tour*, about his later experience, in which he recalled that in 1973 'radio-controlled and electrically detonated landmines occurred with alarming frequency – often several in one day'. He thought that with 'better training and [a] less gung-ho attitude' at least some of those killed would be still alive, and arrived back in south Armagh 'keen also to avenge the deaths of the excellent men lost in 1973'. His keenness would have been fully reciprocated by republicans, who remembered this unit's murderous record in Ballymurphy, both during internment and again throughout the summer of 1972.

While the casualty rate dipped generally after Motorman, the UVF/UDA had reversed the trend, killing over sixty Catholics, or Protestants unfortunate enough to be seen associating with Catholics, mistaken for Catholics or even mistaken for associating with Catholics, by the end of 1972. Among the dead were Paula Strong and Clare Hughes, aged six and four, killed instantly when a bar in the Docks area was bombed by the UDA; a young Protestant mother of one, married to a Catholic; and fourteen-year-old Rory Gormley. The schoolboy died and others in the car were wounded when his surgeon father took a shortcut through the Shankill to drop the boys off at school. The children were all too easily identified by the loyalist gunmen from their school blazers and one of the surviving boys said that he had heard someone shout 'There's a car full of Taigs' shortly before the gunfire.

Nineteen seventy-three had opened with the discovery of the bodies of a young couple found stabbed and shot to death in a ditch on the Donegal side of the Derry border, and a Catholic man killed in east Belfast. Following a brief ceasefire called for internal reasons, UDA killings resumed; over five days between 29 January and 2 February six Catholics were shot dead in Belfast. Two of the dead, Philip Rafferty and Peter Watterson, were aged fourteen and fifteen respectively, and as young Rafferty was abducted before being shot, his killers could have been in no doubt at all about his youth. Both were killed by the UDA unit in the Village area of south Belfast led by Francis 'Hatchet' Smith, who was shot dead by the IRA shortly after the killing of young Watterson. One of the most brutal of the killings during this time was that of Paddy Wilson, an SDLP senator, and Irene Andrews, his Protestant secretary, who were found stabbed to death at a quarry on the outskirts of Belfast in June. They had been abducted in the city centre when the killers encountered them by accident while on the hunt for Catholics. Wilson suffered 32 stab wounds and Irene Andrews was knifed 19 times. John White, who would go on to play a leading role as a UDA spokesman at the time of the mid-90s ceasefires, was later convicted of these killings.

As the slaughter continued there was huge pressure on the British from nationalist politicians and the Dublin government to 'do something' about the UDA, and expressions of frustration at their obvious reluctance to move against them. The response to the killings occasionally bordered on the ridiculous, with independent Stormont MP Tom Caldwell perhaps taking the biscuit with his suggestion that they were being organised by communist agents. Indeed, as late as October that year, the publication of *Political Murder in Northern Ireland* by journalists Martin Dillon and Denis Lehane – which firmly placed the blame on loyalist paramilitaries – caused a sensation of disbelief.

Meanwhile, both the IRA and the British continued to cause civilian casualties, both by accident and design. Our errors included two children, nine-year-old Gordon Gallagher, killed when he triggered a booby trap meant for British troops in Derry, and four-year-old Paul Cromie, accidentally killed when the IRA opened up on troops in Andersonstown. In June yet another bombing disaster occurred, this time in Coleraine, when six civilians – all of them Protestants, four of them women, and all aged between 60 and 76 – were blown to pieces, due, it was claimed, to the inadequacy of a bomb warning. Yet again, we excused ourselves and blamed British misrepresentation.

Chapter 12

While the British believed the South was running an agreed bipartisan policy, this was not necessarily so, and in fact the new government proved to be considerably more malleable than Lynch's. Northern policy was run by Liam Cosgrave, Garret FitzGerald and Labour's Conor Cruise O'Brien, respectively Taoiseach, Minister for Foreign Affairs and Minister for Posts and Telegraphs. FitzGerald had long held a view on how matters should develop in the North, one that turned out to be surprisingly similar to that in the British White Paper, while Cruise O'Brien – one of my old heroes and previously an anti-partitionist – was moving towards the unionism he would later espouse, and there were tensions between these two from the outset. The other key ministries were occupied by Patrick Cooney, back then perceived as liberal, as Minister for Justice, and Paddy Donegan, an unreconstructed Blueshirt,[11] who was both personally volatile and virulently anti-republican, as Defence Minister. Soon the British were bypassing the normal channels to deal with him directly, something that was known to and quietly approved by the equally anti-republican Cosgrave.

Though loyalist rejectionists outnumbered the Faulkner unionists, the latter, with SDLP and Alliance Party backing, still had the numbers for an administration, and a new power-sharing Executive was finally agreed by these parties in November. In return, the SDLP accepted

---

[11] The Blueshirts were Ireland's contribution to European fascism in the 1930s. Led by an ex-Garda Commissioner, they were virulently anti-republican and anti-communist and engaged in regular street fights with IRA members. Blueshirts and IRA members fought on opposite sides in the Spanish Civil War and to this day 'Blueshirt' remains a term of abuse for especially right-wing, anti-republican members of Fine Gael.

there could be no change in the constitutional position before the next border poll while a conference was to be held to settle the shape and working details of various matters, including a proposed Council of Ireland. This took place in December 1973 at Sunningdale in England, where the Executive designate and both governments met and struck a deal. Dublin was unwilling to give up its territorial claim on the North, arguing that the referendum that would be required would be lost. Instead, there were solemn declarations by both governments, with the Dublin government for the first time accepting the legal status of the Northern state. The British, for their part, declared that they would support the wishes of the majority of the people of Northern Ireland and that, if a majority should, in the future, 'indicate a wish to become part of a united Ireland, the British government would support that wish', something that remains their position to this day. It was, and is, a declaration without cost since there is not the slightest chance the loyalists would ever agree to such a thing.

Following the seizure of the *Claudia*, the head of the bomb disposal unit in the North had secretly come south to meet Irish army bomb disposal officers with a view to exchanging information. He also apparently met both the head of ordnance and the chief of staff and was promised covert assistance. More formal contacts were also in place and Irish army intelligence reports, to which the MacEntee Inquiry into the Dublin and Monaghan bombings decades later had access, showed that they had met British intelligence operatives in late 1973 and were concerned that, post-Sunningdale, the loyalists might launch attacks leading to civil war. Curiously, following further meetings in 1974, one of them as late as April, they concluded that the threat had diminished. Given that the loyalist strike and Dublin and Monaghan bombings followed almost immediately, it seems that either British intelligence was extremely poor or they were perfectly willing to mislead their Irish counterparts.

By then I believed that the IRA campaign, combined with Orange intransigence, would derail British plans to stabilise the situation. Accordingly, I saw the loyalists as de facto allies who would help destroy any attempt to reform the Northern statelet. Despite the campaign against Catholics then being carried out by the UVF/UDA, it still seemed vaguely possible that sectarian barriers might come tumbling down and we could come to cut a deal with what Brian Faulkner was terming Protestant Sinn Féinism. Relations with loyalism were widely discussed within the cages, and of course IRA policy back then was for four provincial parliaments, with the unionists having a majority within the proposed nine-county Ulster one. While policy was policy, inside Long Kesh we came to no consensus, some thinking an accommodation was possible, but many more believing the loyalists were incorrigible and steeped in a sectarian fascism with which we could never treat.

Certainly there were anti-Protestant bigots in our ranks, but they were restrained by the republican tradition and military policy of non-retaliation against ordinary Protestants.[12] We heard horror stories all the time. When Patrick O'Neill and Rose McCartney were abducted and killed by the UDA in 1972 we were told by those who claimed to have seen them in their coffins that both had been horribly mutilated and the young woman's breasts had been cut off. We firmly believed this and similar reports, and to this day I don't know whether they were true or not, for there was more than enough material from other killings of Catholics to make such stories credible. My own position saw a meeting of the extremes on socialist grounds once we got the British out of the equation, and I believed that meanwhile we should aim to settle the problem over their heads, ignoring them save where we could get at the killers themselves. I was very conscious that I enjoyed the luxury of theorising without consequence. For many of my comrades, the UDA and UVF men we could see in the adjoining cages were the killers who had been personally involved in the vicious campaign against their areas, something I was reminded of when Martin Meehan, in the course of a heated debate on the issue of

---

[12] 'Two for the price of one'? The English controversialist Christopher Hitchens claims in his memoir to have been physically present when Dave O'Connell used the phrase to laughingly dismiss the death of a pregnant Protestant woman in an IRA bomb blast. The same story features in the book written by the IRA informer Sean O'Callaghan, except that he heard it said by another republican leader, Kevin McKenna. I don't believe either man.

retaliatory attacks, noted that as a native of Dun Laoghaire rather than Ardoyne, it was easy for me to oppose them.

***

In June, the existing cages had been broken up and my immediate friends and I were scattered throughout the camp. Along with those others with a relatively short time to serve, I was sent to Cage 13, which was isolated from Cages 16, 17 and 18, where the long-termers were sent; those with more than ten years left to go occupied Cage 16. McKee decided that a leadership election was required to deal with the new situation and names were duly submitted. Bobby Campbell standing came as no surprise, but the candidatures of both Joe McKee and Davey Morley were. Billy also stood again. The election duly took place and though Billy McKee succeeded by a huge margin, Joe McKee got close to 70 votes, while Campbell and Morley received just over and under 20 apiece respectively.

I was in Cage 13 with McKee and was pleasantly surprised when he appointed me camp adjutant. He asked Morley to serve as Vice-O/C, a shrewd move since our cage was geographically isolated from the others, which were grouped together and had sight of each other. This allowed McKee to exercise control of the camp through Morley and also had the effect of anointing him as his successor. I think Morley stood against McKee because he considered discipline too weak at the time, but the counterblast to this was the important vote for Joe McKee, whose approach would have been the opposite of Morley's. Joe's vote marked out an area of resentment based primarily on the Falls Road that would slowly fester and come to boiling point when more important figures from that area – Ivor Bell, Brendan Hughes and Gerry Adams – came into the cages, thankfully some time after I had been released. Meanwhile, unlike the Falls Road men, Bobby Campbell continued to clash almost daily with the cage and camp staff and was eventually physically thrown out of the IRA cages, one of only two men to be expelled in my own time there.

The cage staff probably had more impact on our daily lives than did the camp staff, and Cage 13 was fortunate in having Jim Davison as

O/C, a sound and assured leader who would brook no serious nonsense either from the administration or from within. After the comparative helter-skelter of the previous eighteen months, I settled down to doing my time, the prospect of a sudden amnesty, in which it had once been possible to believe, well and truly gone, along with the expectation of escape. In the short-term cage, escaping was no longer the priority it had been, and indeed plans devised in Cage 13 were passed up the line for possible implementation elsewhere.

Because we were the short-term cage, there was a heavier than usual turnover as men were released and new men came in to replace them. In addition, we had a preponderance of younger volunteers, dealt with comparatively leniently by the courts because of their age, and of what we termed 'civilians' – IRA supporters who were doing time, generally for having assisted the local unit by holding weapons in their homes or helping to transport them. These tended to be older men. Aside from McKee himself, Martin Meehan was the only one in our cage with a serious reputation from outside and Martin never caused any problem for the staff, either at camp or at cage level.

We devised the routine. It was one of early rising, compulsory exercise, washing, breakfast followed by clean up, classes and military lectures, lunch, a period of drill, walking around the yard, perhaps more classes, tea, more yard-walking, reading and, in the evening, talking and watching television. Men were kept occupied rather than busy and there was plenty of time for handicrafts and other pastimes. Volleyball and table tennis were available in the cage itself and there was a football pitch, to which the cages had access in turn, and a camp gym housed in a Portakabin. Not long after we were moved to the Kesh I had gone there with some of my fellow prisoners, my motivation the novelty of getting out of the cage for a while rather than any wish to emulate Charles Atlas. As the screw in charge screamed at me not to do it, I snatched at a heavy barbell and felt my back give. It was the start of a recurrent problem that would require surgery in the mid-1980s. Of course I didn't know this at the time and after being half-carried back to the cage by a couple of my comrades, I saw the prison doctor and was sent to bed for a day or two to recover. I was then one of the lucky few who was 'prescribed' a wooden bed board, which meant that for the remainder of my time in Long Kesh I enjoyed a firm surface to sleep on, in contrast to the sagging mattresses and collapsing springs that plagued my comrades.

The days were punctuated by visits and the occasional crisis. Sunday was the worst day because there were no visits and so no news from the outside. The news was important; locals came in and perhaps praised, or maybe criticised, the IRA in their area. This all fed in, to be recycled back outside for explanation, and was an important source of our belonging. We got on, I thought, exceptionally, though perhaps this recollection is sepia-edged and we simply avoided those we didn't get on with. There were those throughout the camp who felt they had been overlooked for staff jobs, or didn't feel they had been offered one at the appropriate level, who engaged in low-level sniping, but we sentenced prisoners were broadly fortunate. Most of the prima donnas were in the internee end, people with big names from outside who, despite their protestations, resented the loss of rank. Jail was a great leveller which allowed you to see people close up and make your own assessment of them, unclouded by reputation.

Conditions improved steadily throughout the rest of 1973 and the first half of 1974. Porch extensions were built onto the huts and they received additional insulation in the roofs, so reducing the through winds and other drafts. The sleeping areas in the longer-term cages were given wooden partitions, which allowed for some privacy, though this was not applied to Cage 13 in my time there. Now in a new clique, with Gerry Scullion from Turf Lodge and Kieran Rice from the New Lodge, we all did a lot of reading. Seamus Keenan, older brother of Colm and Seán, had been in Cage 9 while I was there. He was a Trinity College graduate in English and read good books. Borrowing from him, I read serious fiction again for the first time in years. Seamus had a habit of writing a summary of what he had read, which I thought a great self-discipline, and it's something I regret not having adopted. University lecturers came in from the outside, including Miriam Daly – subsequently shot dead by loyalists during the H Blocks campaign – her husband, Jim, and Hugh Bredin, who lectured on political philosophy and brought an entirely new dimension to my thinking, since I had previously identified the subject with what would be called political science. We had various works on the Latin American, African, Vietnamese and Palestinian liberation struggles and biographies of Mao, Lenin, Stalin and Ho Chi Minh, as well as all the better known writings of Marx and Lenin, and those of Fintan Lalor, John Mitchel, Pearse and James Connolly. Noel Barber's *The War of the Running Dogs*, about the defeat of the Malayan communist campaign against the British, and Paul Henissart's *Wolves in the City*, a study of the latter stages of the Algerian revolution, helped shape my attitude, on the one hand towards the SDLP and other reformist politicians, and on the other towards the loyalists.

I had neither the hands nor the patience for woodwork, but did make some leather handbags, belts, purses and wallets for friends and family. This was trickier than the earlier work on handkerchiefs and wall plaques and involved tracing martial or Celtic images, sometimes one and the same, onto pre-cut leather, which then had to be tooled into shape by depressing the slightly dampened leather along the lines, thus raising the required image, which would later be stained. Much of my work made its way quietly into attics in middle-class south Dublin, which was not the best place to be flaunting republican memorabilia in the latter half of 1973 or the following year.

I subjected my parents to lengthy political rants in my irregular letters, as well as to endless requests for books, and my mother became a regular visitor to the Communist Party bookshop in Dublin. She also went to some of the hunger strike meetings and later visited a couple of the female IRA prisoners in Mountjoy and attended their trials in the Special. It couldn't have been easy and she did fall out with some friends. During the hunger strikes telegrams and other messages had arrived from various men and women who had known me as a child. There were surprises, both present and absent, and my mother would tell me years later of how one British couple from the Malaya days enquired eagerly about my brother and two sisters while visiting Dublin, completely ignoring me, until my mother angrily reminded them that she had four children.

My parents visited every four to six weeks, sometimes with my sisters or brother, and once or twice despite my warning not to come because the danger from the loyalists was particularly high. I developed a new dependence on my mother. When I was in Derry some of the volunteers had asked the girls to get them underwear down town, but I was far too shy for that, and despite the occasional offer from my Derry visitors my mother remained the sole supplier of underclothing throughout my time in jail. Occasionally I'd request other clothes as well. With a fashion sense stuck in the late 1960s, I asked her not to bring me the flared jeans or butterfly collars then being worn outside, but prison seems to produce an internal time-lag and I started wearing both after my release, when butterfly collars were on the way out and straight legs were again in style.

The purist position I had once argued over popular music was long forgotten, though in truth I had had great difficulty from the start in not tapping my foot when Hendrix or the Rolling Stones came on the radio. The music played in the huts in those pre-Walkman days, when everyone had to listen along with you, was an eclectic mix of rock, pop, jazz and 'Irish', the last ranging from rebel songs, through Planxty and Horslips, to Seán Ó Riada. There was even a bit of classical thrown in. The TV watched was what people wanted to watch, with *Match of the Day* and *Top of the Pops* clear favourites, though rank was occasionally pulled to ensure that we got to watch important political or historical programmes. We liked the BBC series *Colditz*, about British POWs held in Germany during World War II, and, being prisoners, we sided with the British. We also had the occasional picture show, favouring westerns and war and gangster movies – anything with white hats, black hats and, of course, guns. For some weeks Jim Davison played *Dear John* last thing before lights out each night, a thumping acknowledgement of where we were all really at, and I too made my way through a couple of unrequitable relationships in my few years in jail. For a time I corresponded with a Derry girl in Armagh prison. We exchanged soft words and handkerchiefs at Christmas, and though I have her print of James Connolly to this day, we never did meet up on the outside.

Though being slammed up was occasionally tough for the strongest of us, it was a point of honour to be able to 'do your whack' without complaining. Back in A Wing men could simply go to their cell during the day if they were finding it hard – the chances of their cellmates being there at the same time were not high – but of course this wasn't possible in the Kesh. To walk the cage on your own was just about acceptable, though everyone would know you were in bad form, and I dealt with the odd episode of despondency in the darkness late at night.

I had asked my mother to send me occasional postcards of south Dublin scenes, lest I forget, and walking around the never-changing tarmacked cage would sometimes dream of striding down Albert Road and into Sandycove, walking the pier in Dun Laoghaire, swimming in White Rock or the Forty Foot, or simply lying on grass we no longer saw. I promised myself I would roll in it; I would bury my face in it, though on release I never did. In my dreams it was summer and the sun always shone. I had a small drawerful of fantasies. I dreamed of escape, of Seán Treacy shaking me awake with an urgent whisper, of marching in a victory parade down O'Connell Street in Dublin as the heaving crowds cheered. I dreamed of daring deeds, heroic deeds, and of aching, suffering ones as well. Sometimes as I lay in bed I would imagine my own death, in the cold or heat, in a border field or on a city street, shot to pieces. I could see my funeral too: Dave O'Connell would give the oration, my friends would bow their heads in sorrow, a guard of honour would loose off a volley as my parents stood there proudly. Women I had never known would weep for me, would press against my dead lips .... Feck it, I was young.

I thought, of course, of girls: Stephen's Green at lunchtime on a summer's day; a yapping, arm-waving tangle of colour; of bare legs and tossing hair and flashing glances. I could see the sleepy smiles on the faces of the hippy girls in UCD, in Iveagh Gardens before the afternoon exams, so beautiful in their gypsy dresses, and I dreamed of dark-haired Derry girls as well.

I thought sometimes of a particular girl: my lying on the grass with her, the sun on her hair, her eyes closing and face softening as I leaned in to kiss her. If I worked really hard I could taste the breeze, could feel her arms around me, the wisps of her hair between my fingers and against my face. I would lie there, senses on fire with remembrance, chest thumping, till, unable to sleep, I would get up and sit on the toilet in the corner of the hut and try to read while I waited for the sharpness of what it was I had produced to blur and disappear. Then, hours later and exhausted, I could sleep, to dream of counter-lives which now could never be. And in the morning light, I would focus anew on the path I had chosen, and resolve once again to harden my heart.

I thought time was particularly tough for the civilians, who tended to be older men with families who could not be expected to have the same level of commitment as IRA volunteers and did not get as much out of the prison experience. For us volunteers, prison was a simple extension of our IRA service, during which we prepared ourselves as best we could for our eventual release and return to the struggle.

Time was tough too for suspended volunteers, the ones who had broken during British army and RUC custody and given information, made confessions or otherwise offended IRA orders, perhaps by recognising the court. Those in the last two categories had nothing to worry about, save that they had let themselves and their cause down. The former were not necessarily in the same position and had little to look forward to on the outside except further disgrace and in some cases physical punishment. I had sympathy for them, but not much. They had been in broadly the same position as the rest of us and knew the rules and the consequences of not keeping to them.

Imprisoned IRA volunteers lose whatever rank they may have held outside and are, categorically, inactive. This did not mean that we had no influence, or that those on the outside were not occasionally anxious to persuade us of the wisdom of their ways. Billy McKee kept a sharp and occasionally disapproving eye on developments and there is no doubt that from time to time the quality of control, in Belfast especially, was very poor, with individuals forced by the attrition of death and imprisonment into roles for which they lacked the capacity. Others, by the same token, astonished with the ease by which they adapted to their dreadful responsibilities.

Occasionally we got things wrong. In August 1973 when Jim Bryson and Paddy Mulvenna were shot dead in Ballymurphy, we blamed the Official IRA. The killings took place during a period of confrontation with the Officials in the area and Bryson and the three volunteers with him believed they were being fired on by them. However, unknown to everyone, the British army were using the flats from where the fire was coming as an observation post. Oblivious to this, the volunteers engaged what they thought were Official IRA men and were then substantially outgunned when British reinforcements arrived on their flank. At the time, most of Ballymurphy believed Bryson and Mulvenna had been shot dead by the Officials, as did we after we debriefed one of the men who had been with Bryson that night. The line from our own leadership was that they had been shot by the British army but, with McKee's approval, I dispatched a furious comm to GHQ advising that if they felt they had to lie to the general public for some greater reason, so be it, but we had no intention of lying to our own men. On other occasions we were right, and one very well-known Belfast IRA man was fortunate his career survived the savaging visited on him by McKee following the shooting dead as an informer of a mentally handicapped boy.

There was no contact between prisoners and the administration except through the staff. A screw was placed in a no-man's-land which acted as a buffer between the cage and the pathways to other cages, the visiting block, doctor's and governor's prefabs, and so on, and when someone was required for, say, a visit, the screw would pass the name to a volunteer, on duty solely for that purpose, who would collect the prisoner in question. The same procedures applied to those seeking medical or dental attention (the dentist's nurse was the object of outrageous lying boasts from returning prisoners), with the result that we had total control within the camp. Contact with the other cages came in the main through the football field which backed onto Cage 13, and to which all the cages in the sentenced prisoner end of the camp, including the loyalists and Official IRA, had access on a rota basis. Our other cages – 16, 17, 18 and then 20 – bordered on each other, making rapid communication between them simple. McKee and I had lengthy discussions at the wire with Davey Morley and other members of the camp staff, as well as lighter, banter-led exchanges with our friends and comrades from those cages.

In the latter part of my time in the Kesh there were two outstanding escape attempts, from Cages 16 and 17 respectively, both of which fell at the last hurdle. In the second of these, six men disguised as a British army patrol, complete with full and accurate uniform made up of various materials – some of which had to be smuggled in – and armed with wooden SLRs produced in the handicrafts hut, made their way as far as the final gate, passing through a number of security checks and managing on the way to fool even their putative regimental colleagues before being caught at the final gate. The postscript to these failures was even better, since both sets of would-be escapers would subsequently break out of the courthouse in Newry in March 1975, having been brought there to face charges arising from their failed attempts.

Given the close conditions in which we lived, it is surprising that there weren't more instances of men falling out. There was the odd row, of course, but a dim view was taken of people raising their hands and I don't remember anything serious. One day, when McKee was absent for some reason, I was alerted to the fact that Jim Davison and Martin Meehan were squaring up to each other and had gone, Belfast-style, to get their boots on for business. When they re-emerged, I stepped in and was able to dissuade them, with neither losing face. I persuaded Davison on the basis that as O/C he would be setting an appalling precedent and flattered Meehan separately, citing his standing in the IRA and the bad example he would be giving. The moment passed, but I dread to think what the outcome would have been if those two had got going at each other.

Billy McKee made some bad calls. We ran our part of the camp and decided who did and who didn't come into the IRA-controlled cages. On one occasion McKee refused to let a young IRA man into the cages, having heard from the outside that he had been sleeping with the wife of one of our men before his own capture. As often happens, our man had no idea his wife was cheating on him and matters could easily have been dealt with by arranging that the offender be admitted to a cage where they would never encounter one another, but this was the standard McKee operated and there was no shaking him. Clearly it was not a comradely act to sleep with another volunteer's wife, particularly in circumstances where he was incidentally billeted in her house, but it does take two and it was harsh and wrong that he should have been deprived of political status for this reason.

In other cases involving sexual indiscretion, McKee was the height of understanding, though one might take issue with the outcomes. There was an instance where the wife of a prisoner had become pregnant by another man and a complex and quite ingenious set of measures were put in motion to ensure, successfully, that our prisoner would come to believe the child was his own. These were dangerous liaisons, with some unfaithful wives not above alleging rape, and the combination of young volunteers and lonely women must have left many painful residues in republican areas throughout the Six Counties. That said, most set a high premium on fidelity, and the vast majority of the women did stand by their men. Indeed, it cut both ways once Cumann na mBan and, latterly, female IRA volunteers began to fill the women's prison in Armagh. In retrospect one wonders, but in any case these were the moral standards applied in the cages in the early 1970s. Kevin Mallon used to tell a (possibly apocryphal) tale against himself about how a GHQ directive had arrived in Tyrone to the effect that any volunteer making shapes at a prisoner's wife was to be kneecapped. As he told the story, he and his second in command had contemplated each other's kneecaps at considerable length before deciding to quietly ignore the directive.

Mass was said every Sunday in the half-hut and was variably attended, with numbers soaring in times of high political development, when expectations grew of a possible amnesty. One of the men acquired the nickname 'Amnesty' and was the endless butt of outrageous, teasing rumour. Perhaps the choicest of these came one morning when we emerged from our huts to see blue-bereted soldiers patrolling nearby, driving some to conclude that the British army had been replaced by United Nations troops. Fortunately there were ex-soldiers among us who very quickly told us that, sadly, these were not UN blue berets but rather soldiers from the RAF Regiment.

Billy McKee, who was a daily Mass-goer and communicant on the outside, was aware of my own position on religion and it was never an issue, though I believe the generally low Mass attendance, particularly of the younger men, pained him. Fathers Faul and Murray were regular visitors to the camp, and McKee spent a lot of time with Faul. Denis Faul seemed to me at that time a straight player, though he was heavily criticised during the 1981 hunger strike, which the then leadership accused him of undermining. He was the author, with Father Murray, of a series of important pamphlets describing British misbehaviour, a brave advocate of civil rights and the rule of law, and an open but – I thought – fair critic of the IRA.

Though McKee rarely allowed his religious views to intrude on his politics, a complete separation was unlikely. At one point he banned the use of Ouija boards, a board game being played in some of the cages in which the players supposedly communicate with the dead. This involves players sitting around a lettered board with a finger on an upturned glass, which then moves to spell out a message from the beyond, and presumably works on the basis of the players' subconscious, or perhaps because one or more of them are deliberately manipulating the answers. In any event, McKee felt sufficiently concerned to get the priests in to, as it were, decontaminate the offending cages.

Interestingly, there was a legitimate angle to the ban in that some were using the board to 'communicate' with dead soldiers who were supposedly then pointing the finger at their killers, so giving rise to obvious breaches of security. Loose talk was frowned upon and tended to occur only tangentially. Martin Meehan had detention papers which outlined the various operations he was purportedly involved in, which were truly numerous, and I remember sitting with him while he went through them, singling out the occasional paragraph and saying 'I never did that', thus including by implication all those operations on which he remained silent.

Chapter 13

At the end of October 1973, republican morale was hugely boosted when Seamus Twomey, J.B. O'Hagan and Kevin Mallon – at the time of their arrests the chief of staff, adjutant general and director of operations respectively – escaped from the yard of Mountjoy Prison in a hijacked helicopter. Twomey and Mallon had been captured separately just weeks earlier amid great fanfare, and the escape was excruciatingly embarrassing for the Dublin government, who immediately placed armed guards at the RTE headquarters, so manufacturing distracting fears of an imminent IRA coup. Twomey added further to the government's discomfort with his widely reported interview with German current affairs magazine *Der Spiegel*, in which he invited the British to get a good night's sleep while they could, as a new offensive was about to be launched 'from land, sea and air'.

Though Twomey's offensive never materialised, and McKee winced visibly when reading the reports, a campaign proper did commence in England, with letter bombs and explosions at underground stations and elsewhere. Responsibility for these was tacitly accepted when the IRA released a statement addressed to Edward Heath, saying that while they had no wish to inflict hardship on the British people, they would strike where and when they could until he faced up to his responsibilities. The day following the IRA statement brought a bombing at a Surrey army base while, in Birmingham, an army technician was badly injured when attempting to defuse a bomb and died the following week. Chelsea barracks – one of the targets on which I had done intelligence in 1970 – was also bombed. There were a number of bombings in London over the Christmas period and, though warnings were given, the authorities claimed that there had been insufficient time to clear the streets and there were some casualties, though fortunately no deaths.

The bombings continued in England as 1974 began with explosions in Birmingham and London, including one at the home of a serving officer of general rank, and a letter bomb campaign directed at a variety of what we would have considered establishment targets. The Home Secretary, Reginald Maudling (who was struck by Bernadette Devlin following Bloody Sunday), was one of those slightly injured by a letter bomb. On 4 February the IRA planted a suitcase full of explosives on a coach ferrying soldiers on the M62. Nine soldiers died, as well as the wife and two young children of one of them, and many others were injured. This incident gave rise to one of the notorious miscarriage of justice cases when Judith Ward, an English fantasist, made admissions against a patently fictitious background and was sentenced to life imprisonment. She was finally released in 1992.

There was great interest during the early part of the year among both republicans and loyalists in the so-called Boal proposals. Desmond Boal – a leading barrister and ex-chairman of Paisley's Democratic Unionist Party – suggested two regional parliaments based on the existing border, in what he called an Amalgamated Ireland. Boal's proposal included a 'national' parliament in Athlone and, being not a million miles away from Sinn Féin's plan for four provincial parliaments, which also placed the national government in Athlone, provided an obvious basis for discussion. The proposals, accordingly, were welcomed by ourselves and were discussed in secret talks with the UVF, then supposedly on ceasefire, attended for the IRA by Dave O'Connell and Brian Keenan in Cavan and later continued in Belfast.

Though the UDA also showed some interest in the Boal proposals, unionists – including William Craig and Paisley – condemned them, and they were also dismissed out of hand as a distraction by the Dublin government. The official attitude was summed up by Conor Cruise O'Brien, who described the proposals as a device to clear the decks for a civil war, in the absence of the British, which both 'sides' separately felt they could win, a mantra he would be repeating for the next few decades.

At the end of January, and in partial response to these hopeful signs, the IRA said it would no longer target off-duty UDR members. The UVF responded by suggesting that sectarian assassinations should now be halted, but the UDA said it would continue to kill those it characterised as 'enemies of the state'. In any event, the UVF was divided during this time and elements of it went on killing Catholics throughout early 1974.

In Cage 13 we were next door to the loyalists and could observe their leader, Gusty Spence, strutting his stuff, much of the time in full UVF uniform. We had little to do with the loyalists and had no respect for them. I have never felt a moment's doubt about the moral difference between the IRA, who were fighting for national liberation and a socialist future – for the most part against a clear enemy using discernible tactics – and the right-wing, sectarian fascism of the loyalist paramilitaries. These were people whose idea of soldiering was the murder of innocent Catholics, who piggybacked to political status on our hunger strike, and, in the case of the UVF, had a leader who had gone walkabout for four months while on parole and was treated like a hero for having shot Catholics back in 1966. Billy McKee sent me to a couple of camp liaison meetings attended by Jim Monaghan for the Officials (not the Jim Monaghan of Provisional fame), Gusty Spence for the UVF and Jim Craig for the UDA, where Spence's main preoccupation seemed to be the negotiation of 'a good, traditional Ulster fry' for breakfast. Craig was a wide boy who had been doing ordinary time in Crumlin Road and who had risen to the top of the UDA pile because he was good with his fists. He was a thug, but a friendly and likeable one, and was shot dead years later by the UDA on suspicion of giving information to the IRA.

On Gusty, I took my lead from McKee and thought him a pompous bigmouth. One night he decided on a rebellion at lock-up time and the UVF men in the cage refused to go into their huts. The governor, Robert Truesdale – who had been Spence's commanding officer in the British army years earlier – turned up in person, riot squad admittedly in tow, to face them down and in they went, meek as lambs, with a couple of defiant backward shouts. McKee would never have created such a situation and, if he had, we would have carried through whatever our threat might have been, and the administration well knew it. The power-sharing executive agreed at Sunningdale took up office on 1 January 1974. Some days later the new arrangements were rejected by the Ulster Unionist Council, which in effect was a vote of no confidence in Faulkner, who was then finished as unionist leader. At this stage Faulkner was going to need a miracle to survive. He wasn't to get it. Instead, Heath called a snap election at the end of February to answer the question of who governed Britain, which fetched the response – as someone once put it – that it certainly wasn't him.

In the North, the loyalist opposition swept the boards, taking eleven of the twelve Westminster seats with more than half of the popular vote, an outcome which dealt a terminal blow to Faulkner and the Executive. Harold Wilson of Labour went on to form an uncertain administration, with Merlyn Rees arriving as the new Secretary of State. This was not a surprise as Rees had shadowed the role, but we viewed him as a chinless hand-wringer and he never looked remotely in control of matters. On his appointment, he announced that he would never talk to the IRA, claiming he had been 'cured' of the idea by his previous two encounters (in March and July 1972). In addition to these, however, he had met us in Long Kesh (while he was shadowing the role), where he had expressed his horror to Billy McKee that the British could be holding prisoners in veritable concentration camps, and he had held a line open to us before taking office. The IRA greeted Rees's arrival with a 90-minute gun battle on the south Armagh border and a 500-pounder outside the Grand Central Hotel – the British army's Belfast headquarters – which wrecked much of Royal Avenue. The IRA returned to the scene again at the end of the month to finish the job, this time planting a 600-pound bomb, which devastated what remained of the street.

The loyalists were now determined not just to stop the Council of Ireland from coming into being, but to destroy the Executive. The Loyalist Association of Workers – which had collapsed in recrimination after the failure of a strike move the previous year – was refashioned as the Ulster Workers' Council (UWC) and carefully targeted the key industries. The loyalist demand – increasingly loud and not unreasonable in the circumstances – was for a Northern Assembly election, and there was an expanding threat of industrial and other unspecified action should such continue to be denied to them.

Following his marginal victory, and fearing the possibility of a new Unionist/Conservative alignment, Wilson began to secretly explore both the removal from Westminster of the Northern representatives and, later, terrified that the British army might find itself being fired on from two sides, a British withdrawal. By now the Dublin government was proposing that the ratification of Sunningdale take place in May, something that Faulkner rejected, arguing that nothing further should occur until there was movement on the Irish promises of an improvement in cross-border security. Though Faulkner was finished, no one was willing to drop the Council of Ireland – far less the commitment to power-sharing. Rees and Wilson proceeded to further undermine Faulkner – and incidentally the SDLP – by legalising both the UVF and Sinn Féin, and then opening direct contact with the Ulster Workers' Council, on which both the UVF and the always legal UDA were represented.

May would be the most significant month for some time and opened with bombs in Belfast, including yet another at the Europa Hotel. The IRA launched a major attack on Crossmaglen barracks, and, in Dublin, the National Gallery of Ireland received a ransom note demanding £500,000 and the return of the Price sisters in exchange for canvasses of nineteen Old Masters taken in a raid on the Beit art collection in County Wicklow. The sisters, Dolours and Marian, were among the ten arrested in Britain for the Border Poll bombings in London and were then being force-fed in an English prison.

On 13 May the UWC released a statement threatening a 'province-wide blackout'. A vote in the Assembly the following day was then the trigger for the commencement of the strike, which kicked off against a background of RUC men and British soldiers talking amicably to those on the loyalist barricades. In the early days barricades were indeed removed, but not until after people had made their first, and failed, attempt to get to work. The strike bit decisively after a day or two, thanks in the main to UDA intimidation, and once it had momentum, it quickly became unstoppable, with important support in key industries, such as the power stations and petrol and gas distribution.

Three days into the strike the UVF attacked the South, planting three car bombs in Dublin and one in Monaghan, killing thirty-three people in the single greatest atrocity of the Troubles. Twelve men, nineteen women and two infants died; in addition, one woman, Colette Doherty, was nine months pregnant when she died (her child did not survive) and Martha O'Neill – whose husband, Edward O'Neill, was killed and whose two sons were badly injured – later suffered a still birth. A great many others were maimed, some of them grievously. The entire O'Brien family – John, Anna and their two infant daughters – was wiped out in the Parnell Street blast. Among the dead were a French citizen, an Italian citizen, four pensioners (including a man of eighty), office workers, and shoppers caught in the Friday rush hour in bombings designed to inflict death and injury on the maximum number of innocent civilians. This premeditated instance of mass murder was greeted by the loyalists with celebrations, though muted ones within Long Kesh, and a UDA spokesman describing himself as 'very happy' when asked for a comment.

The bombings remain unexplained,[13] though it has long been thought that the UVF was acting with the assistance, or at least encouragement, of some section of British intelligence. The Garda investigation was mysteriously wound down after a few months and, despite a series of inquiries, the truth is unlikely now to out. In the latest inquiry, conducted by Paddy McEntee SC, collusion was found to be unproven, or, better put, unprovable. The Garda files were either missing or destroyed and whether this was by design or through carelessness could not be established. Samples and exhibits were either not retrieved at all or also went missing, making forensic examination with modern techniques impossible. McEntee, who had asked for sight of a redacted intelligence document from the British, was politely refused, but was assured that the British official responding had himself been advised by those who examined it that the disclosure would compromise intelligence methods and was anyway not relevant to his inquiry.

---

[13] Although the UVF claimed responsibility in 1993, I don't believe their claim that they acted alone.

As with the blasts in Dublin eighteen months earlier in 1972, these bombs too had the desired effect, with Liam Cosgrave immediately blaming the IRA: 'Everyone who has practised violence, or preached violence or condoned violence must bear a share of responsibility for today's outrage.' This distancing and alienation would be consolidated throughout the latter part of the decade as the South simply buried its head in the sand in apparent agreement that the North's suffering was primarily the result of the IRA campaign, and that the troubles were at all costs to stay confined to the North. Cosgrave made this clearer still a couple of weeks later: 'People in the South are saying more and more that the idea of unity with a people so deeply imbued with violence was not what they wanted.' Unlike the aftermath of Bloody Sunday, there was no recognition, no national day of mourning, for these innocent victims, and, in the cruellest of twists, the injured and the families of the dead found themselves intimidated into silence and, on pain of being seen as IRA supporters, they did not attempt to seriously raise questions about the bombings until the late 1980s. Thus was the bombing treated by the Southern establishment as righteous retribution for the actions of the IRA, who were ultimately the ones to blame.

***

When the British finally did respond to the UWC strike, it was far too late. By then it was so solid that the barricades had been taken down as it was no longer necessary to prevent or intimidate unionists from going to work. On 28 May, with the promise of the collapse of power generation, and the spectre of sewage in the streets, Faulkner's backbenchers decided they had had enough. They demanded that the British negotiate with the strikers and, when the British refused, Faulkner resigned and the Executive was finished. With Faulkner noting that the strike had done more in two weeks than the IRA in five years to 'persuade people in Britain that they should pull out', and the victorious loyalists making it clear that there would be no power-sharing, British, and indeed Southern, policy was in tatters.

Though the final cause was the will of the unionist electorate, it is doubtful that this would have had the opportunity to manifest itself had it not been for the failure of the British government to back its creation and impose discipline on its own armed forces. It is forgotten how peculiar a time this was in Britain: the Monday Club[14] was a power, Enoch Powell – the malevolent Tory figure of rivers-of-blood fame – was on the scene, private armies were being formed, and there was much, not at all fanciful, talk of a military coup. There was a lot of wholly justified paranoia about, and when the London *Times* in March reported the existence of a secret oath-bound organisation called 'For Ulster' within the RUC and UDR – pledged to mutiny in the event of their being ordered to move against Protestants – we saw no reason to disbelieve it. While Rees subsequently took it for granted that the RUC was on the brink of mutiny, rumours were rife that the British army too was refusing to move against the UWC strike.[15] Thus, while Rees and the British government were denying they were talking to the IRA, the army was telling selected journalists of the identity of some of the go-betweens. Indeed, Rees complains bitterly about army information policy in his memoir, though he insists on viewing the army's undermining of him as emanating from lower down the command chain.

***

The war generally, and the bombing campaign in particular, continued before, throughout and after the strike, with soldiers, RUC men and UDR members killed and injured. Among the casualties was a female UDR member, killed in a gun and rocket attack on an army

---

[14] A right-wing caucus within the Tory party.

[15] In early September a junior officer writing in the Monday Club magazine under the pseudonym Andrew Sefton said the army had given the UDA tacit support during the strike because it feared a war on two fronts and suggested 'the unwillingness of the Army to end the UWC strike and the subsequent confrontation between the military and the politicians must be the most significant event of recent years. For the first time the Army decided it was right and the politicians had better toe the line.' Years later the then army GOC, Sir Frank King, confirmed the gist of this when he told an interviewer, 'It was clear even before the strike that the executive was already dead as a doornail.' He also said, 'If Rees had ordered us to move against the barricades we would have said, "With great respect, this is a job for the police. We will assist them if you wish, but it's not terrorism."'

base in Tyrone, where the attackers – reckoned to have numbered up to 40 – had blocked off the various approach roads. Huge bombs were exploded, especially in Belfast, where, in late July, the Europa was hit for the 25th time, while a 300-pounder was defused at the headquarters of the Unionist Party, where Enoch Powell was due to give a press conference following his adoption as the unionist candidate for South Down.

Security restrictions had been progressively stepped up since 1972 and, when the control segment (the supposedly secure city centre) was extended yet again in July, the IRA's response was to plant five proxy bombs at the Europa and various government offices. Shops had long since been required to employ security guards, who conducted further searches on people, and by the mid-70s there was only one point of access into Belfast city centre, which in any case had become a ghost town after dark. Yet still the bombing went on. The British army was quite unable to prevent it, and when the second Grand Central bombing took place, conveyed to the scene by a proxy bomber, Faulkner had raised his frustration with Wilson, referring to the 'sense of bafflement and drift' he encountered when he spoke to those in charge of security.

There was a welcome change from the usual statements from army HQ listing items seized, men arrested and a defeated IRA on the horizon when a defence spokesman in London, quizzed on plummeting recruitment figures, attributed the more than 30 per cent drop in 1973 to 'Ulster', adding that there was 'no use denying it'. Just before the UWC strike, the RUC chief constable had said that not enough people were joining the RUC, and reality was again glimpsed when Defence Secretary Roy Mason conceded that there was growing pressure in Britain itself for a date to be set for withdrawal, and that the people of the North needed to 'do more' for themselves by joining the RUC and the UDR. Though his Ministry subsequently denied any change in policy, the remarks were music to our ears and it is a pity we had not the ability to inflict the level of casualties of the previous years. Mason's words also foreshadowed the coming 'Ulsterisation' of the conflict: the demand that locals take the casualties, which is the perennial resort of the power in a colonial war going badly.

Within the cages these were tense times. The assassination of Catholics was proceeding as usual, and, in addition to those killed in the Dublin and Monaghan bombings, many others died during the May of the UWC strike, including two Protestants mistaken for Catholics. The majority of the killings were in the greater Belfast area, where six Catholic men were killed in a single incident when the UVF bombed a bar on the Ormeau Road. The dead included a Queen's University student, 'rompered' in a UDA club before being taken elsewhere to be shot dead, and an alcoholic homeless man, abducted and beaten to death by the UDA.

Towards the end of June the UDA announced a ceasefire, so that July brought an untypical lull with just two Catholics killed, both by the UVF. Ceasefire or not, a group of loyalist women showed that they could match the ferocity of their men when they battered to death a Protestant single mother in the UDA's Sandy Row club for some unknown transgression, while her six-year-old daughter stood outside crying. The ceasefire didn't last long. In August a thirteen-year-old was shot dead in the New Lodge area by a UDA gunman, and the body of nationalist councillor Patrick Kelly, who had disappeared some weeks earlier, floated to the surface of Lough Erne in Fermanagh. He had been shot dead by the UDA and his weighted-down body thrown into the lake. Just days earlier, his brother-in-law had been shot in the back while in British army custody, minutes after being taken from his home.

Among those killed that summer were a young mother of two, a thirteen-year-old schoolgirl and a married couple, shot dead in Tyrone. Their daughter was also wounded. A serving UDR man was subsequently convicted of this killing. William Craig described these dreadful killings as 'understandable and excusable'. With petrol available only at the whim of the UDA, Long Kesh was virtually blockaded and this, together with the loyalist roadblocks and killings, reduced the normal visiting and provision of food parcels to the point of non-existence. There was rationing within the cages and, during the power cuts, we cooked over giant drums with such fuel as could be gathered. Though wary of the loyalists, we vastly outnumbered them and had contingency plans in place for them and for ourselves in the event of a loyalist seizure of power, or of the camp being attacked from outside – both far from impossible scenarios in the circumstances of the time.

Although the UWC strike monopolised everyone's attention in May 1974, there were other developments taking place. As the loyalists prepared to strike, Brendan Hughes, the then O/C of Belfast – who had escaped from Long Kesh the previous December – was captured in the well-to-do Malone Road area. Found with him were implausibly ambitious contingency plans for implementation in the event of a doomsday situation in Belfast, and these were promptly disclosed to the world by Harold Wilson, who claimed the IRA's real purpose was to foment civil war. Two could play at this game, and Dave O'Connell held a press conference the same day in the course of which he revealed the contents of a private letter from Merlyn Rees to a republican supporter in which he had written: 'Frankly we have not the faintest desire to stay in Ireland and the sooner we're out the better.'

On 18 May the British at last ceased the force-feeding of the Price sisters. They had been force-fed for 167 days. The Home Secretary, Roy Jenkins, also said he believed it would be possible for them to serve the bulk of their sentences nearer their homes, though he added that this would depend on the security situation, and their move home was subsequently delayed following the Birmingham bombs in November. Everyone was terrified that one of the sisters, now dangerously close to death, would die, but their strike – and that of Hugh Feeney and Gerry Kelly, who were arrested with them – continued, as did those of Michael Gaughan and Frank Stagg. Michael, who was also force-fed, died on 3 June, after 65 days, the first hunger striker to die in the current period of conflict with the British. His funeral in Mayo was attended by a crowd of 10,000 and Dave O'Connell gave the oration. Frank Stagg was subsequently ordered off strike only to resume it and die in 1976. After Michael's death, the Price sisters and the others finally ended their marathon ordeal when intermediaries underwrote Jenkins' belated offer, so bringing an end to this shameful episode.[16]

The IRA's relations, such as they were, with the government in Dublin had gone from bad to worse. There was the small difficulty that

[16] Dave O'Connell later told me that Jenkins had been wringing his hands from the time he took office in early March, telling various intermediaries that while the situation with the sisters was appalling, any display of 'weakness' by him would do irrevocable damage to his career. I held a low opinion of Jenkins thereafter.

we didn't recognise the legality of the state itself – republican theology having it that the IRA Army Council is the lawful government-in-waiting – but by early 1974, things were truly atrocious. Political status had been squeezed out of the government in October 1973 following a lengthy hunger strike, but the helicopter escape at the end of the same month had made fools of them. By January 1974, inspired by the measures taken by the Israelis in the occupied territories, Justice Minister Paddy Cooney was toying with the idea of closing down the businesses and homes of IRA supporters. Cooney also called on people to refuse to buy republican publications, and the pressures to publicly shun us undoubtedly frightened many. In truth, the IRA had contributed more than its share to raising the temperature. Despite the existence of General Army Order No. 8, which forbids action in the South, there was inevitably trouble when IRA units were confronted by the Gardaí, whether uniformed or Special Branch. In March, Billy Fox, a Protestant Fine Gael senator, turned up dead after a botched operation in County Monaghan, and an equally botched attempt at covering it up. The IRA went into denial mode but was pinned when a number of volunteers were charged with both membership and the senator's murder in an episode that did the movement tremendous damage.

Meanwhile, an Oxford-educated British woman, Dr Bridget Rose Dugdale, the then girlfriend of IRA volunteer Eddie Gallagher, made headlines in January when she used a helicopter – hijacked in County Donegal – for an airborne bomb attack on Strabane RUC barracks. The Beit art seizure had also been the work of this unit and it is unclear whether or not it had leadership approval. In any event, Dugdale herself was arrested shortly afterwards and the stolen paintings recovered. Then, just two days before the Price sisters came off hunger strike, the same unit, now minus Dugdale, kidnapped the Earl and Countess of Donoughmore, minor aristocrats living in Ireland, who were saved from an uncertain fate by the settlement of the strike. Finally, in August, eighteen prisoners blasted their way out of Portlaoise Prison, among them Kevin Mallon, who had been recaptured, and Eddie Gallagher, who had been arrested just days earlier, in what was pretty much a last straw for the government.

We had an almighty scare in the cages that summer as indications of a widespread British intelligence plan run by the MRF began to come to light. While the destruction of the Four Square Laundry operation in October 1972 was a severe set-back for undercover work, the idea was unlikely to be discontinued, and, as Brendan Hughes entered Crumlin Road prison in May 1974, two men, Vincent Heatheringon and Myles McGrogan, were charged with the killing of two RUC men in an IRA operation in which they could not have been involved. Following debriefs, in which Heatherington was forthcoming and McGrogan uncooperative, Heatherington told his interrogators that he belonged to a 'unit' under British army control which was made up of loyalists and republicans and was involved in sectarian bombings and assassinations. A great number of names and operational details were disclosed, many of which it was possible to cross-check, leaving the IRA within the prisons certain that the essential claim was accurate. The revelations, and the spilling of multiple names, gave rise to a major investigation in Long Kesh as well as in Crumlin Road and in Belfast itself. However, overenthusiastic interrogation, including methods that certainly amounted to torture, led to the making of many spurious claims and produced widespread paranoia within our ranks. As we thought and talked about it in Long Kesh, the unit's structure meshed perfectly with everything that was known of black operations carried out by British forces elsewhere. Many operations which had puzzled us, and of which the loyalists would have seemed incapable, now began to make sense. This episode came complete with a generalised and credible poison scare, with at least one incident of a poisoned chicken being discovered, and for some weeks the water boilers in the huts were kept under observation and the cage and camp staffs took on the task of tasting the prison food before it was distributed.

This was a difficult matter to deal with. We felt we had an obligation to warn nationalists that there were British agents capable of murder within our areas, and possibly within IRA ranks, without causing wholesale panic. In mid-July, the leadership issued a measured statement, revealing that some members of the 'Ulster Freedom Fighters' – a cover name the UDA had been using since mid-1973 – had been Catholics and that it had been established that 'criminals' from both sides had been involved in their operations. There is no doubt that we were flooded with misinformation, and indeed some of those being interrogated confessed that they had made up names on instructions as to what to do if cornered, but suggestions that it was a 'sting' operation from the outset, cleverly designed to produce havoc within our ranks, are simply not true. To my knowledge, the subsequent IRA inquiry never properly concluded. The benign view is that the mass of misinformation simply proved to be too dense to penetrate, and, against a background of extreme unease about the methods by which some of the information was acquired, the investigation was overwhelmed by material and simply petered out, though, given more recent revelations about the extent to which the IRA was infiltrated, one wonders.

***

For reasons that are unclear, relations with the prison administration, which had been in something of a free fall anyway, took a dramatic nosedive that summer, when Billy McKee stood down as O/C in preparation for his release in early September. Following an election he was succeeded by Davey Morley and, though with only weeks left to do myself, Morley asked me to stay on as adjutant, in part because the MRF investigation was underway. Following a visit to the Kesh in May, albeit to the internee end, Bishop Daly described conditions in the camp as 'vile, inhuman and deplorable', and that is what they had become. Though for a time we were refusing to see visitors because closed visits had been reintroduced after an internee had escaped by swapping places with his visitor, the immediate *casus belli* was that the food, without explanation, began to arrive in the cages stone cold. After the usual protests brought no improvement, Morley ordered the food to be thrown back over the wire. The prison administration then retaliated by stopping food parcels, refusing access to the prison shop and preventing the IRA camp staff from communicating with the various cages and with each other.

While there was little difficulty in Morley's communicating with the cages adjacent to him, our cage, and the remand prisoners in Cage 10, were isolated and would have been completely cut off. Shortly before-hand, however, and in anticipation of the crackdown, we had devised a system of communication using coded semaphore signals and, on the very first morning after the change, I climbed onto the roof of one of the huts in Cage 13 with Tommy Mullin, our Christmas hypnotist, and, to the consternation of the soldiers in the look-out posts and the screws outside the cage, dictated a series of responses to the queries and instructions Morley was flagging. We felt very clever.

For us, this was a time of mixed messages from the British: on the one hand, following the UWC strike, hints were coming fast and furious of a new willingness to think previously unthinkable thoughts; on the other, the prison administration was getting stuck into us quite unnecessarily. We were talking to the loyalists both inside and outside the prison and released joint statements about the conditions there. Against the backdrop of events throughout the summer and autumn of 1974, our relations with them within Long Kesh were at the highest point that I experienced.

As my own release date came closer, it was becoming clear that it was only a matter of time until the camp went up in flames. More joint statements were put out seeking negotiations, but the governor was refusing to meet us. Rees himself got involved at one point, promising improvements on food and other issues but, typically, nothing happened.

While in the earlier stages, men had been released from imprisonment only to be rearrested and interned, this had now more or less ceased and, in fact, internees were being slowly released.[17] I already knew I was to report back to GHQ for instructions, which in theory was appropriate, as I was reporting back to those I had left to go into Derry, rather than back to Derry itself. As the date approached, I began to worry about the prospect of being returned to England to face armed robbery charges. I spoke to McKee about it before his own release and, subsequently, a simple scheme was put in place, designed to get me out a day early and so, perhaps, foil any arrest arrangement. My parents were visited in Dublin and told not to collect me, and contact was then

---

[17] Internees had by now been renamed 'detainees' in an effort by the British to remove the stench. Long Kesh had become the Maze.

made with the prison authorities, I believe by a cleric, to say a family member was seriously ill and to ask that I be released on compassionate grounds a day early. However, the messages apparently got confused so that nothing came of it, and at lock-up on the evening of 19 September, I trooped into my hut with my comrades as usual.

Chapter 14

The elaborate arrangements I had expected failed to materialise, instead trailing into something approaching fiasco. I left the cages in a much less emotional state than I might otherwise have been, saved by my apprehensions from the tears of guilty departure I had seen shed by others. At the reception area, I received back the few belongings I had seen disappear into that brown envelope three years earlier: a watch given to me in Fermanagh when my own had packed in, and my battered wallet. In a last piece of pettiness, I was not allowed leave with a couple of wallets that had been given to me as mementoes while being permitted others, the ones refused to me having crossed some invisible line in the mind of the censoring screw.

I went through the final gate with that same sense of vacant concentration that I used to experience, for instance, crossing the border – tensed against my essential helplessness should there be a welcoming party – and went to the car park where I was met as arranged. After a few minutes I realised from the road signs that we were heading for Belfast. This was not the direction I expected to be travelling in, but for the moment I said nothing. When we got there, I was brought first to the Felon's Club close to the Falls Road, a famous ex-prisoners' drinking club of which I was now automatically a member, and then to the Andersonstown Prisoners' Dependants' Club. I declined drink in both places and when eventually my hosts realised we were at cross-purposes – theirs being to help celebrate my release – a car and a driver were organised to take me as far as Dundalk. The trip was uneventful in that we met no checkpoints and I crossed the border with considerable relief into the visibly less prosperous South. There I was taken to yet another republican pub where I was handed on to the locals, who took me to Dublin. Throughout, the driver and I confined ourselves to the kind of small talk then considered mandatory for security reasons.

Arrangements had been put in place between Dublin and Dundalk and I was duly deposited at a bar on the airport road, from where I was picked up and taken to a house where I met Dave O'Connell. Dave, who was balding, was wearing a wig which I thought transformed him. I let him know I was less than pleased with the arrangements, but Dave was not the type to be fazed by a bit of whingeing and coolly observed that I was sitting there talking to him. I gave him the latest on the position in Long Kesh, the MRF investigation and my general impressions of the state of things outside, and he listened carefully. He pressed some money on me, and personally dropped me out to Blackrock where I was to meet my parents, who had by then moved back to Dublin. Just a week or two previously, some Sunday paper had reported that the campaign was being run from the Isle of Man, where it said GHQ was based, and though that was clearly codswallop, it was hard to believe that the leadership was openly working away in the manner that it proved to be. I was horrified at the needless risk I perceived Dave to be taking in ferrying me from one side of the city to the other and told him so.

I met my parents, my youngest sister and the dog they'd called Derry in, as it were, my honour, and went home where we ate – what seemed to me after prison fare – a meal of extraordinary richness. The most striking contrast with prison, though, was that of scale; after the space of Long Kesh, the rooms in this ordinary suburban house seemed claustrophobically tiny and I found myself unnecessarily ducking down as I moved through the doorways from one room to another. I had a beer or two with my father later that night and he canvassed the possibility of my returning to university or perhaps emigrating, but I wasn't interested and he accepted this and told me I was welcome to stay. I was so self-absorbed at the time that it never struck me that this was a major concession on his part, putting himself, my mother and my brother and sisters in the frame for possible Special Branch attention.

On the Saturday I was picked up in Dublin as had been arranged and brought to what was in effect IRA headquarters at the time, a large house on Dublin's northside. Here I met Seamus Twomey and

J.B. O'Hagan, both of them on the run since the Mountjoy helicopter escape in October 1973. I felt I knew J.B. from communications with him throughout the last few months in Long Kesh, while Twomey had quite a reputation by 1974, though I couldn't help remaining mindful of McKee's earlier view of him. Twomey's disguise was limited to longer white hair and a serious moustache, but the latter utterly changed him, making him look like perhaps a professional musician rather than an IRA leader, though he was still a tough-looking hombre. J.B., a gentle soul, looked just like his photographs. Again, there was a lengthy discussion on the position in the Kesh and in particular the MRF scare. At the time Twomey was adjutant general, having been replaced as chief of staff when arrested in 1973 by Éamonn Doherty, an ex-British army paratrooper from County Tipperary, who had the lowest public profile of any IRA chief of staff ever. I met him just once myself before he was arrested in mid-October and believe he was away during most of this time on an arms- or cash-seeking mission. The public generally thought Dave O'Connell was chief of staff, but, though he had the highest profile of any IRA leader, he was in fact director of publicity and exercised his influence within the IRA in his role as chairman of the Army Council, though he would be adjutant general for a few months in 1975.

Meanwhile, I was there to be given instructions and waited patiently for them to get to that point. Twomey told me, to my horror, that they had considered moving me in to reorganise Dublin, but had instead decided they wanted me to work with J.B., who was in charge of communication with all the prisons at that time and was de facto liaison between different HQ departments. In reality he was doing the work of an adjutant general and Twomey was really acting as chief of staff. Twomey told me J.B. was also trying to reorganise the intelligence department, which had not functioned properly since MacStiofáin had been in charge of it before the split. I would be J.B.'s assistant and as a first step would undertake a tour of the border areas over the coming weeks to familiarise myself with the problems and personnel.

J.B. had a Cumann na mBan runner at the time and I accompanied her to Dundalk a couple of days later to meet Brian Keenan from Belfast, who was then director of purchase. Keenan, who was an avowed Marxist, was known in IRA circles as 'the Dog' and I was well aware of his fearsome reputation as someone capable of physically assaulting volunteers who let him down. He wasn't in the house where we were supposed to meet him and I subsequently found him in one of the town's pubs, having been pointed in their direction by the householder. Keenan invited us both to have a drink but, solemn as I then was, I refused. I was using public transport and since it was by then too late to get back to Dublin, Keenan gave me money and insisted that I book myself and J.B.'s runner into the Imperial Hotel. Though we did so, this seemed to me to be an unnecessary expense for the Army and I didn't approve of it. I knew Billy McKee disliked Keenan and my view was certainly coloured by that. I met Keenan only once again when he did impress me in organising the moving of Twomey and J.B. out of the GHQ house, which was expected to be hit by the Special Branch. In fact, they hit one of the call houses nearby and the two men moved back in a few days later. Keenan was arrested a couple of weeks after Éamonn Doherty and was another huge loss to the Army. Later on I dealt with Peter D., then the main contact for south Armagh and south Down and well known to the Branch. Peter was a cantankerous enough 1950s' man heavily involved in the supply lines, whose way of figuring you out was to bring you on a spin to drop off some gear somewhere. You knew your presence was superfluous and that if you hit a checkpoint you were going down for a few years, but if you declined the offer to come along he'd have no respect for you. It was complete idiocy, and I sat in his passenger seat with a bootful of gear on more than one occasion wondering what the hell I was doing there.

At this time Twomey and J.B. were being heavily sought by the Branch. Both lived in the northside house, which was a call house for GHQ, and which they shared briefly with a couple of the young women who had been active in England. Those who knew of it needed no permission to come and go and, in retrospect, it is hard to believe that it took the Branch so long to cotton on to it given that myself and others were operating more or less openly, often driving to within a few hundred yards of the house before dumping the car and proceeding there on foot, even during daylight hours. HQ business was conducted here and there were a number of houses on Dublin's northside which were used for meeting people from the different brigade areas. If he was meeting men from Belfast, Twomey would move out by car or on foot, depending on the distance to the meeting house, and would move back again afterwards, thus preserving security. Twomey couldn't drive and had two full-time assistants, one from Kerry and the other from Tyrone, who were later officially assistant chiefs-of-staff. The two men drove for him and were kept busy running ahead to organise pick-ups and transporting him from place to place and meeting to meeting. Deservedly known as Thumper, from his habit of hitting the table for emphasis, Twomey undoubtedly compensated for his occasional inarticulacy by displays of aggression, but in fact his bark was much worse than his bite and I liked him and had no difficulty with him until late summer the following year. He was also known affectionately, again behind his back, as Towser, presumably for his doggedness.

Over the next few weeks I attended a number of meetings close to the border where IRA men from perhaps four or five areas would be separately assembled. Twomey, myself and whoever else was available from HQ would see the staff and discuss operations and other matters, and there would be a lot of liaising on the side. Naturally enough, I had little to say. Surprisingly, there was considerable backbiting in the south Armagh–south Down area, I suspect because the unit centred on Crossmaglen was showing up the other, more cautious, units. This was so even within south Armagh itself, and one of the Crossmaglen volunteers later told me that their relations with the other south Armagh battalion had not been the same since the death of that unit's O/C, Michael McVerry, who had been killed during an attack on Keady barracks in late 1973.

Monaghan was the locus for meetings with the mid-Ulster people, where no such problems seemed to exist and where the weaker areas could expect help from those that were stronger. Here I met John Green, then O/C of the mid-Armagh unit, who was killed early the following year, and Francis Hughes, who was the second man to die in the 1981 hunger strike. At a similar set of meetings in Donegal, I met up again with Pat Doherty and various others whom I had known in 1971. I also met Kevin Mallon for the first time. Mallon was the third man on the helicopter escape and perhaps the most important

IRA figure then not in prison. He had been recaptured in December – typically at a dance near Portlaoise with some gunplay involved – but had again escaped when he was among the eighteen who had blasted their way out of Portlaoise prison the previous August. At this time he would have topped the wanted list along with Twomey and O'Connell. It was an interesting feature of those years that saw government and security sources contribute to the build-up of personalities; time and again on both sides of the border, amid great fanfare, they would claim an important victory when announcing the capture of such and such, the commander of such an area or the most wanted man within it, so contributing to guerrilla mystique while at once setting themselves up for a fall when the great man escaped.

Then in his mid-30s, as was Dave O'Connell, Mallon was a hard-drinking, hard-talking, seriously hard man with buckets of charisma and an unrivalled capacity to motivate people. He was the closest thing the modern IRA had to a Michael Collins and I was completely bowled over by him. I was billeted with him in Donegal and we sat up well into the night with the man and woman of the house talking politics and tactics while getting pleasantly hammered on hot whiskeys. The following morning we went through the checkpoint on the Ballyshannon Bridge and into the southernmost part of Donegal, Mallon having climbed into the boot of the car a couple of miles earlier. He was on the run and always armed, and seemed to believe this was the best position for an active volunteer to be in. Certainly he gave those who got to 'sleep in their own beds', as he would cuttingly put it, a hard time, and he had a penchant when travelling for dropping in on people in the middle of the night or gratuitously inconveniencing them in other ways as if to underline the charged nature of the times. Mallon was a tough and occasionally ruthless user of people, though those who worked for him adored him. But while he could control his people, the special-forces feel he fed in them – the virtual contempt for the rest of the Army – meant that discipline fell away once he was arrested and these individuals pretty much did as they pleased. Dave was similarly charismatic and was our leader as far as the public was concerned. Though the leadership went through various changes in personnel during the early 1970s, escapes and the then relatively short sentences

handed down in the South for membership allowed Twomey, Ruairí
Ó Brádaigh, Joe Cahill, J.B. O'Hagan, Brian Keenan and Kevin Mallon
to remain at its core. The only one who was ever-present, managing to
elude everyone until July 1975, was Dave O'Connell. This was one hell
of an achievement, especially given his public record of appearances at
funerals, commemorations and Sinn Féin meetings north and south. I
had a number of interesting sessions with O'Connell and Mallon where
a bottle of whiskey would be downed and stories, some of them hilarious, exchanged. Speaking of Gerry Adams, Mallon once remarked that
if the roof was falling in around his head, he'd act as if he had planned
it to fall in exactly that way, and though I wouldn't encounter Adams
in person until the early 1980s – when he did indeed prove to be one
cool customer – I was not to forget Mallon's insight.

***

I had dealt with Derry and Belfast on my own. Because internment
was still ongoing, and I couldn't be sure whether or not I was wanted
in London, I was notionally on the run in the North and asked the
Derry intelligence officer (I/O) to cross the border and meet me in
Buncrana, where half the Derry Brigade had taken up residence in any
case. I expected a good welcome from Derry but instead had a row
with the I/O, who turned out to be under instructions not to talk to
me other than in the vaguest terms – though he refused to tell me just
whose instruction it was. I met him a day or so after Long Kesh went
up in flames in October 1974, and my guilt at being absent from that,
combined with his recalcitrance, left me feeling utterly drained. Joseph
M. was at this time the Derry representative in the leadership and was
my prime suspect. He had been a helpful taxi man during my time
in Derry and, having joined the IRA, had, to my amazement, quickly
climbed the ranks, becoming McGuinness's QM, friend and confidant,
before the two fell out. McGuinness got out of prison in November
and resumed control of Derry, initially as Vice-O/C, and my difficulties with the Derry I/O evaporated overnight.

The reception was much better in Belfast thanks to Billy McKee who,
like McGuinness, had immediately taken over as Vice-O/C of Belfast

under Seamus Loughran, the nominal O/C, shortly after his release. Such had been the attrition rate in Belfast that Loughran was probably the only 'O' left standing when he was appointed that autumn, and I suspect he had been given the job because he was thought to be less likely to be arrested, thanks to his Sinn Féin profile. At any rate, there was no doubt who was calling the shots in the city. McKee was reorganising Belfast and I met a number of his key people, among them some friends from the cages, on a nervy trip to Belfast using borrowed identity papers.

Though Seán Treacy had sporadically tried to teach me how to drive in 1971, I was still unable to. Twomey had made arrangements for me to learn in Donegal and, because I needed to get back to Dublin, myself and the Derry volunteer given the job of getting me there agreed that I would learn en route, and I hopped into the driver's seat where he showed me how to operate the controls. We headed south, through Donegal to Sligo and then onto Dublin, stopping outside each town to change driver since I didn't have the confidence to cope with traffic lights and town traffic. We stayed together for a couple of days, at the end of which I had grasped the elements of stopping, starting and steering, but had also laid the foundations for some thoroughly bad driving habits. For some months after I had acquired a car, I would leave it in Ballsbridge if I had to see someone in the city centre, too nervous and unskilled to consider parking on the quays or around St Stephen's Green, and I didn't subsequently pass my driving test until the late 1980s.

When I first met Kevin Mallon, he had let slip that I was being prepared to take over from J.B., so it was no surprise when, some weeks after my release, Twomey told me that was what was happening. Following Éamonn Doherty's arrest, Twomey resumed his old role as chief of staff and J.B. took over from Twomey as adjutant general. On a routine call I made to the HQ house, Twomey simply told me about these changes and asked me if I would take over intelligence. I said that of course I would and was then briefed by him in his inimitable style: when I asked him what he wanted me to do, he replied that I was now in charge of intelligence and that he'd no more tell me how to do my job than he would expect me to tell him how to do his. End of briefing.

I left the house all but bursting with exhilaration at the responsibility and full of semi-formed ideas. There was plenty of money floating about at the time and Twomey told me to go away and recruit a couple of assistants and then come back and tell him what I needed. Meanwhile, he told me to buy a car, handing me £1,000 in a bundle of £10 notes. The money had come from a robbery in Munster and had spent time buried in a silage pit at some point. As a consequence, every note reeked and I pressed my mother into some literal money-laundering. Without my father's knowledge, she washed the notes, drying and airing all one hundred of them on an indoor line. Still they stank, and so we sprayed them with perfume such that they came to smell equally of pig shit and distilled femininity. There was no difficulty conducting the cash purchase of a four-year-old Hillman Estate; all the better, I was persuaded by a friend, to have the look of a commercial traveller as I toured the country, though the salesman couldn't resist commenting on the pungency of the notes. The same afternoon, insurance was arranged through long-time supporters in that industry, and I was officially on the road as IRA director of intelligence.

Among the intelligence contacts I was given was a man I will call 'the Banker' with whom both Dave O'Connell and Éamonn Doherty used to stay. The Banker, in turn, introduced me to a circle of well-placed people in and around the south Dublin area where I had grown up, most of whom were as clean as whistles. They included journalists, stockbrokers, lawyers and other professionals, a number of whom became quite famous in the course of their careers. It was a fantastic human infrastructure which I was never able to properly exploit and we ended up simply using many of their houses for meetings and to billet visiting volunteers. Meanwhile, the first person I recruited, on either Twomey's or Dave's recommendation, was a young Belfast woman who was then on the run from the North. I set up base with her in the Banker's house and began to accumulate paper files and information on our various targets, North and South and in Britain.

One of the early steps I took was to ask the I/Os in the prisons to send me out all they could pull together from the collective intelligence of their volunteers, and I was being deluged with names, addresses, car registrations and the miscellaneous personal details of RUC and UDR men, loyalist paramilitaries, Gardaí and Special Branch members, all of which had to be sifted and put into some sort of order. One document I sought without success was the list of applicants for membership of the Dublin Brigade, created not long after Bloody Sunday, which I was reliably told contained some 400 names. The vast majority of these would probably have lost interest by late 1974, but I reckoned many would retain sufficient sympathy to assist as intelligence sources. We got ourselves the relevant reference books and street directories, and I arranged for one of the I/Os, who had been involved in the MRF investigation in the Kesh, to come down from Belfast for a few months to work on building up an office, with occasional assistance from various female volunteers who were able to type. Laura Crawford was one of those sent down for a few weeks. A secretary in a solicitor's office in Belfast, Laura would be killed in an accidental explosion with another volunteer almost exactly a year later. Separately, I recruited a Dublin man to go on the road with me. Through the contacts I had accidentally acquired, and more traditional IRA sources, we put together a network from such areas as insurance, banking, the public service, motor registration, and posts and telegraphs, from which it was always possible to acquire further information given a start in the shape of a car number, name or address. I got to know my way around a library and swapped ideas and information with, in particular, the I/Os in Belfast and Derry.

There was considerable paranoia in the South at the time, and in the first couple of months we investigated far too many reports concerning purported British agents, among them some allegedly involved in the Dublin bombings. I learned the hard way of the existence of a few Walter Mitty-esque characters within our ranks and, in the absence of any clear direction from Twomey, wasted far too much time exploring their imaginary leads. We also spent a lot of time being introduced to well-placed people who told us things that were interesting but were of no real value to us. We did try to deliver the bits and pieces of information we were occasionally asked for, but the reality was that the IRA was irredeemably localist and short-termist with little use for a centrally organised intelligence system, and certainly not one based in Dublin, so far from the conflict. In addition, the operations people did their own intelligence, making my own department even less relevant to the Army's real needs.

Security, or counter-intelligence, was then part of the intelligence department's role and much of my own time was spent fire-fighting, assisting investigations in Belfast and elsewhere in the North. In Belfast, we tried, but failed, to get to the bottom of the MRF scare. Heatherington and McGrogan were acquitted in May 1975 and were subsequently shot dead, as were a number of others, including a UDA member shot dead by the loyalists in 1976 on foot of information we provided to them about the killing of UDA leader Tommy Herron.

I always believed that the subsequent establishment of a security department within the IRA in the 1980s was a mistake. This turned out to be the case when it was discovered, far too late, that it had been infiltrated at the highest level by British intelligence. The members of this department were volunteers of long standing, who were deemed to be above suspicion, making them a very obvious target. A second difficulty was that the security people were obsessed with inform- ers. They never took into account the possibility that operations, safe houses or materials had been compromised by other means – i.e. by surveillance, including electronic surveillance – and persisted, even in the face of evidence to the contrary, in believing there was an informer active – something perhaps inevitable in a department constructed on paranoia. I raised both this and the existence of a separate Northern Command with the then chief of staff in the early 1980s, believing the latter put too much distance between GHQ and the local units, but he was not for moving. He was proven to be wrong in respect of both decisions, the second one when the leadership was nearly toppled by a Northern Command coup led by Ivor Bell in 1984, ironically the very prospect that the separate command, meant to ensure the leadership could never again 'betray' the Army, was designed to make possible in the first place.

Chapter 15

However, there was no separate Northern Command in 1974, when GHQ had a direct relationship with units and volunteers on the ground and, as a consequence, a far greater feel for what was going on than would later be the case. In the North there were a number of notional brigade or command structures, as well as the long-established ones in Belfast and Derry. North-West Command, made up of Donegal, Leitrim and part of Cavan, west Tyrone and west Fermanagh, still existed, though Derry was now a separate brigade area. Mid-Ulster consisted of east Tyrone, east Fermanagh, south Derry, south-west Antrim, north Armagh and mid-Armagh, and there was a further command area around south Armagh–south Down. These latter two also contained their respective border hinterlands in Louth, Monaghan and Cavan. This structure functioned only sporadically, depending on who was available to staff it, and existed mainly for the distribution of equipment and finance. Outside the cities we dealt directly with the local unit and, in addition to departmental responsibilities, were expected to act as a sounding board and to relay back local concerns and report generally on each area. We all did a lot of travelling.

People had different ways of moving around and through checkpoints. One of Twomey's assistants wore flashy sports jackets, carried a guitar on the back seat, and must have bluffed his way through a thousand checkpoints while posing as a showband member. Some wore suits and carried the *Irish Times*, while some wore working gear and had the *Sun* tucked under their arm. A few swore by public transport and used it as much as they could, while others developed real or imaginary interests in such things as cars and dogs, and read the small ads with great care to be able to account for their movements. In time, I came to see a significant difference in security culture between the Gardaí on the one hand and the British army/RUC on the other; in the North they were fixated on their records, so that if you had a clean car, clean driver or plausible faked identity papers yourself, you were fine. In the South, though, the Gardaí, particularly in the border areas, would hardly trouble you for your papers, instead questioning you closely on your reasons for being on a particular road at a particular time, an approach that was far more intrusive and effective.

The campaign in England was stepped up that autumn with the first of a series of no-warning bombs in bars frequented by British soldiers, and of course civilians as well, in what was a clear change in operational policy. In early October four soldiers, all in their teens and two of them women, were killed, together with a civilian, when a bomb exploded at a pub in Guildford. More explosions occurred at ex-servicemen's clubs in London and at the Conservative Party's Birmingham headquarters before a bomb was tossed into a pub in Woolwich, killing a soldier and the civilian barman and injuring many others. Indirect casualties of the bombings, along with the British system of justice, were the Guildford Four and the Maguire Seven, framed for the bombings on the basis of suspect forensics and confessions that had been beaten out of them, and not subsequently cleared until 1989 and 1991 respectively.

Off-duty soldiers were targets and they knew they were targets, and, back then, I had little sympathy for either the soldiers or the unfortunate civilians who had been sharing their drinking space. The Birmingham bombs were another matter. The bombings came after British police disrupted funeral arrangements for James McDaid, a volunteer who had himself died in a premature explosion in England. Tempers were high and I for one certainly at first feared that the local IRA had knowingly caused these dreadful casualties – 21 people were killed and a great many others injured. I was appalled and personally ashamed of the bombing, which went against everything we claimed to stand for, and told O'Connell and Mallon exactly what I thought when we met up. Mallon had asked me, straight-faced, what I thought, and I've no doubt this was one of the occasional tests he liked to put people through to see how they responded. In fact, both men were themselves furious, fully recognising not just the damage the bombing had caused to the IRA but its immorality as well. The then England O/C and adjutant had made it home and were debriefed by O'Connell and another member of the leadership at the home of a well-known journalist in south Dublin, to which I had been brought as well for different reasons. I met both men and, though I took no part in the actual debrief, I was later told by Dave that the early indications were that the casualties were the result of yet another failure in the warning system, a succession of phone boxes from which the warning might have been relayed having proved to be inoperable.

After the ban on it was lifted earlier in 1974, the UVF formed the Volunteer Political Party and set its sights on parliamentary elections, but when it did badly it abandoned the experiment and returned to bombing and shooting Catholics. There was also considerable intra- and inter-loyalist feuding, in which quite a number were killed, and, indeed, during the early 1970s, shooting, or the threat of shooting, was the usual manner in which leadership changes took place within those organisations. Though primarily a Belfast city phenomenon, the UVF also had a presence in mid-Ulster, although its units there were of a different calibre to those in the city, typically overlapping with the UDR or RUC and having strong links with British intelligence. The UDA had its strength almost entirely in the greater Belfast area and in Derry.

The loyalist paramilitary organisations were supposedly on ceasefire from the summer of 1974, and meetings took place in Libya between the UDA and the IRA. Talks were continuing in the prisons, and also on and off in Belfast, throughout much of 1975, and there seemed to be many loyalists interested in exploring alternatives to the status quo. Contacts also took place at local level and I later met the local UDA in Derry with McGuinness and one of his staff. This was facilitated by a Protestant clergyman and, though as inconclusive as all the others, it did give us an opportunity to explain ourselves, to assure them we meant them no harm, and that we were out to see an end to the Southern as well as the Northern state, leaving everything up for negotiation. Despite this, there was an upsurge in loyalist killings from mid-September, which also brought the terror into areas previously untouched. Bishop Philbin, the Catholic bishop whose diocese included Belfast, was publicly calling for Catholics who needed the protection of the security forces to support them in turn. The suspicion that the British were quite content to let the killings go on for just this reason was held by more than just republicans and, in late October, John Hume referred to there being a 'despicable campaign', of which Merlyn Rees was part, to use the killings to force a change in SDLP policy towards the RUC.

This new wave of killings resulted in the deaths of fifteen boys and men by the end of October, two of these Protestants presumably shot in error, and included four young men shot dead in the greater Belfast area on successive days. Fourteen Catholics died in November, together with two Protestants mistaken for Catholics. While the bulk of the killings were of Catholic men, the dead included Geraldine Macklin and Mary Shepherd. Both were shot at their separate workplaces, killings which by their face-to-face nature underlined the fact that the loyalists had no difficulty murdering Catholic women as well as men.

This time the loyalist killings were met with retaliatory gun attacks on Protestants in the autumn, in which eight people, one of them a teenage girl, were shot dead. With a dozen or so Catholics dead, these killings began in early November with the shooting dead of a man at his home in Belfast, and the drive-by shooting of another. The IRA did occasionally try to target the actual perpetrators, and UDA leader Jim Anderson was shot and wounded during this period, but while a number of the attacks may have been aimed at the UDA/UVF, the majority were deliberate, nakedly sectarian killings, designed to exercise a counter pressure on the loyalist paramilitaries. And, it has to be said, they began not long after McKee's influence would once more have been felt in Belfast.

***

Following the collapse of the Executive, the British had published a White Paper setting out plans for a constitutional convention to come to its own arrangements for a settlement in the North. Though it insisted that there must be provision for power-sharing and an Irish dimension, everyone knew this wasn't going to happen, and the Convention was viewed by most as very much a final throw of the dice, the failure of which would dramatically shorten the odds on withdrawal.

In November Merlyn Rees said that there would have to be a 'radical reappraisal' if the Convention failed, and though he did add that this would not involve a withdrawal of troops, no one believed him. Even the ex-Prime Minister, Terence O'Neill, was saying that he didn't believe the British would be prepared to continue to pay in men and money for another five years. By then, the South's overarching policy was to avoid a British withdrawal, at whatever the cost, and it later sought and received private assurances from the otherwise non-interventionist Americans, promising to back it in persuading the British not to go. Indeed, a US embassy official who attended the Sinn Féin ard fheis that autumn noted that one of the few points of agreement between republicans and Dublin was a firm belief that the British intended to abandon the North, both quickly and soon.

In December talks took place at Feakle, County Clare between the IRA and a group of Protestant clergymen who were trying to broker a truce. These were attended by the then Army Council, four of whom – Twomey, O'Connell, Mallon and J.B. O'Hagan – were on the run, together with Seamus Loughran, Billy McKee and Ruairí Ó Brádaigh. Although we were already talking to the British secretly, after Feakle the churchmen – some of whom expressed themselves pleasantly surprised at our leaders' good manners – began to exert pressure on both 'sides', and the various moves from that time on were publicly noted. The Special Branch arrived in the course of the meeting but, to their embarrassment, the wanted men had already disappeared. The then Assistant Commissioner, Edmund Garvey, launched an inquiry into the Feakle 'leak' following our statement claiming IRA intelligence had received word that the Branch was on its way. Phones in Garda HQ had been successfully tapped a couple of years previously and, yes, we still had that capacity. Accordingly, Garvey was right to be concerned. At the time, relations between the Special Branch and the headquarters-based specialist unit C3 were not good and Garvey suspected the Branch of being the source of the leak, which was an excellent position from our point of view.

Feakle repaired some of the damage from the Birmingham bombs and I was subsequently strongly in favour of the truce. Only a fool could have been unaware of the reassessment that was taking place in London and it seemed to me to be madness to continue to fight the British for something they might be prepared to concede peacefully. I believed we had a responsibility to the people and to our own volunteers to at least explore the possibilities rather than simply battering on blindly, with people fighting and dying for no good reason. Why wouldn't the British want to withdraw? Even back then, the conventional anti-imperialist arguments for their presence in the North made no sense. We all knew the North was a huge financial burden on the British state, as well as a political embarrassment which they would be delighted to rid themselves of, if this could be done without disgracing Britain further in the eyes of the world.

In addition, a truce made tactical sense for us. The move away from a shooting war and out of the cities had become even more marked from September on, since when ten soldiers had died in the North. Also killed were three RUC members, a UDR man and an off-duty member of the Territorial Army, abducted and shot dead in Ardoyne – the only security force casualty in Belfast at that time. With the exception of a soldier shot dead in Derry, all the shooting casualties were close to the border in Strabane, Newry and especially South Armagh. In December there were also attacks in Kinawley, Crossmaglen and Aughnacloy – all on the border – and though the IRA was now stronger in many rural areas than it had ever been, Belfast, in which we knew the war would be won or lost, was by then on its knees.

After a couple of false starts the terms of a bilateral ceasefire were agreed. These included freedom of movement for IRA members; the cessation of raids, screening and arrests; a progressive withdrawal of troops to barracks; the reserving of the right to carry concealed short arms for self-defence; and the establishment of a liaison system to monitor the ceasefire and ensure that 'misunderstandings' were straightened out. Against this backdrop, meanwhile, discussions on British withdrawal were to take place. As the truce commenced in February 1975, Rees announced the establishing of 'hotlines' staffed around the clock by civil servants to maintain communication with us through 'incident centres' in Belfast, Derry, Armagh, Dungannon, Newry and Enniskillen.

These centres were attended by locals with complaints about the security forces and other matters, and grew in time into public offices, giving us an important physical presence on the Falls Road and elsewhere. They can be seen, in retrospect, to have paved the way for the later growth of Sinn Féin – at that time considered an embarrassment by most IRA members, who viewed it as a not terribly effective support group for the Army. Though not at all opposed to the development of a political movement, I was one of those who saw Sinn Féin as incapable of being the vehicle for it. For me, it was for the old and the lame, for those too cowardly or not capable of serving in the Army. Asked by Twomey shortly after my release what I thought of Sinn Féin, I suggested that it should be disbanded to make room for an organisation like the Northern Resistance Movement, which included Michael Farrell and others whose politics and ability I admired. Twomey showed no surprise; in fact, he thought the suggestion hilarious and proposed that I share it with Dave when next we met.

Tom Hartley ran the main centre on the Falls Road in Belfast. Tom, whom I had come across briefly during his short sentence in Crumlin Road, was the only true Sinn Féiner of that generation. To the best of my knowledge, he never joined the IRA and this never bothered him. He ran an effective centre in which our international and publicity links were expanded and given a solid and lasting base. In the centre, I saw a telex in operation for the first time and marvelled at the technology as I had previously marvelled at the photocopier in London which had allowed me to duplicate IRA training material way back in 1970. Though as director of publicity Dave had run IRIS, the Irish Republican Information Service, which issued regular 'war bulletins' as well as Army statements, the Belfast development enabled republicans to at last compete properly with the British publicity machine in real time.

Much was subsequently made of the purported intelligence benefits of the incident centres to the British. Naturally, the British could, and did, monitor the comings and goings, but there was nothing to stop the IRA from moving its business out of the centres, as should have been the case. I was often in Derry during the truce period and was brought to the centre in the Bogside, practically next door to McGuinness's family home, just once to look it over. The IRA in Derry continued to meet in a variety of call houses, taking all the usual precautions, and on my regular visits there and elsewhere in the North, I saw no weakness or dissolution of the Army. Everyone was aware that we were preparing for a resumption of the war – while hoping it might not prove necessary – and there wasn't an area that was not using the time and relative freedom to reorganise and prepare. But history, including institutional history, is written by the victors, and so the myth that the 1975 truce all but destroyed the IRA has taken root.

***

One morning, shortly after Christmas 1974, I drove out of my parents' house and spotted a Branch car at the top of the road, which proceeded to follow me into Dublin. Back then, the Branch drove a combination of Cortinas and blue Hillman Avengers with very obvious aerials, and were hard to miss. I decided to go on the run, getting rid of the car and acquiring a flat in Dun Laoghaire. It was exciting moving around my own part of Dublin incognito but, after an earlier escape near one of our call houses, I was arrested coming away from a meeting, having lasted barely a month on the run. I was brought to the Bridewell in the city centre where I was questioned by a succession of Branch men, one of whom wanted to fight me. Significantly, it became clear that they were taping phone calls in and around Dave. We referred to him as 'she' and 'her' when setting up arrangements over the phone and the Branch simply couldn't resist letting me know how clever they were by repeatedly asking me how 'she' was. Keeping my mouth shut and my eyes on my spot, the interrogations were no trouble, though I was concerned about the keys I had on me for the flat, which was far too close to where I had been arrested. There were intelligence documents there and I was certainly heading for Portlaoise if they found the flat, and might well be heading there in any case. The Branch were a tough bunch who had been unleashed by their political masters and hated us with a vengeance, and it was no surprise to me when they started beating up prisoners. Mind you, there were two of us in it, and when, having left the IRA later that year, I came back in 1981 to find my old intelligence files intact, I was horrified to see how much time we had spent tracking the Special Branch rather than simply keeping out of their way. Fortunately, they released me.

***

Dublin was furious at the ceasefire development and did its utmost to undermine the prospect of negotiations between the British and ourselves, correctly seeing itself as being sidelined. Shortly before the truce was declared Kevin Mallon was arrested in south Dublin, and J.B. O'Hagan's arrest followed a couple of weeks later. Mallon's removal was a disaster for the Army, in that it removed the key hard man who could have carried the truce through the summer, or had it killed off more decisively than was to actually occur. It also led, in time, to a group of his people spiralling out of the leadership's control as the ceasefire became less popular.

The Southern government were not the only ones who set out to disrupt the truce and, as it first beckoned and then bedded in, loyalist attacks on Catholics increased. Oddly, the loyalist paramilitaries, while accusing the British of surrendering to the IRA, simultaneously held that the truce was a clever tactical device designed by the IRA to buy time for it to reorganise, with a view to launching a fresh offensive later in the year. A dozen Catholics had been killed in gun and bomb attacks by the end of February, eight of them in Belfast, and twenty-five more died in March and April. The dead included seven women and an Indian Hindu married to a Catholic, who was shot dead in the loyalist stronghold of Carrickfergus.

These killings increased the pressure on the IRA, especially in Belfast itself and the Murder Triangle around north Armagh and east Tyrone. The slaughter of nationalists simply could not be ignored and though our instructions were to target only known UVF and UDA men, and intelligence on them was not at all bad, Protestant civilians were dying too. While some of these killings were justified, and others were the result of local errors, in April the IRA bombed the Mountainview

Tavern on the Shankill Road, killing five Protestant men. The bombing was in retaliation for a UVF attack on a Catholic bar hours earlier, in which two men had been killed and many others wounded. The Tavern was a well-known loyalist haunt, and, though one of the men killed was a UDA member, the operation was inexcusable.

Meanwhile, the line of demarcation between the loyalists and the security forces remained blurred. The instances of UVF/UDA membership overlapping with that of the UDR and, to a lesser extent, the RUC Reserve, were staggering, particularly in rural areas, while collusion generally was rife, with the British army and intelligence apparatus, both officially and off-the-books, involved in stoking the fires. John Green had been shot dead south of the border by either the British or a UVF team controlled by them, and the loyalist organisations were so heavily infiltrated by the British that it was impossible to know where one stopped and the other started. Loyalist units, whether controlled directly or used as cats' paws by the British, participated in the slaughter of Catholics in a campaign designed to demoralise and divide ourselves and our support, as well as in atrocities like the Dublin and Monaghan bombings, which brought fear to the South and an indirect suspicion of republicans. Further complicating matters was the emergence of the Irish National Liberation Army following a split within Official republicanism, as it was by no means clear what their intentions were in circumstances where we remained on ceasefire.

During this period I got to know Rita O'Hare pretty well. Already a legend within the IRA, Rita had been hit three times during a gun battle with the British army in Andersonstown, and had recovered from her wounds in the South after a risky border crossing. She was also the mother of three young children and this, together with her red hair and soft features, gave her a status within the movement comparable only to that of the Price sisters. Sometime in February she became involved with the operations people in a planned escape from Portlaoise. Her part of the operation involved her smuggling explosives into the prison visiting area concealed in her body, which would be handed over to the prisoner she was visiting. She was indirectly caught when the prisoner was searched at the conclusion of the visit and the explosives discovered. Rita's children were all under ten, and I later resented the fact that any one of a number of equally qualified women had not been asked to take the risk. Rita was charged and subsequently bailed and over the following weeks I sometimes drove her the short distance to the local Garda station to sign on as her trial in the Special Criminal Court and inevitable imprisonment drew nearer and she made plans for the care of her children. In mid-April she was duly convicted, having been permitted to recognise the court, and sentenced to three years.

At the end of March twelve IRA men escaped from Newry courthouse, and though two were recaptured the others made it across the border. These were the men who were facing charges in connection with the separate escape attempts from Long Kesh referred to earlier, and I knew some of them well. Among the escapers were John Quigley, who took over from me as camp adjutant; Gerry Fitzgerald, who was shot in May 1971 and subsequently freed from the Royal Victoria Hospital by an IRA unit; Larry Marley, who would later mastermind the great H-Blocks escape in 1983; and other experienced volunteers, all of them from Belfast. John was someone I rated highly, having first met him in A Wing. He had never been in Dublin before, and I picked him up on the northside and took the coast road from Sandymount to Dalkey and then along the Vico Road on a beautiful spring day, John in the passenger seat, struck dumb at the view over Dublin Bay, which on its day can compare with anywhere.

It made no sense to send the escapers back to Belfast in the middle of a ceasefire and, as no one else had any use for them, I told Twomey I would take those of them who wanted to remain active. Shortly before, I had also taken on the Belfast Brigade I/O's right-hand man, after he had become compromised in Belfast. This left the intelligence department with up to a dozen experienced activists and from then on we filled a gap for GHQ and were asked to undertake various tasks, regularly backing up or stepping in for some of the Southern units. The result was a decisive shift away from paper intelligence towards operations and we received a large increase in budget together with an allocation of weapons, including a half-dozen Armalites, which were stored in the attic space of the Banker's house and moved back and forth across the country by him and others of his circle in their top-of-the-range cars.

The Crossmaglen end of south Armagh provided a base for much of the counter-intelligence work at the time and we were there regularly throughout the year, particularly with the Belfast I/O. Francis McDevitt (not his real name) was the O/C and was by then on the Army Council. Tom Murphy was also about, and the Murphy home, which straddles the border and subsequently became notorious, was the call house and centre of activity there. The British army gave it a wide berth, and though the Gardaí would drive in from time to time, its large barns and other outhouses where visiting cars could be concealed meant there was little to be learned. By now, whole tracts of south Armagh were effectively liberated zones, where the British army was unable to patrol, save occasionally in force, and where they relied on helicopter sorties, dropping and lifting soldiers who set up brief checkpoints, and on the use of covert observation posts, which were themselves vulnerable to attack. It was not until the mid-1980s that the British attempted to make some kind of mark on the area, with the building of a series of heavily fortified hillside observation posts, and, back in 1975, south Armagh played host to a range of visiting IRA men and activities, from the interrogation of suspect informers to the test-firing of weapons and experimentation with explosives. The unit was able to assist or mount operations at a moment's notice, since there were always volunteers, weapons and stolen cars available. These were country boys and there was much banter around the cultural clash between the showband music of Big Tom and the like, and the British and American rock music favoured in the cities. On Saturday evenings, we got a great kick out of seeing them dressed up in gear no self-respecting city lad would be seen dead in, as they headed off to the local ballroom of romance.

Chapter 16

Some of the detainees released declined to get involved again, particularly in Belfast, and though they made much of their 'opposition' to the truce, my own take on it was that they were unwilling to serve under the local leaderships. Equally, prisoners reporting back on release weren't always welcomed because they were seen as a threat to those already in place. In one command area, a couple of ex-prisoners had found themselves surplus to requirements on release, so much so that one of them ended up attached to the 2nd Battalion in Belfast, which was where I met up with him again. Before his arrest, Kevin Mallon had introduced me to an outstanding contact with whom it was possible to travel in comparative safety throughout the then extremely dangerous mid-Ulster region. My contact had legitimate business there and we were gaining access to important intelligence which I wanted to take action on. In due course, I began to travel into the area on my own to meet the local unit, but, partly because of my own links to the ex-prisoners, I was received with less than enthusiasm and so began to lean on my own contacts there, in effect using them as a separate GHQ intelligence cell, something that was not appreciated locally. There were a few of these little fiefdoms across the North, which saw GHQ and the Army leadership generally as little more than an unquestioning source of arms, explosives and cash. In most areas I struck up good relations with the local unit, but in one or two I relied on ex-prisoners who, for one reason or another, had not been welcomed back.

In January 1975 Joe Cahill had been released from Portlaoise on health grounds. He was pretty quiet for a month or two but that summer became adjutant general following the arrest of Dave O'Connell. As it happened, I needed something cleared at a time when Twomey was

189

out of the country. Cahill was stalling and, fed up with it, I arranged to meet him with a couple of my men and berated him for his inability to make a decision, so making myself an enemy quite unnecessarily. Though Cahill had a fine IRA record, I disliked him from the time of that initial clash and never subsequently warmed to him. In the 1980s and 90s, as the older generation fell away – or followed Republican Sinn Féin into semi-oblivion – I came to view Cahill as a place seeker, a yes man and a virtual mascot behind whom the leadership were able to take cover before the older generation, and the Americans in particular. His tight-fistedness with money, which people affected to find amusing, was a complete pain in the arse and on more than one occasion I had travel or other plans unnecessarily delayed or faced embarrassment because of his game-playing. He was the polar opposite of Billy McKee, who could recognise a move upstairs or sideways for what it was. When McKee lost his position as Brigade O/C in Belfast in the later 1970s, probably deservedly, he declined to go to the States as the IRA representative, and when it became clear that nothing else was on offer, refused to accept the £20 sub that was given to volunteers when funds were available.[18] I met McKee on the quays in Dublin in 1980 with his hands in tatters from labouring. By then in his sixties, and with no previous experience of the building industry, he hadn't thought to wear gloves until I suggested it, since the others on the site naturally enough didn't require them.

Though it is not possible to remove anyone from the Army Council, I believe that McKee stood down voluntarily when it became clear that the post-Twomey leadership had no confidence in him as O/C of Belfast. Ruairí also stood down soon after the hunger strikes in 1981, not willing to continue being in a minority of one on what were essentially Sinn Féin positions on federalism and the like. Dave never regained the Council place he had lost when jailed in 1975, though his co-option onto the Army Executive in 1980 would cause ructions. Joe Cahill, by contrast, held onto his power and prestige until the end, his

---

[18] Introduced at the time of internment to compensate volunteers suddenly unable to pick up the dole, the sub had continued long after internment ended and all the full-timers went back on the dole, making this perhaps the first State-subsidised insurrection in history.

view and his vote predictably with the majority. The other old hand, Seamus Twomey, I liked a lot, and though I had a number of stand-up, table-thumping rows with him, he bore no grudges. He was certainly decisive, though in retrospect I'm not sure how troubled he was by the need to decide. I never saw him agonise over a hard decision as I had seen McKee do, far less weep having made it, as I also once witnessed McKee doing.

I had a couple of relationships with republican women during this time, one of them of fabulous intensity, but, in the spring, re-involved myself with my childhood sweetheart, who had married someone else when I was in Long Kesh. Though it's hard to say whether I was cause or effect, within weeks she had decided to leave her husband of less than a year. We moved in together, and her presence in my life, and of other friends from school and university, meant I never lost touch with my southside, middle-class roots. I was perfectly conscious of how the North was playing out with my family, and among all the apolitical and non-republican friends with whom I continued to socialise in an increasingly bifurcated existence, and this backdrop coloured my responses when I had a final run-in with Twomey that September.

***

Incidents on both sides threatened the truce from the outset and, in late February 1975, an English policeman was shot dead in London. It became clear when British police found a 'bomb factory' in an abandoned flat, which they linked to both the killing and previous IRA attacks, that the policeman had been shot by us. Somehow we got away with it. After the courthouse escape in early March, the army in Newry searched the cathedral and other locations and were told by the local command that there would be a resumption of military action, effective forthwith, for a breach of the truce. The Newry Command were quickly rapped over the knuckles by the leadership, which told them they were under orders to do nothing unless and until they received instructions to the contrary from GHQ. Newry was not then a strong area for us and, interestingly, it tended to be the weaker areas that did the most bitching. There was a lot of whingeing about the truce, as there was about everything else – lack of weaponry, finance, targeting policy and so on – but complaining about your superiors is a fact of life in any organisation and I didn't take much notice of it.

On Good Friday I drove up to Carrickmore in County Tyrone, passing in and out of sometimes quite fierce snowstorms which alternated with blasts of bright spring sunshine. I crossed the border without incident and drove into this small village where I met up with some of the locals and Dave O'Connell, who was to give the oration there on Easter Sunday. There was a scare that weekend over a possible loyalist attempt on Dave's life and the way in which it was dealt with by the local unit was impressive. Though deep into the North, and without the natural advantage that a border hinterland gave Crossmaglen, this small area was the same in producing a succession of strong units over the quarter century of war. By contrast, the equally republican area around Bellaghy in south Derry was never the same after the break-up of the unit centred on Francis Hughes and Dominic McGlinchey.

The Easter message from the Army, which Dave would have drafted, referred to tightening limits on our collective patience and said the IRA 'will settle for no permanent agreement which does not include a programme of planned and orderly withdrawal of the English establishment from our country'. In Carrickmore, both Brendan Hughes (not the Belfast one) and Kevin McKenna, well known IRA men locally, appeared in uniform on the platform with O'Connell and one of them read out the Army statement. O'Connell himself referred to the fragility of the truce and said that if peaceful means fail 'we will not be found wanting in employing more direct and more decisive means for securing our objectives'. In Belfast, Twomey, true to form, was a good deal blunter, confirming in his own speech that the truce was 'under very severe strain' and if our demands were not met by negotiation, then it was 'back to war'.

The ceasefire was not popular with the right-wing press in Britain, nor with a few of the army regiments, some of which did their best to subvert it locally. In early April, the then British commander in the North, Frank King, publicly criticised it when he told an audience in Nottingham that, but for interfering politicians, they would have had the IRA beaten in a matter of months. While it is unclear whether or not King gave direct orders to begin to lean on us, the speech obviously gave the troops on the ground some kind of green light, and house searches, which had dwindled to nothing after the ceasefire announcement, were again taking place in Belfast. In response, McKee ordered downtown bombings causing considerable damage, in return, we said, for that caused by the British army in those searches. The British were contacted with a claim of responsibility in which we referred to new IRA orders governing defensive and retaliatory action, and, in a slick rephrasing of the British mantra, warned that IRA actions would be 'related to the level of activity' by British and loyalist forces. Meanwhile, the occasional shot was being quietly discharged, unclaimed, in the direction of RUC patrols, to ensure that they kept out of our areas.

By then, the leadership was anyway privately warning us that a return to war was likely. After Easter our negotiators were told that Twomey's demand for a public declaration of intent to withdraw could not be met, because this would itself produce circumstances that would make it impossible to leave. The British were urging us to accept that progress had to be slow, and that we should be jointly aiming to create the circumstances out of which 'the structures of disengagement' could grow. My own translation of this, based on occasional informal briefings, mostly from Dave, was that the British were telling us they were prepared to leave, and were exploring the possible ways in which this might be done without plunging us all into civil war.

There have been suggestions, bumped up by the leadership that took over in the late 1970s, that the British followed a policy of deliberate ambiguity, giving the IRA negotiators meaningless assurances about their intentions and stringing them along generally while they prepared measures to defeat the IRA. It is not at all clear that they were that clever, or our negotiators that stupid, and if it were indeed the case that withdrawal was never on the cards, the British fooled everyone else as well; the Southern government certainly believed that the torpedoing of British policy by a recalcitrant Convention would lead to withdrawal, and that the IRA had been given assurances to that effect. Indeed, Garret FitzGerald believed that only a chance meeting that summer between himself, Jack Lynch and the British Foreign

Secretary, James Callaghan, who was on holiday in west Cork, saw off the threat of withdrawal.

Permission for targeted retaliatory action had been built into the process from the start, and when Shane Doherty was arrested in Derry and shipped off to England to face charges in connection with a letter bomb campaign, the IRA there had had enough. While the arrest alone was a breach of the truce, Doherty had also been very badly treated in custody and, in response, the IRA set up an operation in May in which an RUC man was shot dead. The killing looked like derailing things, at least temporarily, and was described by the British as disproportionate, which it probably was.

Derry was plagued by a difficult army regiment – even the Dublin government complained about it – and the local IRA was anyway losing patience. At the end of June, Martin McGuinness spoke at a commemoration there and confirmed that we were still negotiating with the British to secure a declaration of intent to withdraw, and that, if this was not forthcoming, it would be back to war until it was. In July, on the same day as O'Connell was arrested in Dublin, the IRA in Derry planted three bombs which badly damaged the Crown buildings. In a statement the Derry Brigade said the bombings had come after numerous warnings and inconclusive dialogue through the centres. The situation in Belfast was also deteriorating with the paratroopers back in town, and a Scottish regiment there, as always, behaving badly. Things were also very bad in the prisons where the sentenced prisoners were recommencing protests and it was obvious to everyone that things were going downhill fast.

Still more significant developments were taking place elsewhere. In south Armagh, the IRA had fired warning shots at the army on more than thirty occasions as they tried to use the ceasefire to conduct operations they would not have dared to try before. In early June an IRA volunteer was shot dead while planting a bomb at a bar in Bessbrook and, in mid-July, the IRA killed four British soldiers in retaliation. There have been suggestions that south Armagh was inclined to do its own thing, but, to my certain knowledge, these are rubbish. There was no way south Armagh was out of control and I am quite sure this operation was discussed and approved at leadership level. The attack brought to five the number of claimed and deliberate IRA actions since the truce began and was obviously the most serious. Talks were suspended for a month following this shooting, and though both the IRA and the British said the truce was still holding, the feeling on the ground was that it was on the way out and that it would be business as usual by Christmas.

***

During these months I averaged about 1,000 miles a week on the road, regularly making journeys such as that to north Donegal and back in a day. I had an easy enough time at roadblocks, both north and south, and became relaxed about encountering the British army on the road. The UVF/UDA, and by extension the UDR, were of concern to me long before the Miami Showband killings, but while I avoided travelling across the North at night, and did so very nervously when it was necessary, the fact that the killings took place on the main Belfast to Dublin road – where I would have felt safe at any time – came as a shock. Once, not long afterwards, when on the road from Belfast to Derry, I exchanged glances with John Hume, who was travelling in the direction of Belfast, both of us having been required to slow down by some obstruction. Hume looked very nervous as I caught his eye, as indeed he was entitled to be with perhaps the best known nationalist face in Ireland.

Meanwhile, the sectarian blood-letting continued and as the number of dead Catholics mounted, the IRA got tougher, particularly in north Belfast where Protestant men were now being shot dead in situations identical to those in which Catholics were dying. Roy Suitters, whose name appears on the UVF roll of honour, was shot dead at his shop in front of his teenage daughter on 10 June. The following day, a young Protestant was shot dead as he sat on a wall. Two men were then killed as they stood talking at a street corner, and another shot dead as he finished work at a garage close to the city centre. On 12 July a UDA man was abducted and later shot dead in Ardoyne.

Other UDA and UVF men died during this period, both in their own accidental explosions and as a result of internecine feuding, as did a number of INLA and Official IRA members in their own bitter feud. This ran from February to June, and, together with a second flare-up between the IRA and the Officials later that year, added to the growing mood of despondency in nationalist areas. On 13 August, the IRA launched a bomb and bullet attack on the Bayardo Bar, a UVF haunt that had been hit many times previously. The doorman and his brother-in-law were shot dead before the bomb was placed. A third man and a woman were killed in the explosion, which also injured up to 60 people, and another woman died from her injuries some time later. The bombing was denied by the IRA, but no one believed them. A few days later Brendan 'Bik' McFarlane, who would later be O/C in the H-Blocks during the 1981 hunger strike, appeared in court having been arrested driving the get-away car and, later again, two other IRA men were arrested and charged with the killings.

***

In the May election, the anti-power-sharing unionists had won 47 of the 78 seats, leaving the Convention dead in the water. Again, we urged the British to declare their intent to withdraw, to enable the Convention to have a context for its proceedings. There was widespread speculation that the crisis would come in late summer or early autumn, when the British would have to reject the inevitable majority report, and, in mid-September, a meeting took place at which the British finally confirmed their acceptance that the Convention had failed. They told McKee and Ó Brádaigh that they would let it play itself out, after which there would be a short-term return to direct rule followed by 'the transitional period' for withdrawal. But by then the gap between what Merlyn Rees was saying publicly and what we were being told privately had become too wide to bridge. Though the report from the Convention in November finally, and formally, closed off the possibility of resurrecting Sunningdale, by that time the other strains on the ceasefire had become too much. And with the consequent firm change in British policy towards the close of 1975, everyone settled down for the resumption of what would be a long, long war.

Meanwhile, Brian Keenan had come out of prison as Dave O'Connell went in, and a number of key operators had gone missing. Twomey believed they were now out of control and doing their own thing, and instructed me to have them arrested and brought before him. We raided a number of houses in and around Limerick, Tipperary and the Midlands, where we knew they had bases, missing Eddie Gallagher and Marion Coyle by minutes on one occasion. They in turn threatened to shoot us, while Twomey received complaints about the raids from the republican supporters whose houses we had hit. Twomey and Cahill tackled me about them just before a GHQ meeting that September. I defended myself and my men and, under continuing pressure from them both, impulsively told Twomey he could stick his job. Twomey asked me to write out a resignation note and I did so there and then. However, he had intended I would stand down as director of intelligence and accept whatever else I was given and was genuinely shocked when he realised I had written out a resignation from the IRA and asked me to reconsider. I refused, feeling that I had been put in an impossible position. Both my unit and I were being threatened for carrying out the instructions of the chief of staff, who was now failing to back us in following his instructions. Either way, I had had it, especially since by then I was pretty sure the 'rogue unit' had approval for what they were doing from some within GHQ itself.

At the beginning of October, Gallagher and Coyle kidnapped Dutch businessman Tiede Herrema on his way to the Ferenka plant in Limerick. Subsequently the outrageous demand was delivered for the release from prison of Kevin Mallon, Rose Dugdale and James Hyland – outrageous because it was disgracefully personalised. Perhaps it was a reflection of where we were at, for the organisation was in any case going to hell in a handcart. Coincidentally or otherwise, things had gone rapidly downhill following Dave's arrest. In Belfast, sectarian assassinations had reached appalling heights, while tensions with the Officials were so badly handled by Billy McKee that there was an explosion in feuding at the end of October in which eleven died. Volunteers were now on the run, not just from the British army and RUC, but from the UDA/UVF and the Officials as well– all of which were out to kill them. These were uncertain, rudderless times and the return to war duly took place without me.

I thought briefly of reporting to McGuinness in Derry, or even McKee in Belfast, but I was also upset that no one had come after me, and by the time some moves were made to get me back, I had definitively removed myself. I made arrangements to hand over what was the Army's car and, as I had no money at all, within days it was no longer possible for me to go to see anyone. Because of my background, it was relatively easy to switch out. Most republicans are thoroughly tied in; their families and social milieu, their very geography, keeps them there, and they stay on, forever, in some diminished capacity. By contrast, all I really had to do was not go to places that I had been going to, particularly north of the border. Much of my south Dublin network, meanwhile, went into something resembling hibernation until I rejoined the IRA some years later.

***

The American philosopher Richard Rorty somewhere advises writers against wistful endings, so here goes. One way or another I had had no money of my own since I left college in 1970 and, save for that short period in London, had been the responsibility of the IRA. I had no idea what to do and for the next few months I relied on my parents and my girlfriend, with whom I lived in something approaching bliss for six to eight months, until that too began to unravel. It was a bruising time, well captured when I was sent by the labour exchange to my first job interview and found the foreman unable to distinguish my having been in Long Kesh from my having been in any other prison. To him, I was just another ex-con looking for a break. For a month or two I worked in a warehouse, stacking pallets and delivery trucks, until I was let go one night when I was unable to do the sporadically offered overtime.

In early 1976, I sent out a scatter of application forms looking for work, all but longing for an undisturbed routine in suit and tie, for Nietzsche's 'miserable ease'. There were few replies and no offers. I refused to use the republican infrastructure through which I could probably have landed a job. In retrospect, this was wise; I later learned there are a lot of people who get a kick out of having a pet IRA man around. Unoccupied, and removed from the mutually supportive circle in which I had lived since 1970, with the days of certainty, comradeship and absolute commitment a vanishing memory, I became less sure of my position and realised how little I really knew of Irish history or of the world around me.

Through my girlfriend I met people who were Labour Party or Official supporters, people who had not the slightest respect for where I had been and were at best inclined to view me as an unfortunate dupe who had taken revolutionary rhetoric too seriously. I had extraordinary encounters with men my own age who told me they had joined the Officials to gain political experience, or because a future in the unions or the media was more assured than if they had joined Labour. I listened to such sentiments in disbelief, first that anyone could hold them, and secondly that they were unashamed to declare them. It seemed incredible that this world of role-playing could exist, while 60 miles up the road people were being shot and blown to pieces. The Provisionals were condemned out of hand while every two-bit Third World liberation struggle was lauded, no matter its methods, in an ongoing parody of college politics. The incidence of adultery within this circle also shocked and appalled me, and was one more indication of the moral swamp in which middle-class Dublin was sunk – though it was the mendacity rather than the sex that outraged me. Meanwhile, my relationship with my girlfriend was haunted by the spectre of our teenage years, and, bewildered at the speed with which my own self-image was dissolving, I waited for this, too, to disintegrate.

There was a short addendum to my five years in the IRA. In July 1976 the IRA killed the British ambassador, Christopher Ewart Biggs, and a female civil servant in a landmine attack in Dublin. I was arrested in the general round up and vigorously questioned by detectives from the then emerging Heavy Gang. While I wasn't touched, it was tough, with plenty of banging and shouting. At one point a couple of detectives told me they were going to take me up the Dublin mountains and shoot me and, while I didn't believe that for a moment, I was in a very uncomfortable position, where, for the first and only time, I was trying to account for my movements and satisfy my interrogators while refusing to answer any questions about the IRA.

Feeling used up and demoralised, and needing to prove myself against a set of new and different standards, I had meanwhile begun to think of going back to university. Someone my girlfriend knew with university connections had told me how to approach UCD, where I applied to study history and philosophy. My application was accepted a day or two after I was released by the Branch, and for the remainder of that long, hot summer of 1976, I worked as a housepainter, having responded to an ad in a shop window. Then I knuckled down to scrape a living and do my degree and, replacing Pearse and Connolly with Kant and Wittgenstein, forgot all about the Republic.

Postscript

I rejoined the IRA in the spring of 1981 as the hunger strike, in which ten men died, reached fever pitch. Over the following years I held various positions North and South. I know plenty, but of leadership strategy and the machinations that led to the 1994 ceasefire, I know nothing at all.

Though the IRA is a top-down organisation, it was only in the 1980s that I noticed it. Gerry Adams can, as they put it in Belfast, 'shite-talk' with the best of them, but if you were stuck in a room with him he tended to flick through a newspaper rather than chat you up, like Dave O'Connell and the others used to do.

The IRA is run by the Army Council, the seven-man body that republicans consider to be the *de jure* government of Ireland. The Council is the power and, in wartime, generates its own membership, selecting replacements for those who die or are imprisoned. It appoints the chief of staff, invariably from within itself, who in turn selects his GHQ staff and, at least in theory, the command and brigade O/Cs, who then name their own staffs. But staff officers are functionaries, and busy ones. No less than the first time around, I got buried in the everyday detail of whatever it was I had to pull together, leaving strategy to the leadership.

By the early 1980s the Army had changed. The chaotic impulsiveness of the 1970s, when each January was greeted as starting out the 'year of victory', had given way to a long-war strategy. The British, too, were there for the long haul. Following the ending of the 1975 truce, they had adopted the dual policy of Ulsterisation and criminalisation, with the RUC taking the lead and processing arrested IRA volunteers through the courts, mainly on the basis of confessions beaten out of them. A new, young, Northern leadership, some of whom I knew, had displaced Dave O'Connell and Ruairí Ó Brádaigh at the head of the movement. Though I thought the sidelining of Dave and Ruairí was a mistake – and the subsequent bad-mouthing of both men unforgivable – I accepted that the movement should be led from the North. Retaliatory attacks against civilian Protestants had meanwhile ceased, replaced by targeted operations against the killers themselves. The new leadership was openly left-wing and the movement's federalist policy was on the way out. From my point of view, there was little there not to like.

Internment was long gone and very few individuals were on the run. The leadership and volunteers operated more or less openly, with RUC/British army and Garda surveillance, together with their informers, an obvious problem. Many IRA members were married with families, and those with responsibilities outside the areas where they lived made their way off on Monday mornings and came back home to relax at weekends before setting off again, for all the world like travelling executives. Operations and other IRA work were meticulously prepared and carried out. The safety of the volunteers – rightly – was paramount. The war was conducted slowly and painstakingly, as the Army paced itself.

Following republican election successes during and after the 1981 hunger strike, the two-stroke strategy – that of Armalite and ballot box – was born, and then the IRA convention of 1986 cleared the way for republicans to attend the Dáil. I supported these moves at the time, but I was wrong. This was not a political strategy, but a narrowly electoral one, dividing the movement's energies at a crucial time, establishing different attitudes towards the two partitioned states, and setting up that deep contradiction between fighting and looking for votes which then unfolded in the way it did.

In early 1987 I was asked to go into Sinn Féin, with a continuing, though slighter, IRA role. Agreeing to this was a mistake. I was unsuited to the work and, though I was head of research for some years and sat on the Ard Chomhairle for a couple of these, they were wasted years, alive with the absurdities of the two-tier strategy. I recall, for instance, completing a detailed policy paper on the health service in the South in the very week, in November 1987, that the IRA Remembrance Day blast in Enniskillen killed eleven civilians; a twelfth died in 2000, having been in a coma since the explosion. The tensions multiplied and, by the early 1990s, I had had enough.

I knew something was up but never what. I didn't formally resign from the IRA but simply wandered off in December 1993, when republican leaders began reinterpreting a clear British restatement of the loyalist veto in the Downing Street Declaration of that year as possibly meaning something else. In August 1994 the IRA declared a ceasefire. As republicans ran a victory cavalcade up and down the Falls Road – and I wondered if perhaps they had beaten the British after all – Bernadette Devlin was one of few who got it right: 'The war is over; the good guys lost.' I watched the later developments – the Good Friday Agreement, the establishment of the power-sharing executive, IRA decommissioning and all the rest – in stunned disbelief and from the sidelines.

The prospects for middle-aged Arts graduates looking for their first real job are not good. With inside help I got freelance work as a sub-editor with the *Irish Press* before landing a full-time post with the paper some months later. Following the collapse of the Press group in 1995, I wrote features and news analysis pieces on non-Northern issues for various papers in the South on a freelance basis. In 1998 Seán O'Callaghan named me in his book, *The Informer*, as having been a GHQ officer. Soon afterwards, Tom Murphy from south Armagh, whom O'Callaghan also named, took a High Court libel action against the *Sunday Times*, which had described him as an IRA leader. O'Callaghan gave evidence for the newspaper, repeating the charges against Murphy which he had outlined in his book. When Murphy took the stand he denied knowing either me or any of the others O'Callaghan had named, only for the newspaper to call a Garda witness who gave evidence that Murphy and I had been arrested together close to the border in 1984 and held on suspicion of IRA membership. Murphy lost his action and, with elements in the press pursuing me, I knew my journalistic career was over. I took up where I had left off in 1970, studying Law and qualifying as a solicitor. The roundabout route – my father, who died in 1996, would have found it hilarious. Since then I have worked as a criminal defence lawyer, bumping into Special Branch detectives professionally, in the courts and while attending Garda stations to advise clients in custody. I remember some of the Branch men well from the old days, and, though I'm sure they remember me too, no one has ever said a word.

I had a bit part in the failed Irish revolution. But I was there, and did what was asked of me. Family and career were delayed, but I got there. Hundreds of other IRA volunteers were killed, or damaged, or had their lives blighted by up to two decades of imprisonment. I met some of the finest men and women of their generation, and held beliefs I would have died for in a heartbeat. And that can't be all bad. Would I do it again? I say yes, but, really, that's just a position. And one hardly consistent with the truth that the outcome of a quarter century of war was not worth a single drop of anybody's blood. Was it all then a futile, useless waste of lives? Probably.

I firmly believe ours was a noble effort, its faults in the main the result of what Mandela, I think, called 'the fallibility of the combatant', though it did sometimes slide into barbarism. But the success of an undertaking must be judged against its reasons for beginning and its end, and, thus seen, the IRA failed utterly, its closing position on how to achieve British withdrawal and Irish unity by then identical to that of the successive British governments it fought against.

As to why it failed, this is my view: From way back, but even more from the time I rejoined in 1981, the IRA's priority was the acquisition of heavy military equipment. 'Getting the gear in' was the Holy Grail that would allow the Army to forcibly expel the British from Ireland, its absence the excuse for our every failing. That time arrived with the Libyan arms shipments of the mid-1980s, following which the IRA was meant to launch the type of offensive that could only have been dreamt of previously. But the IRA was unable to deliver. It got its chance, was given every opportunity, until, with no end in sight, and mounting IRA casualties at the hands of the British and its loyalist satellites in the UDA and UVF, the leadership decided to cash in its chips.

But there's no shame in failure, and these were their chips to use. For sure, I've since jumped up and down and shaken my fist at the television at the sight and sound of republican spokespeople and, yes, Gerry

Adams is a mendacious, lying bastard. But what else could he be? For the movement could never have been taken in the direction that he took it without a bit of dissembling. 'The owl of Minerva spreads its wings only with the falling of the dusk', says Hegel, only when 'a shape of life [has] grown old' can it be understood. Perhaps Adams' genius was to see it had grown old before the rest of us, and to then have taken things in the sole direction left. Or, perhaps, as Kevin Mallon once joked, Adams simply stood there, in the enveloping mess, and acted as if he had planned it all along – and then it just came to seem that way.

With the Berlin Wall down and the Balkans showing us what civil war in Europe really looked like, it was, one way or another, time for the war to end. But as to what the leadership did then – with political credit built upon the deaths and imprisonment of countless IRA volunteers and nationalists killed by the security forces and loyalist murder gangs – that is something else. Four decades on from where it began, the principle of unionist consent has been accepted by the Provisionals, and Martin McGuinness is Deputy First Minister at Stormont, in the same power-sharing executive that was on offer way back in 1973. A British departure, an end to partition and Irish unity are as far away as ever they were, and the dream of a socialist republic in Ireland is finished.

How could it be that the IRA has disappeared into history having settled for the very outcome it had set out to oppose? I remember conversations long ago with Pat Ward about the equivalence between the Catholic Ancient Order of Hibernians and its Protestant marching counterpart, the Orange Order; between Green and Orange Tories; and between nationalism and republicanism; the former our enemy no less than the unionists. I do not know how it happened, but, somewhere along the line, the movement lost its republican soul and became that collection of soft-left nationalists who now help to administer British rule in Ireland.

But that – as we might have said in Earlsfort Terrace back in 1969 – that's dialectics.

Sources and Further Reading

I used the *Irish Times* archive extensively to jog my memory of distant events, as well as the CAIN conflict archive at cain.ulst.ac.uk, and those issues of the *Derry Journal* covering my time there in late 1971. The three volumes of Richard Deutsch and Vivien Magowan's *Northern Ireland: A Chronology of Events* cover in some detail the years 1968 to 1974, while David Barzilay's four-volume *The British Army in Ulster* give events up to the close of 1980 from that army's perspective. Conventional histories of the 1970s include Thomas Hennessy's *The Evolution of the Troubles 1970–72* and Alan Parkinson's *1972 and the Ulster Troubles*.

Lost Lives, by David McKittrick and others, is an invaluable account of every death that occurred in the course of the conflict, while his *Making Sense of the Troubles*, written with David McVea, is probably the best short book on the period. Tim Pat Coogan's *The IRA* and J. Bowyer Bell's *The Secret Army* are standard histories of the IRA, particularly pre-1969, as is Richard English's *Armed Struggle*. Colonel Michael Dewar's *The British Army in Northern Ireland* and A.R. Oppenheimer's *IRA: The Bombs and the Bullets* give a British view.

Tommy McKearney, an ex-hunger striker, has written an analysis of the IRA war, *The Provisional IRA: From Insurrection to Parliament*, the title of which says it all. Ex-IRA man Anthony McIntyre's *Good Friday: The Death of Irish Republicanism* has another giveaway title and comes complete with a cover picture of Gerry Adams in black beret at an early IRA funeral. McIntyre (and others) meanwhile highlights Provisional mendacity daily in his blog at thepensivequill.am.

Peter Taylor's trilogy, *Brits*, *Loyalists* and *Provos*, cover the respective combatants. Henry McDonald and Jim Cusack have written books on both the UDA and the UVF (titled simply *UDA* and *UVF*), while McDonald, this time with Jack Holland, has also written the standard on the INLA, *INLA: Deadly Divisions*. Reading it, I am truly thankful that I was turned down by the Official IRA in 1970, as I would almost certainly have ended up with the INLA, and been caught up in the internecine bloodletting in which that organisation tore itself apart in the late 1980s and early 1990s. *Official Irish Republicanism* by Sean Swan and *The Lost Revolution* by Brian Hanley and Scott Millar meanwhile both do a good job on the Officials.

Peter Taylor's *Beating the Terrorists* documents the early years of the criminalisation strategy, which culminated in the H-Block hunger strikes. On these, Thomas Hennessy's recent *Hunger Strike* has all the British documents, and a British view, and while Richard O'Rawe's two books, *Blanketmen* and *Afterlives*, courageously tell the story from the inside, I remain unable to believe that republican leaders knowingly sacrificed the lives of the final six for electoral advantage. *Ten Men Dead*, by the British journalist David Beresford, is a book I am unable to revisit without tears in my eyes. It reminds me vividly of why, having been asked, I rejoined in 1981, leaving UCD, where I was doing a Master's, for a second time.

British journalist Robert Fisk long ago wrote the definitive book on the UWC strike, *The Point of No Return*, while John McGuffin's *Internment*, the same author's *The Guinea Pigs*, and *Political Murder in Northern Ireland* by Martin Dillon and Denis Lehane are others that have stood the test of time. Anne Cadwallader's recent *Lethal Allies*, on security force collusion in the murder by loyalists of Catholic civilians in the mid-Ulster area, definitively covers ground previously traversed more speculatively by others.

On the government side, there are many memoirs and biographies and other texts. Among those I have found useful are Dermot Keogh's biography of Jack Lynch, Garret FitzGerald's *All in a Life*, Ken Bloomfield's *A Tragedy of Errors*, and *Crisis of Confidence* by Anthony Craig.

There are some half-decent memoirs by RUC men and British soldiers, among them the books by Morton and Styles referred to in the text, Johnston Brown's *Into the Dark*, Alan Simpson's *Duplicity and*

Deception, A.F.N. Clarke's *Contact*, Colonel Steve Smith's *3-2-1 Bomb Gone*, and Ken Wharton's *A Long Long War*, a compendium of testimonies from solders who served there.

There are also various local histories; the best I know of are the Ardoyne Commemoration Project's *Ardoyne: The Untold Truth*, *Ballymurphy and the Irish War* by Ciarán de Baroid, and Eamonn McCann's *War and an Irish Town*, the classic on Derry.

Seán MacStiofáin's *Memoirs of a Revolutionary* was the first memoir to come from a contemporary IRA man and suffers from the same fault as both of Gerry Adams' books, in that it is simply not truthful. At this point I should add that while mine is the truth, it is not the whole truth and cannot be, on pain of possible prosecution and imprisonment, something which firmly underlines the fact that we lost the war. For both that and other reasons, there will be no truth commission, certainly not a truthful one, and while it would be fascinating to read the honest memoirs of Adams, McGuinness, Pat Doherty or other leadership figures, this ain't ever going to happen.

Not unless from beyond the grave; *Voices from the Grave* is the title of Ed Moloney's rendering of the Boston Tapes, based on interviews with the now-dead Brendan Hughes and UVF leader David Ervine. Moloney is also the author, with Andy Pollock, of a book on Paisley, titled simply *Paisley*, and, by himself, of the more recent *Paisley: From Demagogue to Democrat?* He also wrote *A Secret History of the IRA*, a superb work, though I think it is overly Belfast-centric, and do not entirely share his view of Gerry Adams. It is a fact that right up until the ceasefire of August 1994 the IRA was fighting, and between mortar attacks on 10 Downing Street and the devastation of London's financial centre, that decisive blow against the British was always just around the corner, bringing consequences not even Gerry Adams could have controlled. The 'peace process' was, in my view, simply Adams' Plan B, to cover for the eventuality of an IRA failure, but there's no way he could have, or did, *make* the IRA fail. And he was the only one who even *had* a Plan B.

Elsewhere, Shane O'Doherty, who is mentioned in the text, and who I remember as a mad young lad in Derry, has written *The Volunteer*. There is a good biography of Ruairí Ó Brádaigh by the US academic

Robert White, but none yet on Dave O'Connell, while I'm told Billy McKee (now in his mid-90s) has declined to assist a host of would-be biographers. Maria McGuire's *To Take Arms* is worth a read, as is Sean O'Callaghan's *The Informer* and Eamon Collins' *Killing Rage*. Collins was subsequently battered to death, it is assumed by either the IRA or by republican supporters.

There are biographies of a number of republicans, some produced by the movement, and others, on Joe Cahill, Martin Ferris and Martin McGuinness, coming from outside. None of those I've read are terribly good. The one on McGuinness, incidentally, by Liam Clarke and Kathryn Johnson, credits me with saving him from arrest on the night I disappeared into custody back in 1971, something for which, apparently, I retain a small fame in Derry. Mind you, on visits to both Derry and Belfast in recent years, none of my old comrades was in any hurry to buy me a pint on that account.